NEXUS

The International Henry Miller Journal

Thanks to Valentine Miller, Henry Tony Miller, and George Boroczi, Ph.D. for their continuing support of *Nexus: The International Henry Miller Journal*.

Nexus seeks manuscripts and photo-essays that explore any aspect of Henry Miller's work and life. Submissions on the life and work of Miller's friends and associates are also encouraged. International submissions must be written in English with bilingual quotations. Please direct all manuscript submissions (two copies, MLA style, anonymous) to: Dr. James M. Decker, Editor, *Nexus: The International Henry Miller Journal*; 1028 SW Adams #108; Peoria, IL 61602. Electronic submissions are encouraged. Please email: <jdecker@icc.edu>.

Subscriptions are available to individuals and institution at $15 per issue ($25 overseas) postage included. For pricing and availability of back issues visit our website: www.nexusmiller.org.

Questions, please contact: jdecker@icc.edu
Website: www.nexusmiller.org

Nexus: The International Henry Miller Journal is a member of CELJ, The Council of Editors of Learned Journals.

ISSN 1543-0456

NEXUS

The International Henry Miller Journal

Volume Twelve	2018

Henry Miller's *Self-Portrait as Chinese Student*, 5/57
(From the collection of Maurice Bassett)

Editors' Note

As the Miller Notes toward the end of this volume suggest, scholarship on Henry Miller continues to diversify, although much of it still focuses on obscenity (particularly as it relates to *Tropic of Cancer*) and biographical matters. Some exciting new veins of criticism and scholarship are being mined, however, as one can explore in the following pages. Further archival scholarship and textual criticism will help provide new generations of critics with crucial context, while new theoretical approaches and attention to works other than *Tropic of Cancer* will give the field more breadth. To encourage such scholarship, we are pleased to announce the *Nexus* Award for New Scholars. To compete for the award, unpublished writers should submit their essays on any subject pertaining to the Villa Seurat Circle to <jdecker@icc.edu> by 1 June 2019. The winner will receive $500, while second and third place will receive $250 and $100 respectively. Winners will also appear in a subsequent volume of *Nexus: The International Henry Miller Journal*. Submissions will be reviewed by a panel of Miller experts.

In the current volume, Eric D. Lehman offers a second installment of letters from June Corbett to Henry Miller. The letters contain many references to June's ongoing health and money problems, but they also reveal June's interest in Mao Zedong and provide a brief counter-narrative to Miller's version of events concerning both Jean Kronski and Anaïs Nin. Wayne E. Arnold follows with some important archival research on *Aller Retour New York* that sheds light on Miller's efforts (and non-efforts) to publish it after its initial appearance. John Clegg then examines how Miller and Djuna Barnes confront the idea of degeneracy in order to create life-giving art, while Finn Jensen places Miller within a vitalistic tradition that includes Hans Christian Andersen. Ida Therén provides an intriguing fictional complement to June's letters, while Inez Hollander Lake ponders what attracted Miller to Hieronymus Bosch's *The Garden of Earthly Delights*. Akiyoshi Suzuki offers some provocative commentary on textual errors in *Book of Friends: A Trilogy*, and Katy Masuga closes out volume 12 with a history and contemplation of the Henry Miller Memorial Library based on a series of important interviews with figures such as Stefan White and Alisa Fineman. Enjoy!

Dr. James Baxter and June Corbett, Fire Island, New York, 1955

Letters from June Corbett to Henry Miller 1965-1972
Part 2

Eric D. Lehman

The previous issue of *Nexus* included June's letters to Henry Miller up until 1970 from Yale University's Beinecke Library. This second batch contains the remainder of the letters from the 1970s, other than a few undatable letters. Those will be published in the subsequent issue, and may include new insight into June and Henry's long-ago split in Paris.

This grouping of correspondence, which includes letters from Bill Allen and Jim and Annette Baxter, concerns June's retirement from the New York City Department of Welfare and her impending financial needs. The suggestion from June's friends is that Miller increase his stipend to her in order that she can live with some dignity. When reading them in sequence it seems like a concerted effort to squeeze the famous author, with June pointing out her needs without specifically asking, while their mutual friends do the hard work (the Baxters lay it on a little thick). We know that Miller was generous to a fault when it came to women, and though June had long since passed out of his life, he continued to partially support her, increasing the amount of his regular checks to $125.

There are only a few letters after this event. Always interested in socialism, June now develops an affinity for Chairman Mao. Her letters become less frequent, and her health continues to deteriorate. We can assume that Miller's payments continued until June leaves New York for her brother's house in Arizona in 1977.

It is important to note that Yale's designation of the letters as going from 1965 to 1972 is incorrect in that June's letters go to at least 1974.[1] I have kept all misspellings and spacing issues as found.

Sept 10 '71
Bill Allen
329 E. 88 St NY 10028
Subject: June

Thanks for letter – I am not sure how clear my previous letter was.

Main point is that ONLY Dr. Baxter (in my judgment) has the confidence etc of June to handle this matter. NOT I – inspite of my affection even risking offending her by this correspondence. She is very fond of me but in a secondary way; we say hello and make vague plans every week or two…I even think I do not have her latest phone number.

In short, my one suggestion is that Baxter ask her to visit him for a general check-up, his own spontaneous idea. This I believe will lead him to judging that she should go into retirement regardless of the finances. (She has wanted to but finds she cannot afford to.) Perhaps he will find that I'm wrong.

Second step – HOW MUCH would retirement cost as compared to remaining on job??? MY hypothesis is that this is a MINOR AMOUNT which could be supplemented without major sacrifice.

Baxter knows me not at all – at very most he would remember June inviting me to one cocktail party chez lui which I failed to get to. Hence my humble recommendation that you contact him yourself direct.

Devotedly,

Bill Allen[2]

212-LE4-7408 = home

Retiring from City job is a mess – so much so that after trying I RESCINDED. They let you squirm a few weeks or months before the pension starts coming in; meanwhile they give some vague percentage. Incompetent in handling my own life, I feel without self-confidence in handling others'.

(Much of June's trouble stem from a gross injustice which even the least well-intentioned boss could have obviated. For pension they do NOT include a long period when June did full-fledged office work but did not receive SALARY – she was considered a sort of apprentice on a dole. But it is years too late to correct the error.)

I will be most careful with our address and am so concerned with your health and privacy that I resist a desire to review perhaps forgotten phases of your own past – gathering in Brooklyn Library, art show at Gentle-Gove St., Robitailled, Stettner, Dal Brown, Moricant….If you get around to a definitive autobiography it might

be advisable to gather notes from your devotees – each will give a
quite different picture!!!!

James E. Baxter M.D.
435 East 70th Street
New York NY 10021

September 23, 1971

Dear Henry:
You are characteristically – and legendarily – warm and compassion-
nate in inquiring about June's welfare.

Annette and I flagellate ourselves for having been kept by all kinds
of responsibilities from seeing June as often as we have wanted to.[3]
She stayed with us here in the apartment last Friday night, and we
all went out to our place on Fire Island for the rest of the weekend. A
lovely time, for all of us. She remains an unbelievably enchanting
and enigmatic woman.

She's stayed on her job for a year after usual retirement for financial
reasons, feeble – although not too feeble – as she is. She must retire,
at the latest, next spring. Annette and I will help her, as we have
through the years. When the cost of living in New York and our
expenses were both more reasonable, we could be pleasantly
impulsive. But however much our outrageous Manhattan expenses
these days cramp our style, we will see to it that she gets some
regular help from us. If you could add something to that monthly,
even modestly, I know she would accept it gratefully and willingly.
She's not in a position to reject it; and her old treasured memories
would surely incline her to think of it as an echo of the time when
you, with her at your side, were beginning an assault on American
complacency, inanity and stupidity that has now risen to full tide.
(June, you'll be pleased to know, is continuing to abet that assault, in
the limited ways that she can. Your torch is fully aloft in her weary
arms.) She remains dedicated in the most thoroughgoing sense to
your work, and to you.

And are you, Henry, still intact after this latest surgical indignity?
It's a tribute to both you and the surgeons. We think of you plunging
always onward and wish you were closer, to tell us about it.

With love from us both,
Jim and Annette

Henry: - Our children have grown up hearing June talk about you. And they never tire of listening to her. She looks tired but has amazing reserves of strength.[4]

Dear Henry –

Annette + Jim forwarded me with your book on Christmas – it was a great surprise.

I'm leaving the office this June, it's going to be a hardship for me.

The rent is sky high – the telephone, light + gas have been raised. The so + so in Washington + our governor are a pain of ------- -------

New York is the highest state + city taxed and it seems nothing moves them.

The lowest bracket meets all the needs everything.

I believe we first met in the fall I seem to have forgotten exactly when.

Sorry to hear of your hip problem – Do you need an operation?

Why don't you consult a Chinese doctor one who can apply the needles – I do believe in them.

You know so many people – how about it.

I'm sure they would do you a lot of good and I understand there is no ill affect nor do you know that anything has been administered.

Good luck + please do what I suggest. Its safer.

Love, June[5]

Jan. 21, 1972[6]

Dear Henry –

Read your article in the Sunday Times as always found it informative + good.

The review of your book by the critic in the same issue was as always lacking in comprehension.[7]

Your note asked me whether I had received a Christmas present, I didn't, but I understood from your previous notes that you do not believe in Christmas, after all I do not send you anything.

I have been freezing for the last nine days, something wrong with the boiler and we haven't had heat or hot water during that time.

I'm retiring in June.

Don't know how I'm going to manage, but the important thing is my health. Everything else is not on my mind.

Do hope that your health is much better. Be good and do only what you want to

All the best, always for you

June

Dear Henry

It has been very miserable in New York since the first week of October.

I had a relapse after Christmas, a very sore infected throat, a nasal drip that first never stopped, temperature and body aches and pains.

I only returned to work last Thursday, and not feeling all well – the weather took a turn for the better on Friday, still better Saturday and today. And if it continues I will be improving I hope. Your check on Christmas was a very pleasant surprise and on January 28 the lithograph of your watercolor really was the gentle, thoughtful, beautiful self that made me recall dreams, promises, etc, etc. That has been the moving light for living.

I hope that starting July, I will be a little more of my old self, and I promise that if GO you will tire of the mail you receive from me.[8]

Much love to yours, please keep well and always yours,

June

March 8, 1972

Dear Henry,

I'm sorry to be so long in replying to you about June. When we saw her last, a few weeks ago, we went over her finances with her, and here's how they stand. Her current income from her job is, after deductions, $90 weekly, or $360 monthly. She said that her brother added $100 and that you added $50, which totals $510 monthly. Her expenses are:

Rent	$110
Lights	16

11

Telephone   <u>9</u>
$135 plus food, etc.

After retirement, instead of $360 salary, she expects to receive $260 - $210 from Social Security plus $50 from her New York City pension. Thus, if you and her brother were to continue as before, her monthly income would be $410 rather than $510. Her travel expense would be somewhat reduced, but she would of course be grateful if you were in a position to augment what you so generously send her.

When we've seen her, we've continued to put as much conversation as we could on tapes – for whatever posterity. Physically she grows somewhat feebler, but her voice is still dark green velvet, her memory and perceptions astonishing, her enigmas deeper and her confidence more defiant. She will stop smoking Camels when the air she breathes and the water she drinks ceases to be polluted.

We gave June the autobiography at Christmas; we think she was pleased to see the photos of her. Let's hope the new operation has something substantial to offer your arthritic hip. Please keep us posted, and come to see us when you can.

With love from us both,
Jim and Annette

April 26, 1972

Dear Henry,

Thanks for your recent note. We've been in touch with Bill Allen and he's joining us here for dinner next week. Whether he will feel himself able to assist with June's finances will be uncertain until then; we'll sound him out. If he can't help, we'll do our best to supplement your generous increase. We're reasonably confident that June will accept anything, and be able to get along on what we project.

Stay out of the hospital as long as the California sun and your legendary resilience permit. We confidently expect you to outlive us all, in a time when simple survival is almost all that any of us can hope for.

We'll try to see the Chinese film in the interests of larger survival.

Will be in touch with you after Allen's visit.
With love from us both,
Annette

May 1, 1972[9]
Dear Henry

The cape is charming, delighted with it. I'm very moved that Hoki and you presented it to me. I wanted to write you for weeks but I dragged myself to work and home suffering a bad cold that settled in my throat and shoulder and gave me a painful time for the last five weeks.

It just beginning to feel a little better + the weather has improved.

I hope that you can forget about the operation. I'm relieved that you are postponing it indefinitely.

You should enquire of your Chinese friends about a doctor from Peking to give you acupuncture.

I have been reading books published in Peking by Mao tse-tung and I'm really impressed with these works.

Mao-tse-tung is a brilliant man, born Dec 26, I believe he is just one year younger than you, sound and a realist.

Do think about it.

I'm unimpressed by our doctor and hospitals they are mechanics – and not to [sic] good as such –

Haven't seen the Chinese film, but hope to soon.

Thank you + your charming wife for thinking of me.

All my love, always

Good health + don't fall for our doctorette.

June

5.30.72
Dear Henry,

We've had Bill Allen here for dinner + I must say he's a very unusual fellow indeed – wise + funny + ingratiating. He sees June frequently if not daily, + his considered opinion by the phone this evening is this: June has told him that she doesn't want to ask for specific amounts of financial assistance until the moment she retires – in mid-June – when she allegedly will be in a better position to assess her circumstances. Bill has told her that you are discretely waiting with your generous offer + that he + we are also ready to help. I suspect your $125 is just right. The next move is theirs, + we'll promptly pass it on to you. Bill says she looks fine.

Happy Father's Day!

Love from us both, Jim

13

6/26/72
Dear Henry –

What with the lousy weather, which affected my breathing + arthritis pains in my back – I put off writing + telling you how delighted I was to receive the $125 check.

It was good of you to treat me so generously I'm sure it will be of great help.

I'm retiring as of the last day of this month June 30.

Although I'm still to receive a salary for 26 work days of accumulated annual days + then 36 more days of pay for terminal leave a bonus. It will take five additional pay checks sent to me in bi-weekly form.

I still do not know what little bit I will get after that but you can rest assured it will barely amount to much.

It takes the City forever to determine what I'm to get.

That's how the damned system works.

The only thing I'm sure of is your help, my brothers assistants + Social Security.

None of which I can get immediately – not until my terminal leave is over.

I'm pleased that you lack the courage to go to the hospital.

Just read in the New York Times of a man in Russia who is 167 years of age + who celebrated his 88 years old grand son's dousing early.[10]

I believe that you can do as well if you only will forget all depressive ideas.

I haven't seen the Chinese film yet. Hope to when I see it screened again.

Good health + do not worry about the insomnia. So long as you get several hours of rest.

All good for you + always my love
June
Your letters are the only uplift I have – I really look forward to them.

April 29, 1973

Dear Henry –
The special delivery postman delivered the painting + pen + ink sketch April 27 towards evening delightful.

Whenever I receive a book or your watercolors or sketches you give me a present of yourself, it makes my days, weeks, months worth while (all other times I'm not living – hardly going thru the emphysema + rheumatic heart pains + the weather hasn't been of any help.

I don't believe I've written to you for four months.

Haven't acknowledged your book "On Turning Eight" nor the Mexico border.[11]

I write you daily in my mind but during my half-alive waking hours + at night my mind turns to my neglect + troubles me until I doze off.

Very pleased to hear that the doctors are not operating. I'm all for that.

Do you know it's all up to you.

I do know that other than working hard you know how to abstain from harmful things + so you will live as long as you want to, that is so long as anything still stimulates your days + nights – I hope that will be for a long time.

All my love + best to you
Always, June

I understand that the Chinese leader "Mao" is exactly one year younger than you, from the same day, month.

Aug 24, 1973

Dear Henry

Have been ill for many months, paralized with arthritis, rheumatic heart, emphysema, barely able to function.

As you can see hardly able to write properly.

Just manage to go out to pick up some groceries, daily.

It seems I should have left work a year earlier.

My rent has been raised again. It seems I will have to put up with it.

I manage so far.

Received your etching, but no watercolors.

Always happy to receive them.

Good life to Tony, his bride, Valentine + you dear Henry

Joy to you,
Always, June

2/20/74

Dear Henry

I omitted telling you that I phoned the Distributor about your film – he told me that he hadn't received a client + house to show it in - to phone him in a couple of months – I promised to phone him within 30 days each month.[12]

Of course I will write + tell you when I see it.

All your Valentines, birthdays, may be good

The best of all

June

I forgot to mention it but you look formidable in the card, more than ever like what your father should have looked like than you.

Dear Henry

I tuned in to Merv Griffin and heard and saw you, and you looked younger, more beautiful than any one on the program[13]

It comforts all my belief that you are the saint, the master I believed in.

Everything I believed in is true but your interrogator seemed to overwhelmed, confused, limited.

Nevertheless I was delighted to see + hear you, even though I'm aware of the limitations of your audience.

He has endeared himself if only that you were on the program.

Your voice was strong – suspect it seemed to have retained its youthful beauty.

I do hope that you make sense.

I'm not strong right now but perhaps just seeing and hearing you will improve my health.

I believe you are going strong.

Please let me know of anything you do.

Always the best, June

Dear Henry,

This is to write you, not to say nonsense, but to talk to you.

Griffin was shrewd he sensed where his bread was buttered, and you did not force the crap.[14]

It was a show, and you entered into the spirit with grace and charm.

But enough of this.

For me you were you.

I am not attempting a psychiatric analysis + for my bread + butter, it means nothing to me, I am saluting you, Henry, as I would Dostoyevsky, Hamsun, Pique, and the lesser lights. But with equal grace awake as Sartre, who has the love and touch of truth, again I'm ranting to much.

You have the all, I must not debate you. I do understand + love yourself,

June

I have written nothing, just a salute to a great dream

Following are the remaining, undated letters from June Corbett to Henry Miller held by Yale University's Beinecke Library.

Dear Henry

I'm relieved that you're out of the hospital + that it was successful – whatever that means.[15] Mainly I'm happy that you are yourself again. That insatiable curiosity, the enthusiasm for the many interest your ability for exhilaration are more comforting to me than all that nonsense in the medical + surgical world of material detergence + surgical parts in business, business, etc.

Be yourself and everything will be good –

You are to important to many in this world of those who count

I loved your Chinese signature quite attractive. I must get hold of Chinese alphabetic script – not to be left in the dark

You always add surprise, beauty, the exceptional and delightsome + those are rare moments.

The best to you

Always

Forgive my finishing this in pencil my pen went dry.

Dear Henry

Received your letter at Eds, delighted to hear from you, at least I didn't work. It was a nightmare I was living thru.

I really have no idea.
I hope that you make sense of all that has happened.
I don't.
All my love, always,
June

Dear Henry

The painting is exquisite – your sense of all that is.
I'm delighted to have it.
It raised my feeling a great deal.
You always respond to my needs + seemed to be aware of the flaws.
My health is not to good. I think mainly I'm forced to put up with neighbor problems overly much.
Find I'm burdening you with silly nonsense.
Forgive me.
Please be well and live forever.
For me and many thousands you are always young, beautiful and necessary.
I hope that you may always be active + your enthusiastic self.
All my love,
June

Dear Henry

The watercolors arrive via private mail and the many books and cards thru N.S. mail followed several days later. All a great surprise and a moving joy.
It floored me to receive so much of your work it recalled the early days of being swarmed with your joys, work dreams ----- et al.
I sell odds + ends here, there;
The paintings are like a childish dream of release, form technique unlike the perfection of your writings, which for me are poetry, beauty of style, imagination, discipline, creation. The greatest of Americans fall short of your ability, beauty, perfections.[16]
You are the master.
Yours is the chaos of today, even tomorrow but you are not to blame for the cause. Only the way to the future.

With all my admiration, love for your work.
Thank you for sharing so much with me,
Always my best,
June

Dear Henry-

Involved in procedural nonsense due to illness, with the personnel department + no stamina or strength to do more than get up go to work, etc.[17]

I suppose I should have had extended leave to recuperate after all that was withdrawn from me.

Your watercolor is delightful always react to your work as I do with a Klee. The loose leaf beautiful gotten up and very exciting prints arrived from Rotterdam.

Always very happy to get anything of yours.

Do thank Connie Combs for the effort in your and my behalf.

Take good care of yourself
All the best, June

Henry –

This is to explain more that I simply acted as a buffer of the world surrounding you – I tried at the time to explain I could not understand Anais or anyone's interference – I could not + still do not understand your accepting much – for me it dropped you, my Anais. I'm trying to put into words much of what it all meant to me.[18]

It is as if the world fell apart. I'm not writing to the great man but to Val who I assumed a protective cover.

I still am unequipped to write and explain anything. For me the world dropped.

I sit through the nights with a stranger who assumed a privilege of nonsense, who used the excuse of making love to me but lacked the understanding – all.

As I have said before as I am not Dostoyevsky, nor Hamsun, And I'm not attempting to explain just to clarify a long attempt at silence. For me its Goldman, le roi, Mailer

But I still love Picasso, Vincent van Gogh, etc. –

Dear Henry

When I left with Jean for France I was running away from a situation that had reached its peak.

I no longer could take the all night attempts to analyze my silence, I had thought that you knew me well.

And then to discover in France that Anais had entered an alliance with you that had eliminated all of our inherent understanding.

And all that + looking at your manuscript it all seemed so meaningless.

You see I'm your worst critic it was not the style that baffled me but the results.

I could not accept the name + the work.[19]

I still hate the Zionists the American world with few exceptions.

I wish I had strength enough + youth to give of myself to China.

I mean Mao Tse Tung's China, I believe in Mao.

He like you has much to give

All the best,

I still make no sense,

June

Notes

[1] YCAL MSS 472, Box 7, Folder 77, Henry Miller Papers, Series IV. Correspondence, Corbett, June ("Miller") / 1965-1972, undated.
[2] Bill Allen met Henry Miller back in the 1930s in Paris, and later coincidentally worked at the New York City Department of Welfare with June, both as statisticians of sorts. See Kenneth Dick, *Henry Miller: Colossus of One*, 210.
[3] Apparently, Miller had asked Annette Baxter, author of *Henry Miller: Expatriate* (1961), to help June by visiting her as early as, and possibly earlier than, 1961. See *Always Merry and Bright: The Life of Henry Miller* by Jay Martin (Capra Press, 1978), 459.
[4] Handwritten by Annette.
[5] This letter could come before or after the next one. Her references

to taxes in New York is probably an indirect appeal for money, which is the primary concern of both her and the Baxters' letters this winter and spring.

[6] The envelope is stamped January 23.

[7] *My Life and Times*; By Henry Miller. Illustrated. 208 pp. New York: Playboy Press. $17.95. One of America's glories, with 50 books and 80 years behind him," Anthony Burgess, *New York Times*, January 2, 1972.

[8] The only way to date this letter is by her reference to July, when she will no longer be working. It could come before the previous letter.

[9] Possibly not May, month is obscured.

[10] "Early" is as close as I could get to this word, though "recently" would make more sense. Dousing probably refers to baptism.

[11] She means "On Turning Eighty," Village Press (1973). The "Mexico border" is a little more obscure, though it likely refers to a lithograph of one of his watercolors.

[12] It is not clear which of Miller's films she is referring to – perhaps *Quiet Days in Clichy* (1970), *Tropic of Cancer* (1970), or one of the more recent TV documentaries.

[13] Miller's appearance on *The Merv Griffin Show* in October 1974 places this letter.

[14] Again, this second reference to *The Merv Griffin Show* allows us to place this undated letter here.

[15] This could be any number of surgeries or hospital stays. However, this letter likely comes in early 1973.

[16] Contrast this beautiful tribute with June's criticisms of the 1930s.

[17] This letter likely comes from the 1960s, but could be nearly anywhere in that sequence.

[18] These last two undated letters are the most interesting, since they directly address the "love triangle" with Anaïs Nin. In this first one, she attempts to explain her behavior before their split in Paris.

[19] This last letter includes a startling explanation from June of her behavior, and is of incredible value to Miller scholars. It is also valuable in itself, as an expression of a woman's point of view. Of course, it may be somewhat undercut by the declarations that follow.

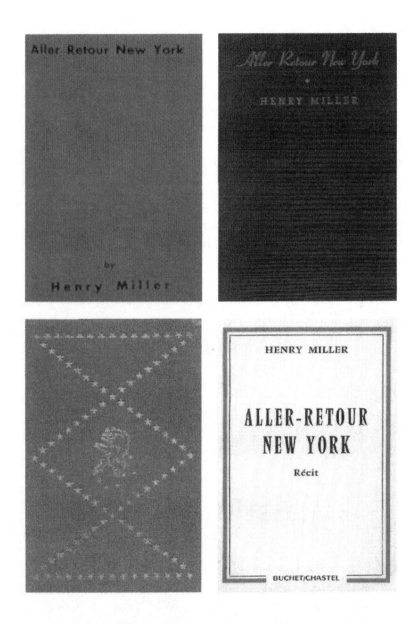

Top (l): First Edition (Paris: self-funded), 1935;   First American
Edition (Chicago: Ben Abramson) 1945.   Bottom (l):   First French
Edition (Lausanne, Switzerland: La Petite Ourse) 1956;   Second
French (Paris: Éditions Buchet/Chastel) 1962.

Never to Return: *Aller Retour New York* and Henry Miller's Shelved Epistle[1]

Wayne E. Arnold

On the 3rd of January in 1935, Henry Miller boarded the French Line *SS Champlain*, temporarily leaving Paris for New York City. While there, Miller continued his prolific writing, putting the finishing touches on the manuscript for *Black Spring* (1936). By May, he was set to return to France aboard the Dutch liner, *Vandeem II*. This short hiatus from Parisian expatriate life impacted Miller in various ways, but perhaps most significantly it revived his antipathy for New York City.[1] Shortly before setting sail for Paris, Miller began writing a departure letter to his friend Alfred Perlès who was living in Paris's Villa Seurat. Since Miller was to be shortly reunited with Perlès he continued writing the letter beyond his departure; following his bitter observations of New York City, the letter proceeds to his observations of the ship's Dutch passengers and finally concludes with Miller embracing his much-loved Paris. The epistle to Perlès was never mailed, as by the time Miller returned to Paris he realized that it was workable as a standalone publication. After some revising,[2] 150 pamphlets were self-published in October 1935 by the Obelisk Press and entitled *Aller Retour New York*. Dedicated to Perlès, Miller boasted that he now held the record for the longest letter written between the two men.

Often an overlooked publication, the background on the composition of *Aller Retour New York* has been noted and generalized by many Miller biographers. What has not been thoroughly explored is why, after its initial Paris publication, *Aller Retour* would appear in print only once in the United States during Miller's lifetime—and at that, privately printed in 1945. Miller considered the letter to be a "thing in itself," as he told William Gordon (Gordon and Miller 4). It was meant to stand in its own historical place. Due to its rather mysterious history, I undertake here to reveal the behind-the-scenes story from the initial publication in 1935 to the first official American publication of *Aller Retour New York* by New Directions in 1991. Archive materials reveal that Miller made attempts to republish the work and was at times frantic to have readily available copies for

---

[1] Primary source material by Henry Miller appearing in this article appears by special permission of Agence Hoffman – Paris, acting on behalf of the Henry Miller Estate.

sale or for personal reference. One critical fact that needs to be acknowledged is the concern over anti-Semitism[3] in the text, raised by select individuals after the 1945 private publication. Possible backlash over anti-Semitism deriving from *Aller Retour* remained in Miller's mind for several years and at times led him, or his publishers, to dismiss efforts of republication (Decker 161n13). The purpose of this research, however, is not to examine the content of the text but rather to follow the long and winding trail of letters surrounding *Aller Retour*, originating with the initial release and ending with the New Directions publication in 1991. What is revealed is an intriguing glimpse into both Miller's business practices as well as his intricate network of friends and publishers.

Five parts in the life of *Aller Retour New York* will be detailed in this article: the first publication in France; the second publication through Ben Abramson in 1945; the 1956 French translation and publication; a failed publication effort in the 1970s; and finally, the 1991 publication by New Directions, commemorating the centennial of Miller's birth. Throughout the first four stages, Miller wavers between actively promoting the publication and standing in reserved defense of the work.

The Short Road to Obscurity

Anaïs Nin offered the funding for the initial printing of *Aller Retour*, allowing Miller to self-publish through the Obelisk Press. It was printed under the Siana Series, a project established by Nin and Miller.[4] Upon returning to Paris in the summer of 1935, Miller was evolving into an established writer—even if on the periphery—bolstered with the 1934 publication of *Tropic of Cancer*. While *Black Spring* is usually considered his next significant work, *Aller Retour New York* was indeed his second publication of considerable length, albeit written after the composition and editing of *Black Spring*. Even though Nin provided the funds she was not enthused with Miller's letter, recording in her diary, "I consider [it] unimportant, but there Henry shows his lack of values and critical faculty. He is in love with his letters to Emil, et al.—all that represents his philosophy of imperfection, the cult of the natural" (Nin 117). The appearance of *Aller Retour* was extremely banal, unlikely to attract much attention with its bright red cover on which the title and author were plainly stated; the quality was also poor, being "printed on thin paper," as noted in the front matter. This thin paper was a publishing choice made by Jack Kakane, owner of Obelisk Press, who calculated that by using the thin "Indian paper," *Aller Retour* "could be posted by first-class mail" (Kahane 202), thereby broadening the potential audience base. At 152 pages, it was not intended to be a fully developed text and successfully marketing it proved difficult. In the Winter of 1935, Obelisk Press first advertised *Aller Retour* in their "Notes and News" flyer. The booklet was listed as "limited and signed" and available for 40 francs. By Spring of 1936, *Black Spring* was in the spotlight but the flyer notified readers that there were "still copies left of Henry Miller's extremely amusing little travel book, *Aller Retour New York*," now available for 35 francs (see Jackson, *Ephemera* 88, 93).

An important fact for future events, Obelisk Press made only one printing of the booklet. After this initial batch, for the next few years Miller anticipated a reprinting. Writing in early May 1937, Miller informed James Laughlin of New Directions that a "new illustrated edition of *Aller Retour*" would shortly be underway for 1938 (Miller and Laughlin 9). In the 1938 publication of Miller's *Max and The White Phagocytes*, the publisher's statement lists *Aller Retour New York* as being available in its "second imp." (*Max* 8). During that same year, Miller wrote to Francis Steloff of Gotham Book Mart that the book "is being reprinted in a regular Obelisk format—1,000 copies. At 30 Francs, I believe (about one dollar!)."[5] Miller was expecting Obelisk Press to print the next edition even as late as June 1939 (Miller and Nin 163).[6] Whatever the reasons (poor sales prospect being likely) Obelisk Press did not reprint, as Miller confirmed to Judson Crews in September 1946.[7] With only 150 originals, in the coming years *Aller Retour* would become a highly sought after Miller publication.

On Miller's end, sales for *Aller Retour* were promoted through subscription blanks, which Nin helped Miller post to various individuals. Marketed as No. 1 of the Siana Series, the booklet originally sold for 35 Francs, or $2.50, according to the publicity flyer—slightly cheaper than the Obelisk list price. Printed in October 1935, it was touted as "A Travel Letter by the author of *Tropic of Cancer*, a hilarious view of the recovery" (Jackson, *Ephemera* 85), a sarcastic reference to post-Depression New York City. Recipients of the flyer could detach the bottom portion for return, requesting one or several copies of the travel narrative. Miller also used the flyers as means of introduction to important figures in the Surrealist and Dada movements. For instance, he sent both Tristan Tzara and Andre Breton personal letters along with the *Aller Retour* flyer (Aleksic 151).[8] A key recipient of the first edition would be the

Gotham Book Mart. The inaugural communication between Miller and Steloff was accompanied with a copy of *Aller Retour*, in late 1935. Along with making his introduction, Miller's opening letter was also an attempt to boost the book's image:

> Dear Sirs:
> This limited edition of *Aller Retour New York* is being published at the author's expense, limited, as the announcement says, to one hundred copies. If you wish to order a few copies will you kindly communicate directly with Mr. Jack Kahane of the Obelisk Press. [...]. The book, *Aller Retour New York,* will be mailed post free, first class, in a sealed envelope. I might add that I am writing you at the suggestion of Mr. James Laughlin IV who has promised to have this *travel letter* published in serial form in the *Harvard Advocate*.[9]

The correspondence between Miller and Francis Steloff would continue for the next 35 years, but it is noteworthy that it began with Miller's self-promotion of *Aller Retour*. It soon became clear, though, that there existed no market seeking to buy a long-winded letter from one friend to another. Nin, due to her financial involvement of both *Aller Retour* and *What Are You Going to Do About Alf* (1935), lamented, "I predicted how people would feel about helping Fred [Perlès], for whom Henry wrote that humorous begging letter [*Alf*]. No response. His *Aller Retour New York*; no subscriptions to cover the expense and the response feeble" (167); Nin further noted, "people criticize *Aller Retour* as of little value" (177). Others in Miller's circle, including Herbert Read, Michael Frankael and Walter Lowenfels also seemed to hold low esteem for the missive, considering it unrepresentative of Miller's potential. Without sales, Miller was left with a stack of the booklets. So, in his typical Miller fashion, he got active and over the course of 1935-36 he started mailing and giving away copies of the pamphlet, signed in some cases, to various people.[10] Apparently, with the continued expectation of a second printing, Miller eventually sold or gave away all his copies of the little red book. The last reference to *Aller Retour* being mailed to the United States appears in May 1938 when Miller sent Gotham Book Mart an invoice for a shipment of books that was currently being held up by customs.[11]

A few partial republications of the 1935 edition, however, did appear elsewhere. The most important prepublication exposure for *Aller Retour* came from the aforementioned *Harvard Advocate*, in September 1935. The *Advocate* was edited by several students, led by John Slocum;[12] included among the ranks was James Laughlin, soon to become the founder of New Directions. The *Advocate* published the first eleven paragraphs of the text under the title "Glittering Pie,"[13] with the editors cautiously removing any potentially objectionable material. This partial publication led to the most notorious public incident to surround *Aller Retour*. One month after the publication of the *Advocate*, a former *Advocate* editor and Harvard graduate of 1902 wrote to *The Harvard Crimson*, the daily magazine of the university, expressing his disbelief that the recent issue of the *Advocate* had not been banned for indecency. Drawing attention to Miller, the former editor wrote: "the letter from an 'Expatriate', called 'Glittering Pie' is the smuttiest of vulgarity. Never, since its founding in '66, has the advocate printed such un-Harvardian trash" ("To the Editor"). The printing of this letter was an unfortunate choice by *The Harvard Crimson*, as the Chief of Police, Timothy Leahy, read the complaint and immediately set out to find a copy of the month-old *Advocate*. The very next day, the Chief banned issues of the *Advocate*, claiming that it contained articles considered "very obscene and vulgar" ("Police Ban"). Specifically, the Chief found objectionable the stories by James Laughlin and Miller. Concerning *Aller Retour*, *The Boston Globe* reported that the Chief "objected to the description of a song by a Paris dancer, Gypsy Rose Lee, in which Miss Lee is represented as placing a simple Hawaiian word in such way that it is easily susceptible of double interpretation" ("Police Ban"). Twice during the next week, the news about the banning would make the front page; ultimately, five of the student staff were forced into resignation to avoid prosecution.[14] Of the 1500 issues that were printed, 400 were brought to the police in order to be destroyed. The publicity surrounding the ban led to an unsurprising outcome: various Harvard students acquired copies of the *Advocate* and went around selling them for inflated prices of one dollar each, thus making *Aller Retour*—for a very short period—Miller's second sought-after banned writing ("Bootleg Banned"; also see MacNiven 91–92).

Miller kept abreast of the situation in Boston. Writing from the Villa Seurat to Frank Dobo on November 8, he concluded his letter by informing Dobo, "P.S. Just had word that the 2nd installment of 'Aller Retour' in the Harvard 'Advocate' was returned by the authorities in Boston. And this despite the dots and dashes employed. Heigh-ho![15] Miller further elaborated on the Harvard calamity to Lawrence Durrell at the end of November, observing:

"mine wasn't the only offending contribution. Seems a story by Laughlin himself was also responsible for the mess" (Miller and Durrell 8).[16] Significantly, even though the text was confiscated, Miller would be correct in believing that *Aller Retour* had not been officially censored by the government, and that it remained "indeterminate" concerning importation into the United States (Miller, "Four" 7).

Even with his brush with the authorities, James Laughlin risked going back to *Aller Retour* in 1936, with the first edition of New Directions' *New Directions in Prose & Poetry* including an excerpt from *Aller Retour* and *Black Spring*. Another sampling of the text came in 1937, when a partial French version was published in the April edition of *Europe* magazine.[17] Translated by Thérèse Aubray, who would also translate sections of *Black Spring*, the selections cover Miller's disgust for life in New York City then jump to his praise of Paris (Miller, "Aller Retour New York").[18] These reprintings may appear mundane, but I mention them to demonstrate Miller's tenacity in trying to reprint his work, always seeking new audiences and continuously promoting his previous writing. It is this tendency that makes the lack of an official American republication of *Aller Retour New York* during Miller's lifetime an intriguing aspect of the booklet's history.

While one review of the "travel letter" did appear, there were a few unsuccessful attempts to have other sections appear in France in addition to the *Europe* publication. Miller's friend Raymond Queneau was an active correspondent concerning the first publication of *Aller Retour*. During 1937, Miller suggested to Queneau that *Nouvelle Revue Française*, directed by Jean Paulhan, who would later come to the defense of *Tropic of Cancer* (Winslow 253), might publish a 25-page section of the booklet. Miller was also eyeing *Nouvelles Littéraires, Artistiques et Scientifiques* as a possible publication source. Neither of these publications materialized.[19] In 1937, Herbert F. West wrote in the *Dartmouth Alumni Magazine* the only known published review of the text,[20] and one of the first reviews on Miller in America. In the review, West writes that Miller "explains in plain terms why he prefers Paris to New York. He is not one of Malcolm Cowley's exiles who are too apt to be sentimental about themselves as members of 'the lost generation,' but instead is a bitter and amusing critic of the post-war demented world" (9). West's review, however, did little to add to the sales of the booklet.[21]

During 1939, Miller, ever the self-promoter, was proactive in ensuring that the New York Public Library held editions of all his publications. On March 16, 1939, he wrote the library director, H. M. Lydenberg, enquiring, among other things, if *Max and the White Phagocytes* was held in the library.[22] In a subsequent letter, Miller asked more specifically about *Aller Retour*. Writing to Gershon Legman in May 1939, Miller relates that the library now had all of his published works except for *Aller Retour*, with Miller complaining, "that was supposed to have been sent them by the Argus Book Shop man of Chicago—Ben Abramson. I'm beginning to think he's a dreamer" ("Four" 9). By March of 1940, Lydenberg reported to Miller that no copy of *Aller Retour* was at the library, but he was grateful for Miller's assistance in trying to locate a copy for their shelves.[23] Miller's mention of Ben Abramson is one of the earliest references to the Argus Book Shop and *Aller Retour*; as we will see, Abramson would become an important, if not frustrating, figure in the history of the epistle.

Publishing *Aller Retour New York* Stateside

Impending war forced Miller to leave France in 1939; by then he no longer possessed any Obelisk Press editions of *Aller Retour New York*. Even worse, he was without an original manuscript. For the next few years it seems that *Aller Retour* dropped off into the background without Miller giving it much thought. During this time, he spent several months in Greece, wrote *The Colossus of Maroussi* (1941) while in New York City, and traversed the United States working on *The Air-Conditioned Nightmare* (1945). In July 1940, Miller handed over to John Slocum a large selection of his writings for safekeeping; when he did so, he made a list of the contents, but there is no reference to *Aller Retour*.[24] It was not until early 1943, when Miller had chosen California as his new residence, that *Aller Retour* became a major topic of conversation between Miller and more than one correspondent.

An important figure to enter Miller's life during the early 1940s was the young poet Judson Crews. Crews had become familiar with Miller through George Leite's magazine, *Circle*, and for a time he joined Miller in Big Sur. While primarily a poet and novelist, Crews would eventually begin his own small-scale publishing company. In January 1943, Crews wrote Miller concerning possible republication costs for *Aller Retour* and *Black Spring*. Miller was quick to reply, as there was a growing demand for these works from his readers in the United States. He told Crews that there were people desperate to buy *Aller Retour* for any suggested price. Crews had remarked that locating a copy for the publisher was proving difficult, to which Miller showed no surprise as he believed "very few [copies] ever entered the country."[25] In an October 27th letter, Miller again reiterates the desire to find a copy, also making clear that he had been unsuccessfully looking for the 1935 edition since returning to the United States.[26] This situation likely frustrated Miller, and he must have been kicking himself for his lack of foresight in not retaining at least one copy of the text.

Shortly after Crews began talking about *Aller Retour*, Miller brought Francis Steloff, of the Gotham Book Mart, into the search for a copy of the text. After asking if Steloff might be interested in reprinting *Money and How It Gets That Way*, he also added on a second option: "There's also the *Aller Retour New York* which should be done soon; it's a small volume, few copies ever reached America, and it's always in demand." Miller added, "I have no copies of either of these myself. I suppose there's a slim chance of ever getting one, eh?"[27] He would again reiterate the scarcity of the text and his need for both *Aller Retour* and *Black Spring*, stressing, "I want them badly."[28] While staying in Hollywood, Miller informed Steloff that "Ben Abramson would like to reprint *Aller Retour N.Y.* I asked Glen Jocelyn if he could lend a copy but he has none. Wonder if you could dig one up from one of your clients—perhaps [John] Slocum?"[29] Gotham Book Mart served as a strategic avenue through which Miller hoped to locate a copy of the original text, but Steloff was unable to procure a copy and she made sure to lament this predicament to Miller.[30] Reiterating the pressing need, Miller wrote Steloff in February 1943, again suggesting that "[John] Slocum has a copy of *Aller Retour*, I'm sure. And there are other customers of yours who also have copies. Do you keep advertising for it?"[31] Miller's confidence that Slocum held a copy stems back to the 1935 incident with the police confiscation of the *Harvard Advocate*. Yet, these suggestions were to no avail, as by December 23, 1943, he was again requesting if Steloff would be able to locate a copy of the text, imploring, "Please answer!"[32]

In a different arena, Chicago's book selling scene in the 1930s and 1940s was dominated by the Argus Book shop, owned by Ben Abramson. Miller became aware of Argus Books while in France and during the late 1930s Abramson and Miller began a correspondence. While traveling across the United States, gathering material for *The Air-Conditioned Nightmare*, Miller stopped in Chicago in March 1941 and met Abramson for the first time (Jackson, *Writers Three* 22). Shortly thereafter, Abramson would make it clear that along with printing *The World of Sex* (1941), he also wanted to bring out *Aller Retour New York*. Miller and Abramson had previously discussed *Aller Retour*, as Miller expected Abramson to supply the New York Public Library with a 1935 copy, but Abramson had been unable to do so as he likely did not have a copy of the text. As early as February 1943, Miller and Abramson were going so far as to discuss the type of binding in which *Aller Retour* might appear, either cloth or paper.[33] Even a year later, in letters to Miller during January 1944, Abramson was reaffirming his commitment to this publishing project. What would continue to be a stumbling block would be securing an original copy of the Obelisk Press edition.

While Miller had been searching the United States for a copy of *Aller Retour New York*,[34] he had learned the whereabouts of a few copies. Unfortunately, the task of getting a copy in-hand for Abramson proved time consuming and arduous. To Crews and other correspondents, Miller noted that he knew of an individual with an available copy,[35] but he never mentioned the person's name. While the exact identity of who provided the 1935 printing to Abramson remains uncertain, there are a few likely candidates to consider. Among those Miller had requested to keep a look out for the book was James Laughlin, the former *Harvard Advocate* editor and now owner of New Directions publishing company. Laughlin owned an original copy that Miller had sent him in 1935. In December 1944, Laughlin wrote Miller that he had received word from Abramson concerning a possible American publication of *Tropic of Capricorn* as well as a request for Laughlin's copy of *Aller Retour New York*. At the time, Laughlin was on an extended business trip at his ski lodge in Alta, Utah, and was unable to send Abramson the book, but promised to do so when he finally returned to the East. Another person to consider at this time was Anaïs Nin. Years later, in 1949, Nin was planning on relocating back to New York City; much of her book collection had been on sale at a book store in San Francisco and had not been sold. Among the rare books that she sent to Kathryn Winslow (owner of M: The Studio for Henry Miller, in Chicago) was "*Aller Retour New York*, original edition. $8" (Winslow 232). In the correspondence taking place between Miller, George Howard and Nin in the early 1940s, concerning certain pornographic writings, Nin may have been made aware of the need to provide Abramson a copy of the original text and may have therefore loaned him her copy. Elsewhere, two letters from Abramson to Miller in late 1943 and early 1944 express frustration with Huntington Cairns, the U. S. Federal Censor who provided advice to the Treasury

Department on which books should be banned from being imported into the United States. Cairns had promised to send along his copy of the booklet, but Abramson notes that he "seemed rather reticent because being an official with the Government he hesitates to send a book which is illegal to send."[36] A fourth and most likely candidate to supply a copy of the book was the aforementioned George Howard, friends with Miller and J. Rives Childs and an avid collector of erotica. Abramson and Howard had spoken on the phone in January 1944 and Abramson reported to Miller that Howard's copy was unfortunately hidden away amid a large assortment of boxes in Abramson's own basement, and that not much could be done about locating it.[37] In March 1944, after the shipments of these boxes to Howard, Miller would write to Howard's wife, Eleanor, enquiring if she had sent the book to Abramson, and if not, Miller wanted to know if they might have it typewritten and sent in that form, presumably skirting around the issue of mailing contraband books.[38] In April, Eleanor struck upon the idea of requesting the Library of Congress to send photostats. Miller loved the solution, but added for safety that if the Library of Congress would not supply the photostats, would Eleanor handle the situation?[39] It does not seem likely that the Gotham Book Mart secured a copy of the text for Miller as the letters with Steloff infrequently reference *Aller Retour*; specific mention of the text does occur again on August 20 1944, when Miller tells Steloff that the book has been proofed and that he is expecting shipment very soon.[40] Whether Abramson received an original copy or photostats of *Aller Retour* remains unclear as it appears that some of Abramson's letters are not included in the University of California, Los Angeles collection.

Nevertheless, by the middle of May 1944, Miller wrote Crews that Abramson now had a copy of *Aller Retour*, delivered "from a friend of mine," and it had been sent on to the printer for proof setting.[41] Once Abrams had the copy of *Aller Retour*, things started to move more quickly. Abramson's original idea was to bring out two editions. The first 100 would be printed on special quality paper and signed by Miller. These would be sold for $10 or $12.50, a rather steep price for the time. The rest of the copies would be sold for a street price of $5.00. The eventual printing was for 500 regular hardback issues with no slip cover, sequentially numbered with no signature, and printed by Nate Roth of Chicago, but bound in New York. Even with apparent printer issues, Miller had a proof copy by June 6th, 1944; but then trouble with Roth resurfaced. By November,

Roth was also engaged with printing J. O. Bailey's *Pilgrims Through Space and Time* (1947), which subsequently held up the printing of *Aller Retour*. Due to an unforeseen medical emergency with Roth—a hernia operation—things continued to be delayed and in April 1945, Abramson was still waiting for Roth to send the 500 copies.[42] More setbacks ensued, including concern over how to mail the copies to Miller without losing them to the police. May rolled into June with no book in hand. Things started to move in the right direction, however, as Miller wrote Crews on June 26th that he had just finished reading the proof of the new book. Finally, in August 1945, Abramson had 100 copies of *Aller Retour* on hand, but it would not be until November of 1946 that the binding company would finally provide the next 400 copies, all printed for private circulation (Shifreen and Jackson 51–52).[43] Of those 100, Abramson had already secured several orders through his mailing catalogues, but he was reluctant to fill every order until he had the remaining 400 books on hand.[44] These issues aside, from August 1945 to November 1946, whenever Miller made purchase requests for *Aller Retour*, Abramson's stock of 100 remained sufficient to meet these orders.[45]

Due to the printing delays and the rather expensive price for the book, Miller began looking to print a cheaper, pamphlet version through Judson Crews, with the help of Walker Winslow.[46] In July, 1946 Miller suggested that Crews contact Abramson about the possibility of getting permission for printing a mass market edition.[47] For a few years Miller and Crews had pondered whether *Aller Retour* was officially a banned book, with Miller telling Crews in 1944, that "to tell the truth, there is very little which is objectionable in *Aller Retour*."[48] Finally, in September 1946, Miller replied to Crews's continued questioning, "Why don't you write Huntington Cairns yourself and see [if the book is banned]. I think he is still the unofficial censor"; Miller concluded with, "No, I don't think he banned the book."[49] Crews was concerned that releasing a publicly available version of *Aller Retour* might bring legal repercussions. Abramson, however, was not keen on the idea of a cheaper version, as he was contemplating printing one himself as well as a combined version of Miller's *Aller Retour* and Alfred Perlès response letter, "Aller Sans Retour London" (1946). With the slow sales and continued publication woes, by October 1946 Miller conceded that Crews had "better drop the idea for the time being—I guess Abramson would mind."[50] The slow sales of the Abramson edition meant that Miller would not find justification in the 1940s to pursue publication elsewhere in the United States.[51]

Two significant historical points arise concerning the reception of the second edition of *Aller Retour New York*. The first is the serious and legitimate claim of anti-Semitism that surfaced shortly after the printing. In the emerging post-Holocaust environment, negative sentiment toward Jewish people was in decline, "with the most significant change occurring from 1946 to 1951" (Dinnerstein 151). In this environment, it did not take long for Miller to begin hearing about anti-Semitic accusations leveled against *Aller Retour*. Perhaps the most damning criticism to Miller came from Albert E. Kahn,[52] in his now infamous January 1945 *New Currents* magazine article entitled, "Odyssey of a Stool Pigeon." Kahn attacked Miller and his work (without specific mention of *Aller Retour*), labeling him "a fascist, anti-Semitic propagandist and a former labor spy" (Kahn 3). Similar claims followed — perhaps fueled by Kahn's article — and in November 1945, Abramson wrote Miller that he was gathering together the negative feedback from a handful of booksellers who were accusing Miller of anti-Semitism. While Abramson does not mention that *Aller Retour* was driving this backlash, it does seem that some booksellers were furious that Abramson had been printing and spreading Miller's works, with one of the booksellers likening Abramson to "being a combination of Judas, Hitler, and the monster of Nuremburg."[53] For a period, this negative feedback became Miller's primary focus.

Miller was concerned for both his reputation as well as being misconstrued as anti-Semitic. It was probably very shocking for him to receive a letter on January 7, 1945 that directly tied these rumors to his publisher, New Directions. Immediately after reading the letter, Miller wrote to James Laughlin, quoting from the letter he had just received while complying with the sender's request for anonymity:

> 'I was talking with a young Jewish bookseller last week about your work and after a little hemming and hawing he said he had been told you were violently anti-Semitic and was it true? I have run into this before and I am sure you have too. However, there is one angle which *is* a bit startling! He told me his informant was a bird named George Stewart (I think), a salesman for New Directions! This ND emissary told him that Laughlin had refused to publish some book which you had submitted because of its anti-Semitism.'[54]

Importantly, Miller goes on to reference Kahn's article as helping to stir up these rumors, especially after Kahn's work had been reprinted in the January edition of *The Daily Worker*. Miller requested Laughlin to try and determine what was going on and to hopefully calm things down, concluding his letter with, "I will soon be regarded as America's No. 1 Jew-baiter."[55] It must have been a long wait for Miller before he received Laughlin's January 20th reply from Norfolk, Virginia. In the letter, Laughlin immediately responds to Miller's questioning, admitting that he had heard the claims, noting at length: "As far as I can tell it springs from something in *Aller Retour* [...]. The talk seems to be being pushed by somebody because Stewart, the salesman, reports that he has run into it in several cities." Laughlin defended Stewart, whom he believed tried to squash such rumors since, if Miller were to be considered anti-Semitic, that would hurt Stewart's commissions. Additionally, Laughlin denied that he had avoided Miller's works: "The story of my having refused some book of yours for that reason is new to me — possibly invented by whomever it is who is spreading the rumors."[56] The claim against Miller affected him deeply, and many of his letters around this period (1946 specifically) touch on his disquietude over being labeled an anti-Semite.[57] From this point forward, *Aller Retour* would be tinged with the fear of it being labeled anti-Semitic and the subject would repeatedly reappear.

Lack of reviews was the second negative impact on this new edition of *Aller Retour New York*. Since the book was privately published, there was no openly public promotion. Nevertheless, Abramson was proactive in trying to secure a review for the book, having sent Edmund Wilson a copy of the text. Wilson had briefly corresponded with Miller in 1939 after the appearance of his review for *Tropic of Cancer*.[58] Yet, Wilson was not keen on reviewing *Aller Retour*. In May 1946, Abramson wrote Miller that he had spoken with Wilson concerning the text. Wilson, Abramson explained, felt that Miller's works were appearing too quickly in succession. Abramson defended Miller, noting that there was a backlog of his works that had yet to see American publications. For his prolific writing, Miller should be praised rather than avoided, Abramson believed.[59] Regardless of this argument, Wilson remained firm, and there is no record of any published review according to Shifreen's *Henry Miller: A Bibliography of Secondary Sources* (1979). Without the needed publicity in the literary magazines, Miller and Abramson depended on their customer mailing lists to promote *Aller Retour*.

Sales for *Aller Retour* were relatively meager, selling far slower than had been hoped. Over the next several years, Miller and Abramson continued their correspondence, which included notes on the sales of the book. Perhaps due to the complications in the business relationship between Miller and Abramson, Miller wrote a detailed letter to Abramson on July 1st, 1949. In the letter, Miller requested to know how many copies of *Aller Retour* were still available. He also provided his personal opinion about the difficulties over the sales of the publication, noting:

> The way I feel about the two books [*World of Sex* and *Aller Retour*] which I presume are now nearing exhaustion is that it hasn't been worth while. If we can not get on to some fresh and more concrete basis, then I would prefer to see the editions run out. I have no particular new publisher in mind. I may not even look for one. But I do know I would rather see them out of print than carry on the way we have.[60]

Miller felt frustrated in dealing with Abramson, a feeling he had expressed in letters to Crews and Laughlin. In Abramson's reply, he explains that his motives for publishing Miller's books had been for monetary profit, but neither book had been able to repay the publishing expenses involved. Additionally, after moving to New York State, the Argus Book Shop had since declined from the prominence it once held in Chicago, consequently hurting Miller's sales. At the end of July, Miller reiterated his desire to let the editions run out, with no new editions intended for press. Letters dated in late 1951, April 1953, and February 1954[61] record a total of 18 copies of *Aller Retour* being mailed directly to Miller for resale. Through the Abramson-Miller correspondence, it becomes clear that the 500 copies printed in 1945/46 were slow movers, and an apparent loss of investment for the Argus Book Shop. When Abramson died in 1955, it is not clear how many copies of *Aller Retour* were still available, but it is certain that the publication was selling less than 50 copies a year.

Interim I: Distant Lands

Between the Abramson pressing in 1945 and the French version in 1956, Miller continued to consider *Aller Retour New York* for future publication. The specter of anti-Semitism certainly caused Miller and his publishers some concern, but it quickly becomes clear when reading the letters after 1946 that Miller did not find the text completely reprehensible. While the Argus Book Shop did hold copies of the text into early 1954,[62] Miller had been in communication with foreign publishers concerning the text. Two specific examples include interest by the German publisher Esto, to whom Miller wrote in July 1951, suggesting both *Aller Retour New York* and *The World of Sex* as possible publications since Miller held the copyrights.[63] In 1954, Meredith Weatherby, who represented Miller's Japanese publisher, Shincho Sha, wrote to Agence Hoffman requesting a copy of *Aller Retour* be sent to Japan.[64] Shincho Sha already provided a large selection of Miller's works printed in Japanese and were looking to expand due to increasing interest from their reading public.[65] Neither of these publications came to fruition, yet these efforts again demonstrate Miller's diligence in trying to republish the text for a larger audience through an international distributor.

Aller Retour to France

Slow sales of the American edition of *Aller Retour* did not prevent Miller from pursuing publication in the country where he was most successful and respected: France. As early as 1948, Miller was corresponding with Maurice Girodias, of Olympia Press, to determine if it would be feasible to print *World of Sex* and *Aller Retour New York*, as they had not been published in the French language.[66] Girodias had been slow in responding to Miller's request, and there was a bit of pressuring on Miller's part to get an answer. "I asked you several times, but no answer: what about the other books due for publication — will you be going ahead with just the same?" Miller wrote, "And what of 'The World of Sex' and 'Aller Retour New York' [...]. Will you be able to absorb all these within a 'reasonable' period — or do you want to permit some of them to be allocated to other French publishers?"[67] Miller was also a bit peeved about the inability to receive his royalties from Olympia Press, so it is no surprise then that he would look elsewhere, eventually finding a venue in Switzerland through Guilde du Livre. In July 1953, Miller wrote to Perlès that he had contacted Albert Mermoud at Guilde du Livre "about 'our' *Aller Retour*. Said if no go, to send it to George [Belmont], who is quite sure he can place it — even if taken by Guilde, may find French reprint editor — they often do this with Guilde books."[68] Mermoud went with Miller's suggestion to reprint *Aller Retour*; due to Miller's popularity in France, the work was first edited by Miller and then translated into French. According to Shifreen and Jackson, the French version of the third edition of *Aller Retour* was published on February 25, 1956 — reprinted in a fourth edition in 1962 — and translated by Dominique Aury (Shifreen and Jackson 53). This expanded and revised French edition was issued in a sizeable quantity of 10,300 copies;[69] additionally, Miller prepared a special preface and a postface for the publication. The postface was again a letter to Alfred Perlès, written over several days in May, 1954, from Big Sur. It would eventually be published in its original English form as "Reunion in Barcelona" (1959). It bears little connection with *Aller Retour* except for its recipient. In contrast, it is the preface to the 1956 edition that highlights some of the troubling publication history originating with the 1945 version.

Yet to be published in its English version, the preface to the French edition of *Aller Retour New York* is an important document concerning Miller and the topics written about in the travel narrative. Surprisingly, it does not seem Miller made any attempt to publish the English version. Originally typed in English, the six-page preface has two differing versions with distinct altercations from the first to the second, final draft.[70] From my perception, the first draft is written with a more personal tone. Comparing the two drafts reveals some of the mannerisms by which Miller smooths out his writing; however, the major differences in content appear on the first page with Miller almost immediately addressing the accusations of anti-Semitism:

> There is only one element of the picture about which I have misgivings, and that is the harsh, prejudiced references to the Jews. I am not an Anti-Semite. I have frequently been accused of being one, because of certain passages in other of my works [*sic.*] which were blatantly caricatural and offensive. I have really no excuse to offer for my attitude. I must confess that I did wage a debate with myself, on the eve of this publication in French, as to the validity of deleting the most flagrant passages reflecting on the Jews. I concluded, however, that it was better to leave the text unaltered and let the reader judge for himself whether I am to be condemned or not.[71]

Crucially, this paragraph in the first version is entirely crossed out after the word "Anti-Semite"; in its place, Miller handwrote sentences that more closely match the second version of the preface. Once finalized, Miller's new section would read as follows:

> There is one element of the text about which I have had misgivings, and that is the harsh, seeming unjustifiable references to the Jews. Of my own volition I have consequently toned down some passages and expunged others. I am not an anti-

Semite. I am not anti-anything, though I have caricatured, ridiculed, fulminated, bombinated and blasphemed to my heart's content throughout the great body of my writings.[72]

Apparently, Miller's fear of being labeled anti-Semitic carried on from the 1945-46 incidents surrounding Abramson's publication. To go through with the French publication, Miller felt compelled to modify the text in order to reduce any potential backlash.

Another marked departure between the preface versions comes in the penultimate paragraph. Miller concludes by reiterating his disgust with New York, claiming that he wants nothing more to do with it. Looking back to 1940, after returning to New York City from Greece and Paris, Miller recalls how shocked he was that he could so quickly fall back into the depressing doldrums that had caused his original flight to Paris. The initial draft of the preface gives insight into how Miller found solace in New York in 1940: "If I had not found a few intimate friends, such as Abraham Rattner, Bezalel Schatz, Emil White, Ephraim Doner, all painters and all one hundred percent *Kosher*, I would now be stark mad."[73] Noticeably, Miller was trying to establish his numerous friendships with Jewish artists to help reduce the impact of the anti-Semitic sections of the original text. After he had modified the text, however, the second version of the preface replaces these sentences to focus on 1940 and his difficulty in dealing with his homeland and the failing health of his father: "From the heights I was thrown to the depths, depths blacker than any I had known in the days of youth. When finally I succeeded in tearing myself away, a difficult task since my father was then dying, when finally I set out to have a look at the rest of the country, I found that all America was nothing but a nightmare — 'an air-conditioned nightmare.'"[74] There are other slight differences between the two drafts; interestingly, the sentences in the first draft, calling attention to the anti-Semitism, shift the focus to his other publications. This diversion suggests that Miller (while certainly aware of the negative impact) was not pinpointing *Aller Retour* as the sole source — or even the significant source — of the anti-Semitic claims arising in 1945 and 1946.

One final aspect worth noting in the drafts of the preface and the postface are the composition dates. Both the draft and the published version of the postface are dated as having been started on May 1st, 1954 and completed on May 19th (Miller, "Reunion" 13, 33). In contrast, the first draft of the preface only states "May 1954," whereas the second draft is dated "May 21, 1954." After these dates,

Miller made multiple grammatical edits as can be attested by the three copies in the archive folder at University of California, Los Angeles. Significantly, these given dates mark when Miller began and completed writing, thereby placing the composition of the preface after that of the postface. I mention this disparity in dates to suggest that the preface was an afterthought, a needed clarification for the contents of *Aller Retour*. As Miller wrote the postface and considered a republication of the text, he must have had misgivings concerning a potential public outcry. The preface and postface were written a year and half before the book would be published in Switzerland, but by November of 1954 Miller was requesting Perlès to bring with him to Big Sur "the Preface & Postface to *Aller Retour* — I have two strong nibbles from foreign publishers and no carbons of either here."[75] It is clear from the preface and the revisions to the text that Miller was taking the steps he felt needed to ensure that the French version of *Aller Retour* would not stir up the painful memories surrounding the 1945 version.

Interim II: Memorandum

Following the third and fourth editions, the next years were relatively quiet concerning *Aller Retour New York*, and during this time, Miller enjoyed the successful sales of the French edition of *Aller Retour*. In 1957, Miller received a letter from Miron Grindea, editor of the long-running *ADAM International*, based in London. Grindea asked Miller to provide a text for an upcoming issue of the literary magazine. Miller did not have anything readily available, replying to Grindea on June 16th that he was thinking of sending on the postface to *Aller Retour*, which up to then had only been published in French. Miller suspected that the length of the postface was too long, and perhaps as a result, nothing by Miller was published in the magazine during 1957.[76] A year later, Miller worked with The New American Library to have the postface, now titled "Reunion in Barcelona," included in *The Intimate Henry Miller* (1959). While The New American Library did publish "Reunion in Barcelona," it was first published two months prior by John Rolph of Scorpion Press in February 1959 (Shifreen and Jackson 317). Rolph had been in contact with both Miller and Perlès concerning this little publication. In his letters, Rolph informed Perlès about the project and asked him to provide a companion piece: "Henry suggests you might have something to offer us — of similar length or round about 40 pages. I wondered whether you would like to do a letter in reply to the 'Aller Retour' one? — It would make a nice sequel."[77] Due to an outdated mailing address, the letter to Perlès failed to arrive in time to be included in the Miller publication, but Rolph's prompting for a sequel to "Reunion in Barcelona" encouraged Perlès to write "Reunion in Big Sur," which was published in in a separate Scorpion Press booklet in 1959.

At New Directions, James Laughlin, who was now assisted by Robert MacGregor, began rereading the text in 1961. On May 25th, Laughlin sent MacGregor an in-house memorandum, with the subject: "Miller's 'Aller Retour.'" In the memo, Laughlin wrote, "I now see why it was that I declined to publish it for him earlier. It is because it contains a number of references that might well be interpreted as anti-Semitic."[78] Laughlin was certain that Miller held no such position, but the reading public might construe things differently. Instead of being anti-Semitic, Laughlin considered the possibility that Miller was employing humor or imitating certain stereotypes he had witnessed in New York City. Laughlin deliberated bringing the piece out in an anthology or some other format, suggesting that "if [Miller] would clean it up a little bit in that respect, it is a rather amusing piece of writing—more or less just a long letter, attacking New York and American life."[79] The very next day, MacGregor wrote Miller and conveyed Laughlin's thoughts, with the assumption that Miller would want to rewrite sections of *Aller Retour* if it were to be brought out in the United States (Miller and Laughlin 194). By June 20, Miller had nixed the idea, with MacGregor approving and suggesting they put the project on hold for the time being. A few other letters that year imply that Miller preferred to leave *Aller Retour* unrevised and unpublished for a modern American audience.[80]

One More Attempt to Return: A Millerite Emerges

Except for an intriguing publication effort that took place in the late 1960s and into the early 1970s, the French version might have been the last significant event in the history of *Aller Retour* until its fifth edition published in 1991. During this period, however, an interchange began between Miller and an individual who took it upon himself to seek out a new publication of *Aller Retour*—until all avenues were pursued. I would classify the correspondence between G. William "Bill" Arnold[81] and Miller as that of a prolonged case of fan mail, spanning over 15 years.[82] Starting in the early 1960s, Arnold began writing Miller while a University of Massachusetts student, praising Miller's work and requesting various items for his personal collection. After graduating, Arnold worked as an adjunct professor at Massasoit Community College in Massachusetts and continued writing Miller. In 1966, Arnold's conversation became more focused on the historical background of Miller's time in New York City during the 1930s. He would soon come to view *Aller Retour New York* as the most important book in Miller's oeuvre, and in his opinion, this period represented Miller at his prime; Arnold felt the lack of readily available copies meant that there was a pressing need to give American readers the real Miller found within *Aller Retour*.

In June 1966, Arnold began questioning Miller about his 1935 trip to New York City, asking him to "spill the beans" about his psychoanalysis practice.[83] He also informed Miller that the Gotham Book Mart was sending him a copy of the 1945 publication of *Aller Retour* for $7.50. Once in his possession, Arnold began encouraging (in some cases pushing) Miller to consider republishing the book in America, and by early July he was lamenting that no biographies mention the book in detail.[84] Arnold made himself very clear: "*Aller Retour NY* has jewels sprinkled throughout which will shine through the blackest historical cellophane. Not even that could wrap it in! *Aller Retour NY* should come out in paperback."[85] Throughout the letters in 1966, Arnold expresses his enthusiasm, even suggesting he write an introduction to the text in order to properly place it in 1930s milieu; concerning the republication efforts, he offered "to do any leg-work if the idea appeals to you."[86] Reminiscent of the discussion between Miller and Crews in 1946, Arnold believed a cheaper version of *Aller Retour* should be available, something less than $1.00. He lamented that the reprinted section of "Glittering Pie" did little to bring to life what Arnold believed was Miller's most valuable "period piece." In response, Miller seems to have tried to diffuse Arnold's enthusiasm for the project by informing him that, "I'm waiting for Grove Press to bring out 'Aller Retour N.Y.' It was published in a revised edition, with a preface by me, some years back. I lost my copy and haven't been able to find another yet."[87] While Arnold's letters are often charged with a bombastic flair, he does occasionally make valid observations. In these early letters on *Aller Retour*, he aptly highlights that, "Written as it was in letter form it generates warmth not found in other American pieces [of that period]. It would not only broaden an understanding of your writing—but offer another dimension to the 'depression' writing written with downcast, heavy heart, no hope, fatalistic finality."[88] During the mid-60s, Avon Press was producing cheap reprints of 1930s literature, such as Nathanael West's *A Cool Million*, and Arnold felt that Avon would be a sure bet for Miller's book. This prodding seems to have revived Miller's interest in the book, but it would take a few more years to receive Miller's blessing on the undertaking.

Nearly two years passed with Arnold only mentioning *Aller Retour* once in 1968. By this time, Arnold had become acquainted with Jon and Louise Webb, of Loujon Press and discussed his project with them. On January 14, 1968, the Webbs wrote Arnold saying that they would be interested in printing *Aller Retour* but that they were only in the market for limited print editions, which would defeat the purpose of a mass market version.[89] Arnold conveyed this message to Miller on January 17th, also lamenting that *Aller Retour* had not yet appeared from Grove Press. During the interim between 1966 and 1968, Arnold had written an article for a graduate seminar in American Literature, entitled, "Henry Miller: Man Against the Crowd." This manuscript, he believed, would provide historical context for *Aller Retour* and serve as a meaningful introduction to the text. After multiple revisions, Arnold mailed the text to Miller on December 6th, 1968, considering it "my justification of a re-print — arguing that *Aller Retour* is the most socially conscious book of the 30's and by an American of the Decade."[90] If Miller refused, Arnold asked him to send the introduction on to a publisher as Arnold believed his introduction held merit and he wanted to see it in print. Unfortunately for Arnold the dispatch of the text was ill-timed, as it was returned on December 13th. Miller's secretary, Gerald Robitaille, informed Arnold that Miller was unable to read the manuscript due to a recent bout with pneumonia, and while Miller would like to see *Aller Retour* reprinted, he had no publisher to recommend for the publication. One glimmer of hope for Arnold appeared in that Miller acquiesced — without yet reading — to the idea of Arnold's essay serving as the introduction to a potential reprint.

Additional letters between late 1968 and early 1969 make it clear that Miller was too busy with other work to devote the time he needed to rewrite the text for a new publication. The letters become more pressing during 1969, with Arnold constantly reiterating his willingness to do the leg work in finding a suitable publisher. He also strongly believed that Miller should not rewrite the text, as it would take away the flare of the 1930s that Arnold so valued. At the end of January, Arnold suggested that the University of Massachusetts Press might be interested in bringing out an edition of *Aller Retour New York*. Indeed, through Arnold's initiative, the university press was intrigued, but they did not want to use Arnold's preface. Instead, they suggested that Miller write a new preface with which they might be able to move forward on the project. With a reputable press showing interest, by March 1969 Miller was more enthusiastic concerning the possibility of a new publication. He read Arnold's manuscript with approval and wrote to Arnold requesting the details that UMass Press could offer in terms of copies, royalties and advances on *Aller Retour*. Arnold took charge of the communication with the press, only to report to Miller in May of 1969 that UMass Press had chosen to pass on the book, citing that it was too commercial for their smaller, select publications.[91]

Rejection from UMass Press seems only to have fueled Arnold's efforts in securing a publisher for a project that now appeared to have Miller's backing. Throughout the next year, Arnold undertook the leg-work he had offered to perform. Next on the list to receive the introduction and a copy of *Aller Retour* was Doubleday & Company, a publisher who had a rocky relationship with Miller; they also declined *Aller Retour*, adding, "even if we made an offer he would probably reject it."[92] Knopf Publishers was also added to the rejection list. John Cushman Associates, representing Curtis Brown Ltd., declined in January 1970, considering the subject of Arnold's introduction "too academic for anything but a university press."[93] Letters from Miller during this period make it clear that he no longer owned a personal copy of either the Abramson or the French version, and Miller's lack of a text helped Arnold stoke Miller's interest in having *Aller Retour* readily available.[94]

In February 1970, Arnold began working more closely with Herbert West in an effort to have the Henry Miller/Herbert West correspondence published, roughly 150 letters, an idea to which Miller had also given his written approval. The Miller/West correspondence spanned the 1930s and 40s and covered a variety of topics, including discussion of *Aller Retour*. Arnold and West had formed a cordial friendship and both men felt that the correspondence would prove interesting to fellow Miller aficionados. Arnold visited Dartmouth College with West in late February to examine the 1935 copy of *Aller Retour* and to collate the Miller/West letters in order to approach a single publisher with both projects.[95] Arnold was confident that the Miller/West correspondence would parallel the importance of the Miller/Durrell letters, and he tentatively titled the unpublished work, *An American Correspondence*.[96] Still, the prior rejections were discouraging and Arnold lamented to West that he believed some of the larger publishers had rejected the text because "they want the list by the author, not a single work."[97] While waiting for the photocopies of the

Miller/West correspondence from Dartmouth College Library, Arnold approached an additional publisher with renewed confidence.

When John Cushman turned down the *Aller Retour* project, he had suggested that Arnold try Walker Cowen at The University Press of Virginia. On the second of February, Arnold wrote to Cowen concerning the manuscript. Cowen was quick to reply, recalling his own interest in the text: "Some years ago I asked Miller about reprinting this and he was against the idea at that time. I'm glad that he has changed his mind and that you have taken up the project."[98] As it would turn out, the UP of Virginia would be the closest *Aller Retour* would come to seeing a 1970 publication. After Arnold sent on the photocopies of both his introduction and Miller's text, Cowen replied that if approved by the Board of Directors, an original printing of 2000 copies, no advance payment and standard trade royalties on the book could be offered.[99] Finally, in March 1970, Arnold heard the news that he had been waiting for: The University Press of Virginia would print *Aller Retour New York*—with one catch, however. Due to its length, Arnold's introduction would be dropped from the book. While this news may have disappointed Arnold, Miller's reply to the offer dashed all of Arnold's hopes. Even before UP of Virginia informed Arnold that it would accept the project, on February 27, 1970 Miller wrote the following to Arnold, rejecting their meager offer:

> Frankly, I don't think the proposal by Univ. of Va. Press worth my time and effort. In the first place I would not want book [*sic.*] reprinted *as is.* I made many correction and cuts when I thought Girodias would reprint some years back. I could never retrieve these pages from him, unfortunately. So I would have to do job all over again—and I lack time.[100]

Miller concluded the letter with, "Please forgive me!", obviously aware of the time and effort Arnold had put in to the project over the last three years. Crucial to note here is the difference in opinion between Miller and Arnold concerning the state of *Aller Retour.* Miller was firmly against reprinting the book in its original form while Arnold was arguing for the importance of leaving it intact. This discrepancy of opinion would ultimately be the undoing of the entire project. Arnold reluctantly informed The University Press of Virginia that the offer had been declined by Miller, but he told

Cowen that he would redouble his efforts to convince Miller of the importance for reprinting *Aller Retour*. Miller's rejection did not stop Arnold from moving on to the next potential publishing house, Little-Brown Publishers. This time Arnold was armed with his introduction, the text of *Aller Retour*, the Miller/West correspondence, as well as Arnold's own manuscript for a novel. [101] All were rejected in June, as Little-Brown considered *Aller Retour* to be of insufficient length.

During this period, Arnold continued his attempts to persuade Miller to pursue the Miller/West correspondence, and in May, Miller advised Arnold to contact Robert MacGregor at New Directions to determine their interest in the letters. Following this suggestion, Arnold first chose to phone MacGregor at the end of July to discuss the project. Even though Miller had directly told Arnold that he was not interested in republishing *Aller Retour* in its current state, Arnold went ahead and included *Aller Retour* with the West letters.[102] Surprised at the sudden appearance of these projects, MacGregor queried Miller on August 4th concerning the two projects and the unexpected phone call. Both the Miller/West letters and *Aller Retour* publications appealed to New Directions, with MacGregor noting that, "although we turned [*Aller Retour*] down, I guess years ago, times have perhaps changed and we might be interested now."[103] MacGregor, however, requested confirmation from Miller concerning Arnold, as Miller had neither mentioned Arnold nor an approved introduction text. Arnold's efforts were quickly vouched for and by August 14 MacGregor had Arnold's introduction and the photocopies of both *Aller Retour* and the Miller/West letters.

New Directions' involvement with both of Arnold's projects was the beginning of the end for his endeavors. Waiting on MacGregor antagonized Arnold to no end; it is clear from his various letters to Miller that he believed New Directions had not shown proper respect to Miller as an author, nor had they promoted his work to the appropriate degree—on this latter point, Miller himself had expressed similar complaints to New Directions. From August to October 1970, Arnold heard no reply from MacGregor, so he sent the publisher a reminder. On October 21, MacGregor requested Arnold to allow for more time on each project as there were several other Miller projects of unpublished or out of print materials that needed consideration.[104] Arnold forwarded a copy of MacGregor's letter to West concluding that MacGregor retained "the manuscripts and I assume from the content of his letter that they are not too far away from hard decisions one way or another; apparently, they do not want to give away their option lightly."[105] The reply from New Directions was the official response to Arnold. In contrast, the in-house conversation between James Laughlin, Bob MacGregor, and Miller was a bit more biting. On the carbon copy of the October letter sent to Arnold, MacGregor typed a lengthy note to Laughlin informing him of his opinion on both of Arnold's proposals:

> I'm not overwhelmed by this young man's essay on Miller, and the West letters I've read seem mainly concerned with telling West what's being published, where West can get the forbidden books [...]. Maybe I've missed the meat [...] but these letters so far are no where near as rewarding as those he was writing to me in the same (later) period or probably you earlier. Thought I might try Peter [Glassgold] on *Aller Retour*, for which Henry has been accused of being anti-Semitic, and asking quite frankly if Peter thinks it true. There are some remarks, but I think I'm over sensitive for my Jewish friends.[106]

Following this in house memo, New Directions continued to put off responding to Arnold, focusing attention elsewhere. At the end of December, MacGregor wrote Miller that Arnold was becoming "somewhat impatient," yet MacGregor was reluctant to contact Arnold for a variety of reasons. In his detailed letter to Miller, MacGregor noted that Arnold's essay was "not exactly brilliant" and that "it avoids entirely the possible charge of Anti-Semitism. [...]. Another problem with Arnold's essay is that he seems to me to be trying to prove that you were indeed very much involved in politics." The Miller/West project did not fare well either, as "these letters do not seem to me to be as centrally important in your development as Mr. Arnold seems to think."[107] With these valid arguments, MacGregor was essentially encouraging Miller to reject Arnold's introduction and diminish any value in publishing the Miller/West correspondence.

To MacGregor's letter, Miller replied in great detail. Reminiscent of the letter written to Maurice Giordias at Olympia Press in 1946, on January 9th and February 20th, 1971 Miller wrote two lengthy letters defending himself against those who might choose to label him anti-Semitic.[108] In the January 9th letter, Miller agreed with MacGregor concerning Arnold:

> As for Bill Arnold—I understand how you feel. He's

pushing, I feel, because he wants his name to be associated with mine in some way. I don't remember his essay or intro to "Aller Retour" but do recall it was too scholarly and off in other respects. (Ridiculous that I was ever interested in politics, except during the Emma Goldman period. I have no use for politicians — agree with Buckminster Fuller — and of course, remain an "anarchist."[109]

Concerning the Miller/West letters, Miller considered them not important and suggested that they would be better off published after his death — if ever. These two letters are filled with crucial self-evaluation concerning Miller's relations with Jewish artists and communities. What they ultimately reveal is that this subject remained a very sensitive and personal one for Miller. Bringing out a new edition of *Aller Retour New York* would open wounds that Miller was trying to forget and move on from, and he concluded: "why bother to exhume a book which might rightly or wrongly create a bad impression?" (Miller and Laughlin 247). The republication would ultimately risk encouraging more unwanted attacks concerning his writing — certainly unneeded in the early 1970s, as Kate Millett's *Sexual Politics* (1970) was spearheading the second-wave feminist assault on Miller.

Throughout the Fall of 1970, no letters passed between Arnold and Miller, but Arnold wrote once and twice phoned New Directions, demanding to speak with MacGregor.[110] Finally, on February 16th, 1971, MacGregor composed a two page, in-depth letter to Arnold outlining why New Directions was rejecting both project proposals. The primary concern remained that *Aller Retour* had been, and still was, considered by some to be an anti-Semitic text. New Directions had sent both Arnold's introduction as well as the Miller text to "certain intelligent Jews, conscious of their own history and the place of some of their fellow in American and in bourgeois life generally."[111] While the text was deemed acceptable by the Jewish reviewers, MacGregor felt that Miller would need to address these anti-Semitic claims in order to properly contextualize the text.[112] The anti-Semitic concerns were completely overlooked in Arnold's manuscript, MacGregor noted, thereby making it ineffectual for the task of properly introducing the text. Ultimately, MacGregor concludes, neither the timing nor a sufficient introduction made the publication of *Aller Retour* feasible. The Miller/West letters suffered a similar fate in that MacGregor believed they did not contain sufficient and meaningful new content, as Miller often wrote to multiple people on the same day concerning the same subject. Ultimately, MacGregor felt the letters in the Miller/West correspondence would be redundant with previous publications of Miller's letters.

The letter from New Directions could merely have been another stumbling block in Arnold's attempt to assist Miller in the republication of *Aller Retour New York*. It was, however, the reply that soured Miller's interest in working with Arnold. In an abrasive letter to MacGregor, Arnold — essentially a Miller fan/pseudo-scholar — completely derailed both projects. Arnold sent off a fiery compilation of words, thereby burning his bridges with both New Directions and Miller. The February 19th letter was essentially an attack on MacGregor's professionalism in handling the matter at hand, with Arnold opening in the following manner:

> I just received your letter dated Feb 16, 1971. First of all, let's cut the shit! [...]. I have never received a more childish petulant piece of shit in all my life as your last reply. I marvel you can walk a tightrope as you do in this letter, and also claim to have known "the" Henry Miller intimately [that I have known] over the years. Who gives a shit if you or yours "have known Miller far longer" than I. What is this? — some sort of personality contest you're waging?[113]

Over the course of the next ten pages, Arnold admonishes the manner in which he felt MacGregor and New Directions had dealt with the projects, for selectively choosing which Miller works get published, and even accusing MacGregor of anti-Semitism for raising the issue of anti-Semitism in *Aller Retour*.[114] The letter concludes with Arnold severing any possible ties with MacGregor and New Direction. To ensure that all parties involved knew of his infuriation with New Directions, copies of the letter were sent to Miller and Herbert West. On the same day, Arnold wrote to Miller concerning the exchange with MacGregor and renounced his efforts to find a publisher for *Aller Retour* as he felt Miller had not provided enough persuasive support to see the project through. Arnold also wrote West, stating: "The recent squabble is an illumination; they were entirely impolitic and [un]reasonable about the whole thing. They have given us our 'freedom' to go elsewhere."[115] Miller chose not to reply to Arnold's letter and made no mention concerning Arnold's diatribe in his next correspondence with New Directions. It is clear, though, that by January 18th, 1972,[116] Miller was finished with Arnold. On an envelope from Arnold, Miller wrote a note to his son: "Tony — I'm not replying to this. He writes me often — bit of a well-meaning bore."[117] In Arnold's letter, he mentions that the Miller/West letters have stalled, as some half dozen publishers, including the most recent, G. P. Putnam's Sons, felt the letters were not commercial enough. Arnold ends the letter by expressing his final contempt: "New York's fuckface establishment has about pissed me off to the absolute end!"[118] With the failed attempt of Arnold's well-meaning efforts, the possibility of *Aller Retour New York* being republished in America during Miller's later years came to an end.[119]

Miller's Centennial and *Aller Retour New York*

It is not clear if Miller ever did recover a copy of the 1935 edition of *Aller Retour New York* for his personal collection, or that of the 1945 edition. As noted in a letter to Arnold, Miller had even misplaced his 1956 French version. Occasional references to the book do appear, as in Harry Kiakis's memoir, wherein Kiakis retells a snippet of conversation from 1969: "Joe has a friend who owns an original edition of *Alter Retour New York*," with Miller asking, "Do you think he would give it to me?" (Kiakis 73).[120] No copies of the book are listed in Miller's possession after his death, as documented in *Henry Miller: A Personal Archive*, compiled by Roger Jackson and William Ashley in 1991. Miller was constantly overwhelmed with his

small projects, creating watercolors and giving interviews, so that the last decade of his life left virtually no room for him to return to the long-outdated text of *Aller Retour New York*. Furthermore, in Jay Martin's opinion there was likely very little interest for the text during the 1970s.[121] Miller had reached the peak of his worldwide popularity in the 1960s and by the 1970s, his writing had transitioned into a much more personal and emotional form of writing. *Aller Retour* just did not seem to fit into Miller's current trajectory.

Another twenty years

passed before *Aller Retour New York* began reappearing in letters concerning Miller's publications. With the approach of Miller's centennial birthday celebration, 1991 would prove very active for Miller affairs, with two major biographies and several smaller works being published. In the lead-up to Miller's centennial, Peter Glassgold, Editor-in-chief at New Directions, approached George Wickes in October 1990 to see if he would be interested in seeking out "a selection of small Miller classics long out of print" and preparing an introduction for the selected items. Two initial possibilities were to combine *Aller Retour* with another text of similar length, or alternatively, as Wickes preferred, seek out and "assemble half a dozen fugitive pieces to represent different aspects of Henry Miller."[122] By December, New Directions had decided to go with a small edition under their Revived Modern Classics series. This booklet would be published alongside Frederick Turner's anthology of Miller's works entitled, *Into the Heart of Life: Henry Miller at One Hundred.* Both projects at New Directions were led by Griselda Ohannessian, the vice-president, and Glassgold, as James Laughlin had mostly retired to the countryside.

In early January 1991, New Directions ran into a little stumbling block with the plans for *Aller Retour*, one that would cause a bit of consternation. Millerite Craig Peter Standish had been in contact with New Directions concerning his Miller-related publications. Having been informed by New Directions of the plan to bring out *Aller Retour*, Standish was quick to reply that he was involved with Noel Young at Capra Press concerning a collection of ten unpublished essays by Miller.[123] Predictably, Standish's letter caught New Directions by surprise. Who held the copyright for *Aller Retour New York* was the apprehension between the two publishers. New Directions assumed, correctly, that the copyright was owned by Miller, since he had never officially published the text. As a result of Standish's news, Ohannessian began to pursue information on the copyright with Vincent Gioia and George Evelshin, the representatives for Miller's three children. Additionally, Glassgold initiated a copyright search in February with the Library of Congress. It was hoped that if Capra Press held a non-exclusive lease then New Directions would still be able to publish a reprint of *Aller Retour* for their Revived Modern Classic series.[124] New Directions did not initially contact Capra Press, waiting until May 1991 to do so.[125] In the meantime, they continued forward as planned, drawing up contracts for Miller's children and mailing them on January 22nd. Both *Into the Heart of Life* and *Aller Retour New York* were being rushed to publication in order to make sure, as Ohannessian wrote, that "Henry's birthday candles will be well lit."[126] Ultimately, all of the concern over the conflict of publication rights for *Aller Retour* proved unnecessary, as Capra Press neither had a contract for the text nor did they follow through on the publication with Standish.[127]

Once the copyright issues were squared away, it was basically smooth sailing as the Miller children were on board with the publication. New Directions likely used James Laughlin's 1945 copy of the text,[128] and when Ohannessian returned the text to Laughlin in December 1990, she wrote, "Returning herewith your book. We've made a xerox which we can use for setting copy. [...]. It's a wonderfully fresh Milleresque piece, lots better, I think, than a good deal of his latter burbling and ought to please his fans and perhaps garner some new ones."[129] Due to his previous work with New Directions, Wickes, who by 1991 had been writing about Miller for thirty years, proved to be the fitting person to provide the introduction for the new edition. Interestingly, Wickes makes no reference to the anti-Semitism in his introduction.[130] Considering that this issue had plagued the book for so many years, it is a striking absence in light of the historical narrative of the publication history. Neither is there any reference to Miller's preface for the French edition, which clearly addressed the concerns that Miller and Laughlin had so long held.[131] As it turns out, Laughlin was still hesitant to publish *Aller Retour* in 1991, but the staff (primarily Ohannessian and Glassgold) decided to move forward with the publication (Miller and Laughlin 247-48fn).[132]

Finally published on November 27th, 1991, it had been nearly 45 years since Miller's letter to his friend Alfred Perlès had returned in fresh ink. The publicity statement written by Laurie Callahan for New Directions called *Aller Retour New York* "an exuberant, rambling, episodic, humorous account of [Miller's] visit to New York in 1935 [...]. It is truly vintage Miller."[133] Only one nagging aspect of the publication remained incomplete until 1993, and that concerned the copyright with the Library of Congress. The initial 1991 paperwork had to be reworded in early 1992 to make clear that the first two editions of *Aller Retour* had not been copyrighted in any manner. This change still did not sit well with the Library of Congress, as it seemed to conflict with their records of the Obelisk and Abramson publications. In their opinion, either the 150 copies of the Obelisk Press edition or the 500 copies of the 1945 edition were numerous enough to presume the publishers of either version must have held some form of copyright. In a detailed letter from New Directions in August 1993, Declan Spring wrote the Examining Division of the Library of Congress. Citing Shifreen and Jackson's recently published comprehensive publication history of Miller's oeuvre, Spring laid out how the first two editions of the text were both limited editions and published for private circulation. Spring concluded his letter with a convincing note: "I might add that by this time [1945] Henry Miller had acquired an international reputation. Around the time of these earlier editions, his books *Tropic of Cancer*, *Black Spring*, and *Tropic of Capricorn* were being widely published and read. Surely, if he had intended *Aller Retour* to be publicly published in the copyright sense, he would have arranged it so."[134] Thus, with this final letter, the Library of Congress granted the request and nearly 60 years after penning *Aller Retour New York*, Miller's epistle was finally under copyright of his long-time publisher, New Directions.[135]

Notes

[1]While in the United States, Miller's first American post-*Tropic of Cancer* article was published. A biting critique of the "enormous citadel" filled with a "howling, raging mob" ("I Came" 26), the tone Miller employs toward New York City would continue in his subsequent writings. "I Came, I Saw, I Fled" had been re-titled by the original publisher and Miller would later republish it in *The Cosmological Eye* (1939) in a revised, longer form with the intended title of "Glittering Pie."

[2]In her diary dated August 5, 1935, Nin recounts a morning breakfast with Miller where she gave feedback on *Aller Retour*, recalling that, "Henry, after my criticism of certain too-factual parts of his hundred-page letter to Fred, is piqued, and he adds to it and makes a fine small book of it. […]. We baptized it *Aller Retour New York*" (Nin 125).

[3]It has been noted that while on the *SS Champlain*, Miller was reading Hitler's *Mein Kampf* (Dearborn 175).

[4]Originally, Miller's *Scenario* was slated as the first publication under the Siana label, but Nin disliked the text, considering it too empty; as a result, Nin records, "I suggest we open fire with that letter to gather a group of subscribers around Henry, instead of with the *Scenario*, which is esoteric and limited" (Nin 125).

[5] Miller to Steloff, 29 Mar. 1938. Henry Miller Collection. The Henry W. and Albert A. Berg Collection of English and American

Literature, The New York Public Library.

[6]Slightly earlier, in the beginning of March 1939, Miller queried Gershon Legman to see if he would be interested in a new edition of *Aller Retour*, at 30 francs (Miller, "Four" 7). Miller also wrote Steloff at the Gotham Book Mart at the end of March, reiterating what he had said to Legman, that "neither *Black Spring* nor *Aller Retour New York* (the latter now being reprinted at 30 Francs) have ever been brought to the attention of the authorities at Washington." Miller to Steloff, 25 Mar. 1939. Henry Miller Collection. The Henry W. and Albert A. Berg Collection of English and American Literature, The New York Public Library.

[7]Miller to Crews, 18 Sept. 1946. Judson Crews Papers (Collection 673). Department of Special Collections, Charles E. Young Research Library, University of California, Los Angeles.

[8]Perhaps the first recipient of a personalized copy of *Aller Retour* was Herbert Read, whose copy is inscribed October 1935. Held at Leeds University archives, this inscription "suggests that, unusually for an Obelisk title, the printed publication date is accurate" (Pearson 199). Another copy dated October 1935 was inscribed to Richard Thoma and is held at the University of California, Santa Barbara archives. Thoma, author of *Tragedy in Blue* (1936), worked with Ezra Pound in editing *The New Review* (Bloshteyn 68). Karl Orend notes that Miller sent Joseph Delteil an early version of the manuscript, for what purpose it is unclear ("Reveries" 33). A recipient of a flyer and letter of introduction was the Romanian artist De Hirsh Margules, who would become one of Miller's regular correspondents while he traveled the United States gathering material for *The Air-Conditioned Nightmare*. Based on the intact flyer, Margules never bought a copy of *Aller Retour*. See Miller to Margules, 7 Sept. 1935. De Hirsh Margules papers, 1888-2001, bulk 1923-1965. Archives of America Art, Smithsonian Institution.

[9]Miller to Steloff, No date. Henry Miller Collection. The Henry W. and Albert A. Berg Collection of English and American Literature, The New York Public Library.

[10]Miller still held copies in October of 1936, as he asked James Laughlin to try and find customers for the booklet (Miller and Laughlin 5).

[11] Miller to Steloff, 4 May 1938. Henry Miller Collection. The Henry W. and Albert A. Berg Collection of English and American Literature, The New York Public Library.

[12]Slocum would later become Miller's agent with Russell &

Volkening (Hoyle 43). Miller had sent Laughlin a manuscript section of *Aller Retour* for publication in the *Harvard Advocate*, but it was not until late October 1935 that he sent the published version, also asking Laughlin to try and "dig up any subscriptions" for the text (Miller and Laughlin 1–2).

[13]*Aller Retour* appeared in issue CXXII (September 1935), pages 22-24; it should be noted that this printing appeared one month before Miller had the print edition from Obelisk Press. The title is confusing due to repetition of use, but it should not be misconstrued for Miller's more famous "Glittering Pie," the original title for "I Came, I Saw, I Fled," and found in its complete form in *Max and the White Phagocytes* and *The Cosmological Eye* (1939).

[14]The Assistant District Attorney for the case was Frank Volpe. James Laughlin explained about Volpe in an interview with George Wickes in 1992, recalling, "'I don't think he really wanted to prosecute; he just wanted to get publicity for a while. We got him two tickets to the Harvard-Yale game on the 50-yard line from somebody we knew, and he was very happy with those, so the case just faded away and was never presented'" (qtd. in Wickes xi). In a lengthy section of *The Boston Globe* article, Volpe pontificated on the outcome of the event, and indirectly included Miller among the guilty: "We do not want to send these earnest young writers, these immature attackers of the public morals, to jail. Because, after all, they are inexperienced boys, suffering from delusions of grandeur, and, thereby committing a youthful indiscretion" ("Quit Harvard").

[15]Miller to Dobo, 8 Nov. 1935, Henry Miller Collection. The Henry W. and Albert A. Berg Collection of English and American Literature, The New York Public Library.

[16]In December 1935, Miller wrote Herbert Read expanding on his thoughts about the *Harvard Advocate* debacle:

> This "Aller Retour" was, as you noticed, the first of a Series. I brought it out at my own expense, believing that I had at least a hundred readers I could count on. So far I have had about thirty responses — orders, I mean. If I could afford it I would go ahead with the 2nd number, despite the inertia. But I just can't. So I am biding my time. [...].
>
> Did I tell you that the first installment of "Aller Retour" published in the Harvard "Advocate", brought down the censors? Imagine it — even with the four letter words

excised—they found it filthy and seized the magazine, jailed the editors, etc. A big spread in the Boston papers, where it occurred. One of the papers had me identified with the Harvard undergraduates, "an embryonic writer," etc. who would regret later on, etc. Delicious. (Miller, "Henry Miller's Letters" 13)

There is a conflict here between the Read and Dobo letters concerning the "first" and "2nd" installments. In the letter to Dobo, Miller refers to the *Harvard Advocate*'s publication as the 2nd installment because, I perceive, Miller considered the publication of "I Came, I Saw, I Fled," meant to be titled "Glittering Pie," as the first incarnation of the text, although none of this earlier publication is included in *Aller Retour* (See Miller, *Aller Retour* 1).

[17]Miller would write to William Saroyan on April 23, 1937 about how pleased he was to see this translation appear in the same issue that included an essay by Élie Faure, entitled "Personalism" ("An Unpublished" 25).

[18]In Aubray's copy of *Aller Retour*, Miller inscribed, "'with thanks and gratitude for her spontaneous impulse'" and dated it December 1936 (qtd. in Sipper et al. A23). This date confirms that Miller still possessed copies of *Aller Retour* at the end of 1936.

[19]Miller also makes a brief remark to Queneau that Du Chêne et Stock are interested in *Aller Retour* and *Black Spring*, but nothing progressed from there. For *Nouvelles Littéraires*, Miller had suggested pages 113-119 for inclusion, with the title, "Aboard the S. S. Veendam." Miller to Queneau, 17 Oct. 1937. Henry Miller Collection (Collection MS-2832). Harry Ransom Center, The University of Texas at Austin.

[20]There was also to appear a combined review of both *Tropic of Cancer* and *Aller Retour New York*, written by Cyril Connolly for the *New Statesman* in 1935. Miller read a manuscript of the review, but it was never published (Miller and Laughlin 2; Miller, "Henry Miller's Letters" 13-14).

[21]A little narrative in the *New York Times*, July 13, 1938, makes a passing reference to Miller and *Aller Retour* as well as to Australian author Norman Lindsay, whose book *Age of Consent* (1938) had just been published and would be banned in Australia until 1962 (Thompson 19).

[22]Lydenberg to Miller, 29 Mar. 1939. Box 38, Folder 8, Henry Miller Papers (Collection 110). Department of Special Collections, Charles

E. Young Research Library, University of California, Los Angeles.

[23]Lydenberg to Miller, 1 Mar. 1940. Box 38, Folder 8, Henry Miller Papers (Collection 110). Department of Special Collections, Charles E. Young Research Library, University of California, Los Angeles. Interestingly, it was not until the years 1989 and 1995 that the New York Public Library received two copies of the 1935 *Aller Retour New York*. Held in the Berg Collection, each copy is signed and inscribed: one to Bertha Schrank, the other to Karl Karsden. Both signatures are dated November, 1935 ("NYPL Catalog").

[24]Miller to Slocum, 3 Jul. 1940. Jay Martin Papers. The Huntington Library, San Marino, California.

[25]Miller to Crews, 28 Jan. 1943. Judson Crews Papers (Collection 673). Department of Special Collections, Charles E. Young Research Library, University of California, Los Angeles.

[26]Miller to Crews, 27 Oct. 1943. Judson Crews Papers (Collection 673). Department of Special Collections, Charles E. Young Research Library, University of California, Los Angeles.

[27]Miller to Steloff, 20 Jan. 1943. Henry Miller Collection. The Henry W. and Albert A. Berg Collection of English and American Literature, The New York Public Library.

[28]Miller to Steloff, No date. Henry Miller Collection. The Henry W. and Albert A. Berg Collection of English and American Literature, The New York Public Library.

[29]Miller added, "Ben promises not to mutilate the copy in having it reprinted." Miller to Steloff, No date. Henry Miller Collection. The Henry W. and Albert A. Berg Collection of English and American Literature, The New York Public Library.

[30]Steloff to Miller, 12 Feb. 1943. Henry Miller Collection. The Henry W. and Albert A. Berg Collection of English and American Literature, The New York Public Library.

[31]Miller to Steloff, 26 Feb. 1943. Henry Miller Collection. The Henry W. and Albert A. Berg Collection of English and American Literature, The New York Public Library.

[32]Miller to Steloff, 23 Dec. 1943. Henry Miller Collection. The Henry W. and Albert A. Berg Collection of English and American Literature, The New York Public Library.

[33]While informing Francis Steloff on the project, Miller wrote, "Ben Abramson is now writing me about *Aller Retour*—he would like to bring it out, he says. (claims binders won't do cloth bindings these days—but that *Aller Retour*, being a thin book, could be done in

paper covers.)" Henry Miller Collection. The Henry W. and Albert A. Berg Collection of English and American Literature, The New York Public Library.

[34]Miller would write Herbert F. West in November 1943, asking:

> Incidentally, if you ever hear of any one wishing to get rid of a copy of *Aller Retour New York* or *Black Spring* or *Capricorn*, do let me know, will you? Especially the first-named. How strange this... when in Paris, disgusted with the slowness of the sales on that little opus, I began giving them away—even to strangers. Would sit down and think up names—like Andre Gide or Paul Morand, and send them out. Now for four years I have been searching for a copy unsuccessfully. (Miller, "More Letters" 17)

West would become an important factor in the 1970s effort to republish *Aller Retour*.

[35]Miller to Crews, 18 Jan. 1944. Judson Crews Papers (Collection 673). Department of Special Collections, Charles E. Young Research Library, University of California, Los Angeles.

[36]Abramson to Miller, 13 Jan. 1944. Box 1, Folder 2, Henry Miller Papers (Collection 110). Department of Special Collections, Charles E. Young Research Library, University of California, Los Angeles.

[37]Abramson to Miller, 24 Jan. 1944. Box 1, Folder 2, Henry Miller Papers (Collection 110). Department of Special Collections, Charles E. Young Research Library, University of California, Los Angeles.

[38]Miller followed up his letter with a postcard wanting to know if Huntington Cairns would be willing to send his copy on to Abramson. Miller to Eleanor Howard, 23 Mar. 1944. Box 1, Folder 10, George Howard Papers (Collection 1321). Department of Special Collections, Charles E. Young Research Library, University of California, Los Angeles.

[39]Miller to Eleanor Howard, 17 Apr. 1944. Box 1, Folder 10, George Howard Papers (Collection 1321). Department of Special Collections, Charles E. Young Research Library, University of California, Los Angeles.

[40]Miller to Steloff, 20 Aug. 1944. Henry Miller Collection. The Henry W. and Albert A. Berg Collection of English and American Literature, The New York Public Library.

[41]Miller to Crews, No date (presumably 15 May 1944). Box 3, Folder 8, Judson Crews Papers (Collection 673). Department of Special Collections, Charles E. Young Research Library, University of California, Los Angeles.

[42]The April 24, 1945 letter from Abramson details the printing troubles and runaround he had been experiencing with Roth. Roth did not publish the Bailey book, nor was he able to have *Aller Retour* bound in Chicago. Instead, Roth sent the folded sheets to New York to be completed. Compounding everything, Abramson did not serve as a very dependable correspondent, spending four pages of this letter to bring Miller abreast on his queries from August the previous year. Abramson to Miller, 6 June 1944; 24 Apr. 1945, Box 1, Folder 2, Henry Miller Papers (Collection 110). Department of Special Collections, Charles E. Young Research Library, University of California, Los Angeles.

[43]See also: Abramson to Miller, 18 Jun. 1946. Box 1, Folder 2, Henry Miller Papers (Collection 110). Department of Special Collections, Charles E. Young Research Library, University of California, Los Angeles.

[44]Abramson to Miller, 24 Aug. 1945. Box 1, Folder 2, Henry Miller Papers (Collection 110). Department of Special Collections, Charles E. Young Research Library, University of California, Los Angeles.

[45]Abramson's Argus Book Shop and the Gotham Book Mart were not the only locations offering copies of *Aller Retour*. Among others, the Whyte Bookshop and Gallery in Washington D.C., run by Polly and James Huntington Whyte, also advertised the book in their monthly bulletin of September 1945, listing it under "Essays" with a price of $7.50.

[46]As soon as Abramson had copies of *Aller Retour*, Miller was asking him to send one to Patience Ross in England in order for her to pursue publication of both *Aller Retour* and Perlés's companion piece, "Aller Retour London." Nothing came of this venture as Miller and Ross parted ways in the middle of 1946. Miller to Abramson, 28 Aug. 1945. Box 1, Folder 2, Henry Miller Papers (Collection 110). Department of Special Collections, Charles E. Young Research Library, University of California, Los Angeles. For Crews: Crews to Miller, No date. Box 10, Folder 8, Henry Miller Papers (Collection 110). Department of Special Collections, Charles E. Young Research Library, University of California, Los Angeles.

[47]Miller to Crews, 22 July 1946. Box 3, Folder 9, Judson Crews Papers (Collection 673). Department of Special Collections, Charles E.

Young Research Library, University of California, Los Angeles.

[48]Miller to Crews, No date. Box 3, Folder 8, Judson Crews Papers (Collection 673). Department of Special Collections, Charles E. Young Research Library, University of California, Los Angeles.

[49]Miller to Crews, 29 Sept. 1946. Box 3, Folder 9, Judson Crews Papers (Collection 673). Department of Special Collections, Charles E. Young Research Library, University of California, Los Angeles.

[50]Miller to Crews, 21 Oct. 1946. Box 3, Folder 9, Judson Crews Papers (Collection 673). Department of Special Collections, Charles E. Young Research Library, University of California, Los Angeles.

[51]In Shifreen and Jackson, they list *Aller Retour* as being printed in New York. From Abramson's letters, however, it seems clear that he did indeed stay with Roth and print the book in Chicago. Concerning the numeration, Shifreen and Jackson note that the numbered copies they examined were marked with low-denomination numbers or were not numbered. Some appear to have gone unnumbered; yet, one of my personal copies is numbered #426, and the Amherst College, G. William Arnold Collection holds copy #490.

[52]Kahn wrote a regular column in *New Currents* where he set about "exposing writers and cultural heroes whom he deemed fascist and anti-semitic" (Ferguson 291). Yet, Kahn's career was checkered with accusations of being a member of "smear groups", or those who intentionally tried to destroy the livelihood of individuals they disliked (Flynn 16). Hoyle provides a more detailed background on Kahn, noting that he was arrested for refusing to comply with the United States government (see Hoyle 115–17).

[53]Abramson to Miller, 7 Nov. 1945. Box 1, Folder 2, Henry Miller Papers (Collection 110). Department of Special Collections, Charles E. Young Research Library, University of California, Los Angeles.

[54]Miller to Laughlin, 7 Jan. 1946. Folder 13 of 81, New Directions Publishing Corp. Records, circa 1932-1997 (MS Am 2077 1152). Houghton Library, Harvard University.

[55] Ibid.

[56]Laughlin to Miller, 20 Jan. 1946. Box 37, Folder 2, Henry Miller Papers (Collection 110). Department of Special Collections, Charles E. Young Research Library, University of California, Los Angeles. In 1961 Laughlin did admit to Miller that he rejected *Aller Retour* in the 1940s because of its anti-Semitism (Miller and Laughlin 194).

[57]Miller would write a lengthy letter to Maurice Giordias of Olympia

Press in 1946, extensively explaining his personal position concerning the supposed anti-Semitism in his writings. Included in the letter is an extended exposition on his views of Jews and the current state of the Jewish people, post-World War II. See Miller to Giordias, 10 May 1946. Box 39, Folder 14, Henry Miller Papers (Collection 110). Department of Special Collections, Charles E. Young Research Library, University of California, Los Angeles.

[58]Wilson's review, "Twilight of the Expatriates," was published in the *New Republic* in 1938.

[59]Abramson to Miller, 3 May 1946. Box 1, Folder 2, Henry Miller Papers (Collection 110). Department of Special Collections, Charles E. Young Research Library, University of California, Los Angeles.

[60]Miller to Abramson, 1 Jul. 1949. Box 1, Folder 2, Henry Miller Papers (Collection 110). Department of Special Collections, Charles E. Young Research Library, University of California, Los Angeles.

[61]In the 1954 letter, Abramson mentions mailing Miller 12 copies of *Aller Retour.*

[62]On February 8, 1954, Miller wrote to Gotham Book Mart requesting two copies of *Aller Retour* if Steloff still had any in stock. Steloff wrote back that she was trying to locate copies, but there were "none on hand." Miller to Steloff, 8 Feb. 1954; Steloff to Miller, 5 Mar. 1954. Henry Miller Collection. The Henry W. and Albert A. Berg Collection of English and American Literature, The New York Public Library.

[63]Miller to Lothar von Balluseck, 1 Jul. 1951. Folder 26 of 81, New Directions Publishing Corp. Records, circa 1932-1997 (MS Am 2077 1152). Houghton Library, Harvard University.

[64]Hoffman to Weatherby, 2 Sept. 1954. Folder 13 of 88, New Directions Publishing Corp. Records, circa 1932-1997 (MS Am 2077 2678). Houghton Library, Harvard University.

[65]*Aller Retour New York* (ニューヨーク往復, in Japanese) was not published in Japan until 2013. It was translated by Kobayashi Michiyo and released by Suisei Sha Publishers (水声社).

[66]Miller to Girodias, 30 Sept. 1948. Box 39, Folder 14, Henry Miller Papers (Collection 110). Department of Special Collections, Charles E. Young Research Library, University of California, Los Angeles.

[67]Ibid.

[68]Miller to Perlès, 26 July 1953. Henry Miller Collection, Special Collections & University Archives, University of Victoria. In a letter on August 15, 1953, while Miller was returning to everyday life in

Big Sur after his European trip, he wrote Perlès a downtrodden letter: "Have you had any news yet about *Aller Retour* [...] or anything else? Reading the mags here (the big ones) I'm convinced it's hopeless even to try them." Miller to Perlès, 15. Aug. 1953. Henry Miller Collection, Special Collections & University Archives, University of Victoria.

[69]By the 1950s, Miller had achieved an esteemed position in Europe as a writer of merit, thus the high volume count of *Aller Retour*. That this edition of *Aller Retour* would need to go into a second printing within six years gives testament to Miller's European reputation as well as interest by the French readers in Miller's perceptions of New York City and Paris.

[70]The first draft is held at the Harry Ransom Center, University of Texas, Austin. The versions of the second draft (a total of three copies, each with diminishing grammatical corrections) are held at the University of California, Los Angeles.

[71]"Preface to *Aller Retour New York*." 16 May 1954. Container 1.2, Henry Miller Collection (Collection MS-2832). Harry Ransom Center, The University of Texas at Austin.

[72]"*Aller Retour New York*. 'Preface' and 'Postface' 1954-1958." Box 82, Folder 10, Henry Miller Papers (Collection 110). Department of Special Collections, Charles E. Young Research Library, University of California, Los Angeles.

[73]"Aller Retour N. Y.: Preface and postscriptum." 16 May 1954. Container 1.2, Henry Miller Collection (Collection MS-2832). Harry Ransom Center, The University of Texas at Austin.

[74]"Aller Retour New York. 'Preface' and 'Postface' 1954-1958." Box 82, Folder 10, Henry Miller Papers (Collection 110). Department of Special Collections, Charles E. Young Research Library, University of California, Los Angeles. For a brief, but interesting perspective on Miller's tendency to note his friendships with Jewish individuals, see Karl Orend's *Henry Miller's Paris Years – Reflections on a Paradigm for Biography* (Orend *Henry* 21–23). In a more biting critique of *Aller Retour*, see Gerald Stern's *Stealing History* (2012), in which he notes Miller's tendency to attack Jews, while at the same time, "like Pound, he dilutes and confuses his hatred with his profession of friendship with the many Jews (five?) he knows in New York and Paris" (270).

[75]Miller to Perlès, 12 Nov 1954. Henry Miller Collection, Special Collections & University Archives, University of Victoria.

[76]Miller to Grindea, 16 Jun. 1957, *ADAM International* Papers,

KC/ADAM/FIL/182. King's College London Archives. Miller and Miron Grindea exchanged a few letters over a twenty-year period, but Miller never published in *ADAM International*; in a 1969 issue, Grindea did include two photo reproduction of letters from Miller to both Georges Simenon and Grindea.

[77]Rolph to Perlès, 27 Nov. 1958. Henry Miller Collection, Special Collections & University Archives, University of Victoria.

[78]Memorandum, 25 May 1961. Folder 23 of 88, New Directions Publishing Corp. Records, circa 1932-1997 (MS Am 2077 2678). Houghton Library, Harvard University.

[79]Ibid.

[80]In 1962, Die Arche published the German version of the letter, *Reise nach New York*, translated into German by Marlis Pörtner. Even though this text includes a photo of the 1945 title-page of *Aller Retour*, it is almost certain that this text was produced from the 1956 French edition, as the book includes the preface — but not the postface — of the edited French version.

[81]Bill Arnold is of no relation to the author of this article. Arnold has written several novels, including a romantic fiction set in 1911 concerning Miller, entitled: *Aimee's Secret* (2013).

[82]For the sake of clarity, it must be noted that Miller did write multiple responses to Arnold's letters; however, these were often short and limited to half page letters or postcards. The exchanges by no means reached the intimacy of other Miller correspondences.

[83]Arnold to Miller, 29 Jun. 1966. Box 2, Folder 9, Henry Miller Papers (Collection 110). Department of Special Collections, Charles E. Young Research Library, University of California, Los Angeles.

[84]Arnold's complaint has remained relatively true even into 2018, with only Arthur Hoyle's *The Unknown Henry Miller: A Seeker in Big Sur* (2014) containing an engaging look at the text, devoting three pages to a historical overview of *Aller Retour* (Hoyle 12–15).

[85]Arnold to Miller, 7 Jul. 1966. Box 2, Folder 9, Henry Miller Papers (Collection 110). Department of Special Collections, Charles E. Young Research Library, University of California, Los Angeles.

[86]Ibid.

[87]Miller to Arnold, 13 Jul. 1966. G. William Arnold Papers, Box 6, Amherst College Archives and Special Collections, Amherst College Library.

[88]Arnold to Miller, 7 Jul. 1966. Box 2, Folder 9, Henry Miller Papers (Collection 110). Department of Special Collections, Charles E.

Young Research Library, University of California, Los Angeles.

[89]Jon Webb to Arnold, 14 Jan. 1968. G. William Arnold Papers, Box 6, Amherst College Archives and Special Collections, Amherst College Library.

[90]Arnold to Miller, 6 Dec. 1968. Box 2, Folder 9, Henry Miller Papers (Collection 110). Department of Special Collections, Charles E. Young Research Library, University of California, Los Angeles.

[91]Stein to Arnold, 6 May 1969. G. William Arnold Papers, Box 6, Amherst College Archives and Special Collections, Amherst College Library.

[92]Doubleday to Arnold, 22 Aug. 1969. G. William Arnold Papers, Box 6, Amherst College Archives and Special Collections, Amherst College Library.

[93]Cushman to Arnold, 27 Jan. 1970. G. William Arnold Papers, Box 6, Amherst College Archives and Special Collections, Amherst College Library.

[94]In a fan letter to Miller in 1970, the writer mentions reading copy number 356 of the 1945 edition and that he would be willing to send it to Miller if he needed it for his personal collection. In the margin of the letter, Miller wrote "Yes, send me!" It does not appear that Miller ever received the copy. White to Miller, 1970. Box 72, Folder 3, Henry Miller Papers (Collection 110). Department of Special Collections, Charles E. Young Research Library, University of California, Los Angeles.

[95]In his description of this trip, Arnold records for Miller that he found the librarian to have "some damn nerve" for leaving Miller's collection available on the open stacks, as Arnold believed they should be behind locked doors, due to their extreme value. West owned the original Obelisk pressing, and when Miller visited him in Darmouth in 1944, Miller dedicated the book: "To Herb, nine years later, sitting in his home. Salute to an old friend, a veteran, and a defender of all good things in life," dated November 12, 1944. Photocopy of Miller Inscription, in G. William Arnold Papers, Box 6, Amherst College Archives and Special Collections, Amherst College Library; Arnold to Miller, 28 Feb. 1970, Box 70, Folder 3, Henry Miller Papers (Collection 110). Department of Special Collections, Charles E. Young Research Library, University of California, Los Angeles.

[96]Arnold to Norm [no last name], 28 Feb. 1970. G. William Arnold Papers, Box 6, Amherst College Archives and Special Collections, Amherst College Library.

[97]Arnold to West, 7 Oct. 1970. G. William Arnold Papers, Box 6, Amherst College Archives and Special Collections, Amherst College Library.

[98]Cowen to Arnold, 5 Feb. 1970. G. William Arnold Papers, Box 6, Amherst College Archives and Special Collections, Amherst College Library.

[99]Cowen to Arnold, 12 Feb. 1970. G. William Arnold Papers, Box 6, Amherst College Archives and Special Collections, Amherst College Library.

[100]Miller to Arnold, 27 Feb. 1970. G. William Arnold Papers, Box 6, Amherst College Archives and Special Collections, Amherst College Library.

[101]Attempting to monopolize on the situation, Arnold began including his own unpublished manuscript with the photocopies of *Aller Retour New York*.

[102]Arnold to Miller, 23 Oct. 1970. Box 70, Folder 3, Henry Miller Papers (Collection 110). Department of Special Collections, Charles E. Young Research Library, University of California, Los Angeles.

[103]MacGregor to Miller, 4 Aug. 1970. Folder 74 of 81, New Directions Publishing Corp. Records, circa 1932-1997 (MS Am 2077 1152). Houghton Library, Harvard University.

[104]Arnold to New Directions, 30 Sept. 1970; New Directions to Arnold, 21 Oct. 1970. G. William Arnold Papers, Box 6, Amherst College Archives and Special Collections, Amherst College Library.

[105]Arnold to West, 23 Oct. 1970. G. William Arnold Papers, Box 6, Amherst College Archives and Special Collections, Amherst College Library.

[106]MacGregor to Laughlin on carbon of letter to Miller, 4 Aug. 1970. Folder 74 of 81, New Directions Publishing Corp. Records, circa 1932-1997 (MS Am 2077 1152). Houghton Library, Harvard University.

[107]MacGregor to Miller, 21 Dec. 1970. Folder 74 of 81, New Directions Publishing Corp. Records, circa 1932-1997 (MS Am 2077 1152). Houghton Library, Harvard University.

[108]Due to extended jury duty during this period, MacGregor was slow in responding to both Arnold and Miller. Concerning Miller's heartfelt explanation of personal views on Judaism, MacGregor considered Miller's letter a far more fitting introduction to *Aller Retour* than the "socio-political frame and bias" of Arnold's essay. MacGregor to Miller, 16 Feb. 1971. Folder 75 of 81, New Directions

Publishing Corp. Records, circa 1932-1997 (MS Am 2077 1152). Houghton Library, Harvard University.

[109]Miller to MacGregor, 9 Jan. 1971. Folder 75 of 81, New Directions Publishing Corp. Records, circa 1932-1997 (MS Am 2077 1152). Houghton Library, Harvard University.

[110]Arnold, it seems, told the New Directions secretary that he would "expose" to Miller the inaction of New Direction concerning the two projects. MacGregor was quick to point out that the publisher had been associated with Miller far longer than Arnold, and "that excited and angry phone conversations are reported to me, [...] and threats to expose us to Henry Miller mean nothing." MacGregor to Arnold, 16 Feb. 1971. G. William Arnold Papers, Box 6, Amherst College Archives and Special Collections, Amherst College Library.

[111]Ibid.

[112]Peter Glassgold is fairly certain that there were no other Jewish readers of the text besides himself and that MacGregor was aggrandizing here to make his argument more solid against Arnold's position. Glassgold also does not recall reading Arnold's introduction. Glassgold, Peter. "Re: Henry Miller, Aller Retour New York." Received by Wayne E. Arnold, 2 Feb. 2017.

[113]Arnold to MacGregor, 19 Feb. 1971. Box 73, Folder 14, Henry Miller Papers (Collection 110). Department of Special Collections, Charles E. Young Research Library, University of California, Los Angeles.

[114]Arnold did not hold back: "Fuck your 'certain intelligent Jews'! That book is not anti-Semitic!! You are to *even* hint at it!" Ibid.

[115]Arnold to West, 19 Feb. 1971. G. William Arnold Papers, Box 6, Amherst College Archives and Special Collections, Amherst College Library.

[116]Incidentally, 1972 was the year that the first Argentinean edition of *Aller Retour New York* was published: *Nueva York, ida y Vuelta*, Buenos Aires: Editorial La Pleyade.

[117]Miller to Tony Miller, Jan. 1971. Box 77, Folder 6, Henry Miller Papers (Collection 110). Department of Special Collections, Charles E. Young Research Library, University of California, Los Angeles.

[118]Arnold to Miller, 18 Jan. 1972. Box 77, Folder 6, Henry Miller Papers (Collection 110). Department of Special Collections, Charles E. Young Research Library, University of California, Los Angeles.

[119]There was a very brief enquiry by Scott Meredith Publishers in August 1975 concerning the possibility of publishing *Aller Retour*

New York; however, the relationship between Miller and the publisher was unstable during that period and therefore nothing came of the idea. Frederick Martin to Miller, 9 Sept. 1975. Folder 77 of 81, New Directions Publishing Corp. Records, circa 1932-1997 (MS Am 2077 1152). Houghton Library, Harvard University.

[120]Kiakis's record does not make it clear who is being quoted, but due to context, it does seem that Miller would be posing the question.

[121]Martin, Jay. Personal Interview. 26 Jan. 2016.

[122]Wickes personal memo, 4 Oct. 1990. Box 1, Folder 18, George Wickes Collection (14.106.M), Special Collections & University Archives, University of Oregon Libraries, Eugene, Oregon.

[123]The book was tentatively titled *Henry Miller Times Ten* before being changed to *Octet: The Forgotten Works of Henry Miller*.

[124]Ohannessian to Gioia, 8 Jan. 1991. Folder 63 of 88, New Directions Publishing Corp. Records, circa 1932-1997 (MS Am 2077 2678). Houghton Library, Harvard University.

[125]By June 1991, Glassgold was fairly confident that Capra would not be moving forward with the rumored anthology as he had heard no reply from them nor had he caught wind of anything at that years' American Booksellers Association conference. Glassgold to Wickes, 10 Jun. 1991. Box 1, Folder 18, George Wickes Collection (14.106.M), Special Collections & University Archives, University of Oregon Libraries, Eugene, Oregon.

[126]Ohannessian to Frederick Turner, 7 Feb. 1991. Folder 63 of 88, New Directions Publishing Corp. Records, circa 1932-1997 (MS Am 2077 2678). Houghton Library, Harvard University.

[127]Standish eventually published two thick volumes of tributes to Miller in 1994 and 1996; in the second volume, Standish reveals that *Octet* was cancelled two months prior to the publication date (Standish 522). He also published for the first time Bill Arnold's 1967 introduction for *Aller Retour New York*, "Man Against The Crowd" (see Standish 288–301). Standish would also write a book review of the 1991 *Aller Retour*, published in *The Bulletin of the Henry Miller Society of Japan*, number 7, and reprinted in his self-published books.

[128]Peter Glassgold recalls photocopying the book and believes that it was the blue hardback version, which would be Abramason's 1945 edition. Glassgold, Peter. "Re: Henry Miller, Aller Retour New York." Received by Wayne E. Arnold, 2 Feb. 2017.

[129]Ohannessian to Laughlin, 12 Dec. 1990. Folder 62 of 88, New

Directions Publishing Corp. Records, circa 1932-1997 (MS Am 2077 2678). Houghton Library, Harvard University.

[130]A testament to George Wickes' impact to Miller scholarship is clearly illustrated in his dedication to seeking out, editing and compiling several collections of Miller's vast communications. After editing the highly praised *Lawrence Durrell & Henry Miller: A Private Correspondence* (1963), Wickes struggled to find agreement with Miller over *Letters to Emil*, slated for a 1970 publication. This collection was ultimately shelved, with Miller and Wickes suffering a severance in their friendship due to textual disagreements. In 1989, New Directions — with Wickes as editor — finally published *Letters to Emil*; due to the cordial relationship between publisher and editor, Glassgold chose Wickes to supply the introduction to *Aller Retour New York*. Even before the text was published, Wickes had initiated work on what would become *Henry Miller and James Laughlin: Selected Letters*, published by W. W. Norton in early 1996. To prepare these letters, Wickes had to go through all of the correspondence, including those related to *Aller Retour*. In doing so, he sought out clarification for some of the issues that had prevented the book's official publication until 1991. Writing to Peter Glassgold on December 13, 1994, Wickes queried Glassgold if he was indeed the staff member who had evaluated the text for its anti-Semitism. Galssgold never replied to this letter, as he was out of the office for the holidays. Instead, Griselda Ohannessian answered on December 16, so as to give Wickes a timely reply. It is partially from this reply that Wickes added to the footnote for the collected letters between Miller and Laughlin; however, Wickes also includes the quote: "particularly conscious of his Jewishness." This phrase was not taken from Ohannessain's letter but is a direct quote from MacGregor's 1970 letter to Bill Arnold concerning the rejection of his project proposal. It is impossible to know if Wickes knew in detail the anti-Semitism claims that had haunted *Aller Retour New York* prior to its 1991 publication; it is clear, though, that by 1994, Wickes was trying to fill in some of the historical gaps of *Aller Retour New York*.

[131] In a 2017 interview, Wickes recalls that the theme of anti-Semitism was "in the air" around *Aller Retour New York*; however, he did not remember New Directions making any specific request to address the topic for the introduction. Wickes also relates that in terms of the anti-Semitism, he "did not want to go into that topic" in the short introduction. Wickes, George. Personal Interview. 30 Jan.

2017. Glassgold also confirmed such sentiments. Glassgold, Peter. "Re: Henry Miller, Aller Retour New York." Received by Wayne E. Arnold, 2 Feb. 2017.

[132]Glassgold considers Laughlin's hesitation over the possible anti-Semitism backlash as partly resulting from his years of dealing with the issue concerning Ezra Pound's publications. Clarifying his personal opinion on *Aller Retour* for both 1970 and 1991, Glassgold writes: "I was speaking as an editor and a believer in free expression and the exchange of ideas in what is often referred to as the court of opinion. Or to put more bluntly, you write your books, you have them published if you can, you get your rewards, you take your knocks—and the world is the better for it." From this stance, he held no reserves about publishing *Aller Retour New York*. Glassgold, Peter. "Re: Henry Miller, Aller Retour New York." Received by Wayne E. Arnold, 2 Feb. 2017.

[133]New Directions Press Release, 27 Nov. 1991. Production and promotional materials. New Directions Publishing Corp. Records, circa 1932-1997 (MS Am 2077 2679). Houghton Library, Harvard University.

[134]Declan to Library of Congress, 19 Aug. 1993. Folder 63 of 88, New Directions Publishing Corp. Records, circa 1932-1997 (MS Am 2077 2678). Houghton Library, Harvard University.

[135]Readers might be left wondering what Robert MacGregor may have meant by suggesting that Glassgold was "particularly conscious of his Jewishness." Glassgold himself was amused by this phrasing, and even though MacGregor wrote Arnold in 1970, it was not until the collected letters were published in 1996 that Glassgold read this description of himself. After reading the Miller/Laughlin letters, he wrote a letter to Wickes on July 7, 1996, noting: "I also got a kick out of seeing reference to my 1970 memo regarding *Aller Retour New York*." In references to his "Jewishness", Glassgold observed, "Well, I own that I am, but not in the way he [MacGregor] thought." In a lengthy paragraph, Glassgold goes on to provide Wickes a bit of New Directions history, recalling how MacGregor "was very much a stickler for office rules." It seems that in the 1960s, New Directions only provided a day and half for religious holidays. A fellow (unnamed) Jewish coworker encouraged Glassgold to help each other in getting MacGregor to give additional days for the Jewish Holidays. And, as Glassgold humorously relates, MacGregor "relented, and I found myself, willy-nilly, taking the full three days of the Jewish holidays, and being pegged as a young man of an

especial Jewish self-consciousness, whose opinion of *Aller Retour* presumably represented that of my tribe!" Thus, from New Directions' perspective, the possibility of anti-Semitic kickback, what Ohannessian called the "tempest in a teapot" concerning *Aller Retour*, ultimately proved to be the most significant factor in preventing the American version of *Aller Retour New York* from seeing republication until 1991. Glassgold to Wickes, 7 Jul. 1996. Box 1, Folder 24, George Wickes Collection (14.106.M), Special Collections & University Archives, University of Oregon Libraries, Eugene, Oregon; and, Ohannessian to Wickes, 16 Dec. 1994. Box 1, Folder 24, George Wickes Collection (14.106.M), Special Collections & University Archives, University of Oregon Libraries, Eugene, Oregon.

Works Cited

Aleksic, Branko. "The Unpublished Correspondence of Henry Miller & Andre Breton, the 'Steady Rock', 1947-50." *Nexus: The International Henry Miller Journal*, translated by Karl Orend, vol. 5, 2008, pp. 150–72.

Bloshteyn, Maria R. *The Making of a Counter-Culture Icon: Henry Miller's Dostoevsky*. U of Toronto P, 2007.

"Bootleg Banned Issue of Paper." *The Boston Globe*, 21 Oct. 1935.

Dearborn, Mary V. *The Happiest Man Alive: A Biography of Henry Miller*. Simon & Schuster, 1992.

Decker, James M. *Henry Miller and Narrative Form: Constructing the Self, Rejecting Modernity*. Taylor, 2005.

Dinnerstein, Leonard. *Antisemitism in America*. Oxford University Press, 1995.

Ferguson, Robert. *Henry Miller: A Life*. Norton, 1991.

Flynn, John T. "Smear Groups Fan Embers of Intolerance." *Chicago Daily Tribune*, 13 Jan. 1947, pp. 1, 16.

Gordon, William A., and Henry Miller. *Writer & Critic: A Correspondence with Henry Miller*. Louisiana State UP, 1968.

Hoyle, Arthur. *The Unknown Henry Miller: A Seeker in Big Sur*. Arcade, 2014.

Jackson, Roger. *Henry Miller, His Life in Ephemera 1914-1980*. Roger Jackson, 2012.

---, editor. *Writers Three: A Literary Exchange on the Works of Claude Houghton*. Roger Jackson, 1995.

Kahane, Jack. *Memoirs of a Booklegger*. Obolus Press, 2010.

Kahn, Aflred E. "Odysey of a Stool Pigeon." *New Currents: A Jewish Monthly*, vol. III, no. 1, Jan. 1945, pp. 3–4, 26.

Kiakis, Harry. *Henry Miller in Pacific Palisades: Selections from a Journal*. Nexus: The International Henry Miller Journal, 2017.

MacNiven, Ian S. *"Literchoor Is My Beat": A Life of James Laughlin, Publisher of New Directions*. Farrar, Straus and Giroux, 2014.

Miller, Henry. *Aller Retour New York*. New Directions, 1991.

---. "Aller Retour New York." *Europe*, translated by Thérèse Aubray, vol. 43, no. 172, Apr. 1937, pp. 486–502.

---. "An Unpublished Introduction to an Unpublished Book." *The International Henry Miller Letter*, vol. 2, 1961, pp. 23–26.

---. "Four Previously Unpublished Letters from Henry Miller to Gershon Legman," edited by Karl Orend. *Nexus: The International Henry Miller Journal,* vol. 1, 2004, pp. 1–22.

---. "Henry Miller's Letters to Herbert Read: 1935-1958," edited by James Gifford. *Nexus: The International Henry Miller Journal,* vol. 5, 2008, pp. 3–35.

---. "I Came, I Saw, I Fled." *Artists' and Writers' Chap Book,* The Westchester Arts & Crafts Guild, 1935, pp. 25–27.

---. *Max and The White Phagocytes.* Obelisk, 1938.

---. "More Letters to Herbert F. West." *The International Henry Miller Letter,* vol. 6, Apr. 1964, pp. 17–19.

---. "Reunion in Barcelona." *The Intimate Henry Miller,* New American Library, 1959, pp. 13–33.

Miller, Henry, and Lawrence Durrell. *Durrell-Miller Letters, 1935-1980,* edited by Ian S. MacNiven. New Directions, 1988.

Miller, Henry, and James Laughlin. *Henry Miller and James Laughlin: Selected Letters,* edited by George Wickes. Norton, 1996.

Miller, Henry, and Anaïs Nin. *Letters to Anaïs Nin,* edited by Gunther Stuhlman. Putnam's Sons, 1965.

Nin, Anaïs. *Fire: From "A Journal of Love" The Unexpurgated Diary of Anaïs Nin, 1934-1937,* edited by Rupert Pole. Harcourt, 1995.

"NYPL Catalog." *New York Public Library,* 31 Jan. 2017, https://catalog.nypl.org/search.

Orend, Karl. *Henry Miller's Paris Years-Reflections on a Paradigm for Biography.* Roger Jackson, 2003.

---. "Reveries of a Solitary Old Man and His Angels—Henry Miller's Unknown Book and His Encounter with the Magician, Joseph Delteil." *Nexus: The International Henry Miller Journal,* vol. 7, 2010, pp. 9–50.

Pearson, Neil. *Obelisk: A History of Jack Kahane and the Obelisk Press.* Liverpool UP, 2007.

"Police Ban Issue of The Harvard Advocate." *The Boston Globe,* 20 Oct. 1935.

"Quit Harvard Advocate Board." *The Boston Globe,* 23 Oct. 1935.

Shifreen, Lawrence J., and Roger Jackson. *Henry Miller: A Bibliography of Primary Sources.* Vol. 1, Shifreen & Jackson, 1994.

Sipper, Ralph B., et al. *A Descriptive Catalogue of the Dr. James F. O'Roark Collection of the Works of Henry Miller.* Joseph the Provider, 1982.

Standish, Craig Peter, editor. *MORE! 1944-1996 (The Companion Volume To Henry Miller: A Book of Tributes, 1931-1994)*. Standish Books, 1996.

Stern, Gerald. *Stealing History*. Trinity University Press, 2012.

Thompson, Ralph. "Books of the Times." *The New York Times*, 13 July 1938, p. 19.

"To the Editor of the Crimson." *The Harvard Crimson*, 19 Oct. 1935, https://www.thecrimson.com/article/1935/10/19/the-mail-pto-the-editor-of/.

West, Herbert F. "Hanover Browsing." *Dartmouth Alumni Association*, Jan. 1937, pp. 8-9, 72.

Wickes, George. "Introduction." *Henry Miller and James Laughlin: Selected Letters*, edited by George Wickes, Norton, 1996, pp. ix–xxiv.

Winslow, Kathryn. *Henry Miller: Full of Life*. Tarcher, 1986.

Djuna Barnes and Thelma Wood

"For a hundred years or more the world, our world, has been dying.": Degeneration, Sex, and the Palliative Writing of Henry Miller and Djuna Barnes

John Clegg

Introduction

Considering that the first half of the 20th century was marred by what retrospectively are considered to be the two most grotesque and destructive instances of war ever experienced, it comes as no surprise that the novelistic accounts of the period took up, and professed, ideations of apocalypse. Although the apocalyptic feeling, society's degeneration and self-destruction, was pertinent to the works of writers from the fin-de-siècle to the Cold War, there is no period more ravaged by the thought of personal and societal destruction than that of Late Modernism. For it was a period still interacting intimately with the aftermath of the First World War, while sitting ponderously at the foot of the Second. So strong is the sentiment of apocalypse in Late Modernist literature that various critics and scholars have suggested that, rather than simply being one of many concerns for the period, apocalyptic feeling is the major constitutive factor behind Late Modernist literature (and art). Tyrus Miller astutely recognizes that feelings of apocalypse and degeneration seeped out of society and into the relationship between art forms, stating that "late modernist writing appears a distinctly self-conscious manifestation of the aging and decline of modernism, in both its institutional and ideological dimensions ... It is as if the phosphorescence of decay had illuminated the passageway to a re-emergence of innovative writing after modernism" (7). From the outset, it appears that Late Modernist literature was a paradoxical endeavor; only out of the decline and degeneration of society could the work be produced. Rather than an idyllic, Edenesque creation, the craft of Late Modernism follows the path of Dante; it necessarily requires – and is predicated by – a fall that allows for the subsequent rise. The apocalyptic path that degeneration – a term and ideology present in the minds of the epoch – moves society down is the fruitful ground from which the authors of the interwar period produced literature new and profound.

It is through this interaction, the production of literature as buoyed by the degenerate world, that we then must read, especially in the case of novels self-consciously "outing" themselves in the relationship between art and degeneration. Henry Miller's seminal, obscene novel *Tropic of Cancer* locates itself in, and works through, the problems of degenerate society, degenerate people, and degenerate art that will culminate in a post-Freudian analysis of sex in relation to degeneration throughout the work. Simultaneously, I will produce a co-reading of a novel that could easily be viewed as being directly opposed in political ideology to that of *Tropic of Cancer*, Djuna Barnes' bewildering opus, *Nightwood*. What I will suggest in my reading of these two influential novels, is that they aim their gaze at a degenerative society/people in order to recontextualize and reconstitute human vitality through their artfulness. Before doing so, however, it is important that I contextualize this reading through a discussion of the work of Max Simon Nordau and his seminal text, *Degeneration*.

Contextualization

In order to understand the concept of degeneration – often discussed in relation to the Darwinian theory of evolution as being a decline in species survivability – as it was applied in nineteenth and twentieth century Europe, we must first turn to Max Simon Nordau, the French author most well-known for his work entitled *Degeneration*, originally published in 1892. A moralistic takedown of contemporary art, as well as the societal situation that allows its production, *Degeneration* suggests that social and individual decline are symbiotic phenomena. Nordau states in the work's opening book, "Fin-de-Siècle", that at the turn of the century (19th into the 20th) "there have arisen in more highly-developed minds vague qualms of a Dusk of the Nations, in which all suns and all stars are gradually waning, and mankind with all its institutions and creations is perishing in the midst of a dying world" (2). Nordau, from the very beginning of his work, posits both the natural ("suns and all stars") as well as the social world ("institutions and creations") as degenerating in unison. This doubling of degenerate apparitions at the turn of the century is then once more doubled as it interacts with the individual being. A large part, a majority even, of Nordau's pessimistic moralizing takes issue with the "degenerate art" of fin-de-siècle Europe:

> The poet, the musician, is to announce, or divine, or at least suggest in what forms civilization will further be evolved ... And the more vague and insignificant they are, the more they seem to convey

of the future to the poor gaping souls gasping for revelations, and the more greedily and passionately are they expounded. (6)

It is clear in the multiple doublings of his work that Nordau's viewpoint on societal degeneration depends on an understanding of the world in which its individual elements conspire together. Degenerate art develops out of the degenerate society and thus produces more degeneracy thereafter, while the physically degenerate consume drugs and alcohol due to their moral ineptitude. It is this very sweeping generalization – that there is a loop of degeneration ad infinitum – that the authors of Late Modernism, including Henry Miller and Djuna Barnes, preoccupy themselves with in their work. Though elements of degeneration are palpable in these interwar works, for these authors art, and the contemplative artist, are afforded the ability to exit the cycle and reclaim some semblance of non-degenerate human vitality. Degeneracy therefore becomes the issue from which fruitful artistic production is made. By deftly interacting with the individual entities affected by degeneracy, as conceived by Nordau and his peers, Miller and Barnes utilize the negative destruction of degeneration and produce art as a way out; the mandate of their work is realized through their interaction with that which Nordau sensed was destroying society.

Sigmund Freud, like Nordau, was a thinker interested in the destructive behaviors of society and individuals. Freud, as a psychoanalyst interested more in the psychology of individual beings, interacted with the issue of the ego and the libidinal exertions that free the human from the inward turning of the mind. Unlike Nordau, Freud did not see degeneration as being the mandate of society, but rather the inverse; the manifestation of the complexes of the ego in relation to society. This is not to say, however, that Freud did not discuss the issue of societal discontent; it was just always through the lens of its relationship to the individual. Two of Freud's works that deal with both individual and social degeneracy, though not explicitly, are *Beyond the Pleasure Principle*, and *Civilization and Its Discontents*. Both deal with, to some degree, humanity's propensity towards both death and creation; the Eros of the "pleasure principle" for instance, and its opposite, the "conservative nature of living substance" which is widely known (and which I will refer to) as "death drive" (*Beyond* 43). It is in the texts' similarity to Nordau's conflation of the social and the individual, the organic and the mental, that I see Freud's espoused theories in these texts as significant in a simultaneous reading of *Tropic of Cancer* and *Nightwood* with *Degeneration*. Like Nordau, Freud assimilates his theories into a multivalent application, from the smallest structure – the "protozoa" – right on up to the social body, where "civilization" imposes potentially necessary laws in order to stop the son, to use Freud's example in *Civilization and Its Discontents*. Both deal with, to some degree, humanity's propensity towards killing the Father. Yet, as we see in both *Tropic of Cancer* and *Nightwood*, the degenerate society – in that it itself is bent on its own destruction – is unable to fully mitigate the issue of the individual propensity towards death, real or imagined.

The Historical Mandate of the Degenerate Reading

The degenerate reading of *Tropic of Cancer* can be suggested and explored through a look into Miller's expansive preoccupation with the issue throughout his career. In the essay "The Angel is My Watermark" Miller looks back towards the writing of another book from the contestable Obelisk "trilogy," *Black Spring*: "I was already reveling in the fact that the world about me was going to pieces. From the time that I was old enough to think, I had a hunch that this was so … It didn't matter to me whether I was intact or falling to pieces. I was attending a spectacle: the crumbling of our civilization" (39-40). Miller extends his interest in the degenerate world backwards into "the time that [he] was old enough to think", as well as forwards into the latter half of the 20th century, the period in which this essay was authored. "Angel" is an extended pondering by Miller on his affinity for painting, wherein he places significance not on the reception of art but rather in the act of production itself. He, at one point, positions the production of art against the bureaucratic endeavors of the societal elite:

> in fair weather or foul the men who make the least fuss do more to save what is worth saving – and how much is worth saving, do you ever stop to think? – than those who push us about because they think they have the answer to everything. When you put your mind to such a simple, innocent thing, for example, as making a watercolor, you lose some of the anguish which derives from being a member of the world gone mad. (40)

Miller, in stepping away from his fictional (or more fictionalized) works, seems to theorize the production of art as a way out of the "anguish" induced in the individual by a degenerate world. Moving the locus of artful importance away from "meaning" and into the realm of mindful "production" allows for the individual to "save" some aspect "of the world gone mad." Therefore, when Miller's narrator in *Tropic of Cancer* delivers his extended diatribes regarding the writing of the book being consumed by the reader, we can turn back to essays such as "Angel" in order to garner a non-fictional contextualization of the importance Miller places on the act of creation.

Similarly, Djuna Barnes provides the attentive reader with a suggestion that her work has a more far-reaching preoccupation with degeneration and ability of art – specifically literature – to reconstitute those being affected thereby. Phillip Herring, speaking of the vengeful reasoning behind the authoring of *Nightwood*, quotes an illuminating letter written – on the 14th of February 1937 – by Djuna Barnes for Emily Coleman, wherein Thelma Wood, whose fictionalized stand-in is Robin Vote, is both disparaged and described as being brought to life:

> really what an idiot I was – her stock was so exactly what the young, budding St Louis homosexual would have, de Sade, Chanson de Bilitis, the poems of Wilde, the French texte for anything voluptuouse, the newest movement in german [sic] art, the surrealists, her drawings, worst of all her note books full of "lamb chops so much, candy for Djuna so much" … and sketches of butterflies!!!! …this sounds terrible, I really love her, but I know her now, -- she should be damned glad for Nightwood, and to what I made her. (17)

In referencing the texts of de Sade, and Wilde, along with the compositions of symbolist Debussy, Barnes positions her lover, the one that sits in as the spiritual center of *Nightwood*, beside authors that also worked in and around the degenerate (deviant) sexual worlds of European cultural centers. When she later admits her continuing love for the primary subject of *Nightwood*, that Thelma should be "glad" for "what [she] made her", Barnes suggests that she viewed her writing of *Nightwood* as a means by which she was able to "make" people, at the very least in a way that does not align with the prescribed normative structure of socio-moral prescription.

The textual referentiality of Barnes' degeneration, where authors worked on the problem generations and centuries before, eerily mirrors the intertextuality of Miller's work. Intertextuality, specifically that which pertains to writers working around the issue of degeneration, serves to prop up Barnes and Miller's specific artistic practice as part of a long line of literary preoccupation. In suggesting, whether it be through allusion or reference, that their works are related to those thought of as degenerate (while also thought of as canonical), Barnes and Miller relieve the degeneracy of their own work in favor of utilizing degenerate beings as subject. Sarah Garland notes that "Miller's step across the Atlantic into the avant-garde tradition is a step into a steady stream of apocalyptic prophecies and rhetoric," a degenerative rhetoric influenced by a "continent steadied and sustained by the past [writings]" (199-200). Barnes who was reading and interacting with similarly degenerative texts as Miller, also made the exact same move as Miller, from the heavily industrialized and democratized world of progress that was modern New York to the degrading and elder interwar world of Paris. Both authors dealt with degeneration beyond the work of their two seminal novels, and both seem to have been motivated to make similar artistic and spatial decisions at the same time.

Barnes, in her essay "Lament for the Left Bank" commissioned by *Town & Country*, another piece that helps to contextualize an overarching theme of degeneration, wrote of the similarity with Miller in both artistic and spatial terms. First, suggesting that her characters and community were made up of "the real secret, the secret of that great and fallen country [France]: the open hospitality of the street ... The house holds bitterness, the street does not" (113). Second, in a moment that aligns astoundingly well with Tyrus Miller's idea of "Late Modernism" as apocalyptic in nature, Barnes writes of the ending of an old age and the beginning of a new one, at least as artistry in Paris is concerned: "Stein's star, Cocteau's moon, had set ... Joyce himself was another matter" (116). Ending, it seems, is of utmost importance to Miller and Barnes throughout their work, both artistically and physically, and ending is always centered in Paris. Why is this so?

Paris: A Degenerate Locus Reanimated Through Literature

From a narratological perspective the reader is alerted to the degeneration of Cancer before even cracking the novel open. Taking into consideration Gérard Genette's concept of "paratext", the word "Cancer" – though implicated in the geographical demarcation that is the "Tropic of Cancer" – suggests a second reading wherein a specific place is in fact cancerous. This specific place is, of course, Paris. Miller states on the very first page of *Tropic of Cancer* that: "The cancer of time is eating us away ... We must get in step, a lock step, toward the prison of death. There is no escape" and then subsequently geographically implicates this "prison", alerting the reader that it "is now the fall of [his] second year in Paris" (1). Nordau states Paris is the locus of degeneration in Europe:

> By the frightful loss of blood which the body of the French people suffered during the twenty years of the Napoleonic wars, by the violent moral upheavals to which they were subjected in the great Revolution and during the imperial epic, they found themselves exceedingly ill-prepared for the impact of the great discoveries of the century, and sustained by these a more violent shock than other nations more robust and more capable of resistance ... Thousands lost their reason. In Paris a veritable epidemic of mental diseases was observed ... This explains why hysteria and neurasthenia are much more frequent in France ... it explains, too, that it is precisely in France that the craziest fashions in art and literature would naturally arise. (42-43).

In Nordau's contextualization of his fin-de-siècle degeneration, we see the groundwork laid out for the conditions that can potentially instruct and influence our specific reading of degeneration in *Tropic of Cancer*. France, and more specifically Paris as the seat of governmental legislation, is a place whose being is assaulted by memories of war, this in the context of Nordau's view of the fallout of the "Napoleonic wars", as well as later on in the context of the two World Wars. There seems an imperative here, on the part of Nordau, that war is the major constitutive factor behind the onset of horrific (in his eyes at least) degeneration. In much the same way that war has at its end the destruction of a physical/spatial governmental entity, so too does degeneration have at its end the destruction of a physical being. Paris, by the fact of its long history as a theater of war and rebellion, sows the seeds of degeneration in its citizens, a fact that Miller and Barnes reminisce on many times over.

Throughout *Tropic of Cancer*, Paris and its inhabitants are described in terms of moral and physical degeneration. Death, sickness, and adverse sexual perversions permeate the text, creating a miasma of degeneration that allocates Paris as a specific place with a specific propensity for decay. The decay of Paris implicates its inhabitants that it is oft described through personifying language: Paris "is a clump of decrepit buildings which have so rotted away that they have collapsed on one another and formed a sort of intestinal embrace" (40); Paris has a "poisonous breath of spring" (43); Paris contains "people who ... are dead" (64); and "Paris is like a whore" (209). Paris, I would suggest, in its embodiment of degeneration, serves as the perfect place for both Miller and Barnes to take up the cause of regeneration.

For Nordau, degeneration is precipitated by a warring nation and its "violent moral upheavals"; there is no doubt that Miller, being temporally located in the interregnum between the two World Wars, was witnessing and participating in a society with an acute understanding of the negative effects of war. In one particularly illuminating passage, Miller amalgamates the act of sex with that of war, drawing us closer to a reading based on Freud's two instinctual drives:

> It's like a state of war: the moment the condition is precipitated nobody thinks about anything but peace, about getting it over with. And yet nobody has the courage to lay down his arms, to say, "I'm fed up with it ... I'm through." No, there's fifteen francs somewhere, which nobody is going to get in the end anyhow, but the fifteen francs is like the primal cause of things and rather than listen to one's own voice, rather than walk out on the primal cause, one surrenders to the situation, one goes on butchering and butchering. (142)

By situating both acts – that of war and that of sexual intercourse (and subsequently pregnancy and birth) – as one and the same insofar as psychological recognition goes, Miller implicates supposed regenerative forces as a destructive and degenerate tendency. The "mental diseases" of Nordau's degenerate France are the very mode by which Miller conflates sex and war, thus attributing to his curiously degenerate outlook – wherein, through the interaction between deadly and regenerative drives, a new form of "palliative" libidinal life-giving is created. Interestingly enough, Miller in this stanza also applies an economic imperative to the warring state of sex (and the sexual state of war?); the "civilized"

82

economic imperatives of the modern human troubles the author deeply throughout his work, as it is seen as a means by which his subjects are entrapped in a negative social entity.

Freud, of whom Miller was undoubtedly aware and versed in (he, in *Tropic of Cancer*, calls Freud's work "arcana") (25), discusses how civilization – one that mirrors Miller's economically driven, degenerate one – causes the individual to become disaffected and degenerate in his work, in *Civilization and its Discontents*:

> Life, as we find it, is too hard for us; it brings us too many pains, disappointments and impossible tasks. In order to bear it we cannot dispense with palliative measures ... There are perhaps three such measures: powerful deflections, which cause us to make light of our misery; substitutive satisfactions, which diminish it; and intoxicating substances, which make us insensitive to it. (41)

The fact that throughout *Tropic of Cancer* sex is constantly obstructed and negated by sexual inadequacy, sterility, and disease, suggests that it is one of the discontenting experiences created by a frustrating civilization. Instead of sexual satisfaction then, Miller conceives of art as the "palliative measure" in which he is able to form some sort of satisfactory experience for the inhabitants of Paris, namely himself. War, there is no doubt, is an event dictated by the bureaucratic civilization, one that I have shown previously to be degenerate. War, in entering the sexual lives of the degenerate beings and causing a modicum of sterility, requires a "palliative measure" in order for the individual to constitute life; sexual intercourse has at its end pregnancy and the creation of life.

The "palliative measure" that allows for sex in *Tropic of Cancer* to become once more an act of creation is discussed by Michael Hardin in a passage worthy of an extended quotation:

> By returning to the origin and site of creation [the female reproductive system], the male can appropriate the one power which men, by definition, have been denied, that of giving life. The male cannot undergo the process of actual pregnancy; reproduction for him is either artistic creation or the donation of sperm ... For Miller, the return to the womb may seem primal, but the act itself rejects the possibility of being primal by its

artificiality; what is created will not be a human, but the book he is writing. (132)

It seems, according to this passage, Miller's attention to the creation of life as the writing of the novel is one that mirrors the double drives elucidated upon by Freud in *Beyond the Pleasure Principle*. Freud discusses the dynamics of his two drives and their relation to the "Pleasure Principle" all at once when he suggests that "the life instincts have so much more contact with our internal perception [ego] … while the death instincts seem to do their work unobtrusively. The pleasure principle seems actually to serve the death instincts", which he afterwards corrects, suggesting that the Pleasure Principle "is more especially on guard against increases of stimulation from within" (77). In the case of *Tropic of Cancer*, the degenerate society eliminates the potential for palliative sexual reproduction which therefore causes the characters to turn inward, onto their own egos, and attempt to enact destructive "death instincts" on their own selves.

The warring nature of sex in *Tropic of Cancer* seemingly eliminates the ability for its characters to "produce" in the sense of life drive. They are unable to create anew due to impotence, disease, and the imposition of death. Degeneration has rendered the pleasure principle as one that does in fact "serve the death instincts." The "pleasure principle" in Freud's mind is primarily attributed to the human libido, otherwise known in *Beyond* as the "'sex instincts', which are directed towards an object, [as opposed to] certain other instincts, … described provisionally as the 'ego-instincts'" (61). The sexual desires and drives of *Tropic of Cancer*'s characters are limited by the degenerative body, and these sexual desires are attached to the libidinal "death drive" – which has at its end a symbolic return to the womb – they in turn exhibit an excess of excitation of the ego from within, which limits their ability to reproduce in a substantial manner. The characters are exhibited in a loop wherein the life instincts are unable to flourish due to the complication, and limitation, of libidinal drive outwards onto the object. As it so happens, the character in *Tropic of Cancer* who most obviously displays sexual impotence, the hapless and hilarious Van Norden, is a man who displays the binary between the libidinal and ego instincts both overtly and subconsciously.

Van Norden's inability to enact livelihood due to the sexual malfunction instigated by the degenerative body seems to alter the fundamental nature of his ego, thus causing suicidal ideation: "He wakes up cursing himself, or cursing the job, or cursing life. He wakes up utterly bored and discomfited, chagrined to think that he did not die overnight" (100). The degenerate body is both of his own physical malfunction – a laundry list including rotting teeth (101) and a mysterious sexual illness referred to as "those things" treated by "blue ointment" (124) – as well as that of "moral degeneration", Norma a love interest is "queer" (101). Though Van Norden enacts and endeavors on the prescribed path of "life drive", that of libidinal sexual activity, his degenerate infertility, as well as societal moral infertility, renders it a rather egoistic endeavor which is qualified by the fact that sexual-drive mandates a death driven component, that of the return to the womb. Donald Gutierrez suggests that Van Norden's frustrated palliative sexual drive is indicative of a horizontal egoism which has as its relief the sexual instincts: "Van Norden's sex-obsession, however, is a symptom of a deeper ailment: he is self-obsessed. Caught in the prison of an endlessly frustrating egoism, he thinks sex and women will spring him loose from his torment" (25). It is in the womb that Van Norden's self-destructive ego attempts to annihilate itself, as he no longer is able to enact the physical, libidinal, destruction that is situated at the center of the "life drive." Van Norden, so frustrated with his degenerative inability to consummate sexually, turns towards himself (as ego), through the symbol of the mirror. Miller engenders in Van Norden's ego the degenerative forces which disallow him the ability to create – symbolically or otherwise – life: "In every room there is a mirror before which he stands attentively and chews his rage ... piece of his jaw crumble away and he's so disgusted with himself that he stamps on his own jaw" (127).

I suggest that the return to the womb as conceived by Miller in *Tropic of Cancer*, and the subsequent artistic production as replacing sexual reproduction, is an innately political act that has at its core a humanitarian motive. Looking back into the annals of Miller's oeuvre, Lawrence J. Shifreen notes and analyzes the means by which Miller attempted to alleviate his subjects – akin to Freud's "Discontents" – in his series of "Mezzotints" which "can be seen as the prototype for all of Miller's work" (11). Much in the same way that the pieces contained in *Stand Still Like the Hummingbird* contain insights into the continued/unending preoccupations within Miller's work, the "Mezzotints" – in the eyes of Shifreen at least – center Miller as an author who through his work attempts to illuminate and alleviate "types" of people subjected to the inadequacies of the "Modern" world. Speaking of these represented types in the "Mezzotints," Shifreen sees in the images and tropes of modernity as utilized by Miller an attempted ascendancy on the part of the degenerate being. The machination of modernity, the attempt of the individual to escape through drugs and alcohol, are the very degenerate themes that Miller uses in order to give a new "creative (created) life" to those subjected to the degenerate forces. The New York of the "Mezzotints" is a "sick reality ... a society of one dimensional people whose lives are monotones and who live in a dead world beneath the earth's surface [and] forms the basis for Miller's term "cancer," an incurable disease that eats away at and destroys our society" (12).

Miller speaks of the reconstitution of the degenerate being in a world other than that of Nordau's war-affected reality. At the very beginning of *Tropic of Cancer* Miller posits the narrator (which is the author as well), along with the book, as something outside of the traditional "world" of art. Miller, suggesting that this obvious piece of writing is something other than a book, and he something other than an author, states that: "A year ago, six months ago, [he] thought that [he] was an artist. [He] no longer think[s] about it, [he is]. Everything that was literature has fallen away from [him]. There are no more books to be written, thank God" (1). Therefore, as the author is both the creator and the subject of *Tropic of Cancer*, it seems he is, is suggestive of an entirely separate navigable world; Henry Miller, when he says that *Tropic of Cancer* "is not a book" while also asserting that he – as both author and character, for they are one and the same – is, seems to be allocating new life-giving potential to the work of art (2). Shifreen adheres to this reading of Miller's regenerative qualities in the face of the degenerate world in (Miller's early works) the "Mezzotints", noting that the "living death the workers experience horrifies Miller, who feels obligated to raise man above his meager lot in life" (13).

James Gifford posits that the reconstitutive work of Miller, primarily *Tropic of Cancer*, though often read as an apolitical Quietism, is in fact a pointedly political one, wherein by retracting himself into the world of his "art" Miller is able to produce new possibilities for those degenerative beings of interwar Paris, suggesting that the:

> combination of urban desolation and futile war set contrary to fecund organicism and rural locales would run across the Villa Seurat and New Apocalypse as well as the early San Francisco

86

Renaissance as a shared preoccupation reflecting their common sympathies for pacifism, self-development, and anti-authoritarian quietism. (46)

By ascribing a political perspective to Miller's work, whose locus of popularity lies in the publication of *Tropic of Cancer*, Gifford draws out a potential humanist preoccupation with the reconstitution done by Miller through interaction with Freudian theories. The fact that Miller can be viewed as a political novelist, rather than merely a fecund sensationalist which many critics and readers warily suggest he is, sheds new light on the concept of art as "palliative measure." The act of regenerative libidinal writing as a way out of the degenerate sexual interactions of his subjects seems to suggest that through his "quietist" writing Miller was able to perform a valuable political move. As George Orwell notes in his seminal piece "Inside the Whale" – and what better way to describe a work dealing with a return to the womb than through the imagery of allowable consumption into another being – "Miller is able to get nearer to the ordinary man than is possible to more purposive writers. For the ordinary man is also passive … he feels himself master of his fate, but against major events he is as helpless as against the elements" (4).

Felix – a problematic caricature of the "degenerate Jew" – is the character in *Nightwood* most easily read as degenerate due to the extension of degenerate lineage onto his mentally unwell son, he finds in Paris a place wherein he can locate himself as a degenerate being. Paris is said to be the "right" place for Felix, the prime example of bodily degeneration and, therefore, moral degeneration according to Nordau; "In nineteen hundred and twenty he was in Paris (his blind eye had kept him out of the army), still spatted, still wearing his cutaway, bowing, searching, with quick pendulous movements, for the correct thing to which to pay tribute: the right street, the right café, the right building, the right vista" (9). Felix is kept out of the army by his degenerative eyesight. According to Nordau failing eyesight is a physical sign of degeneration, and "[p]reviously men had recourse to spectacles at the age of fifty. The average age is now forty-five years" (42). Felix moves to Paris searching for the "right" "object" on which to turn his ego, the "right" thing on which to focus himself. Speaking to my idea of *Nightwood* as a reconstitutive novel which undoes some of the effects of degeneration, and this must essentially be situated in Paris, Thomas Heise reveals, through his "mapping" reading of *Nightwood*, that the spatial situation of Paris is to be regarded as the remains of Georges-Eugène Haussmann's renovation of the cityscape. Envisioned as a means by which the city could suppress dissent and spread out undesirable citizens, Haussmann's renovations embody the spatial assertion of control taken up by bureaucratic powers in Paris, which thereafter degrades and diminishes the livelihoods of those considered degenerate. Heise posits that "*Nightwood* is a … defense … mapping the underworld of queer Americans in Paris in explicit sexual and geographical detail … when an imperiled and nomadic queer underworld reterritorializes spaces in the twentieth-century city, dwelling in its degraded, submerged geographies in ways that produce new forms of erotic sociability' (289).

In the chapter "The Squatter" *Nightwood* offers up a symbolic scene of the merger between sex and war. After a large party at the home of Jenny Petherbridge, with guests including Dr. Matthew O'Connor and a mysterious adolescent referred to only as "the child", Robin Vote and Jenny enact a symbolic birth through the act of war. "Jenny struck Robin," we are told, "scratching and tearing in hysteria, striking, clutching and crying" (76), Jenny whose "ego" is so attached to the "objects" of her life – including the degenerate Robin, "tiny ivory or jade elephants", "[s]omeone else's marriage ring" and many other "second-hand dealings" (65-66) – cannot seem to bear the "object" turning on her, civilization, as the bringer of pleasure, causes in Jenny a great amount of discontent. The egoism of Jenny Petherbridge is made disconsolate and reversionary by the abject degeneration of the Parisian metropolis, thus leading to a turn towards symbolic warring, and attempt to destroy that which is meant to bring pleasure. Later on in this symbolic war between Robin and Jenny becomes explicitly sexual:

> Jenny also, as if compelled to conclude the movement of the first blow, almost as something seen in retarded action, leaned forward and over, so that when the whole of the gesture was completed, Robin's hands were covered by Jenny's slight and bending breast, caught in between the bosom and the knees. And suddenly the child flung herself down on the seat, face outward, and said in a voice not suitable for a child because it was controlled with terror: 'Let me go! Let me go! Let me go!' (76)

Ending their fight in an embrace involving the sexualized female breast, and a culmination that is a child wanting to leave the enclosed area of the carriage – the realm of the sexual fight – is suggestive of the fight, as degenerate war, being the interaction that turns into the production of a new being, or life. This is the first instance of any sexual encounter for Jenny seeming to produce some sort of appreciable life, the men of Jenny's past did, not only, not produce children but they died off one by one: "Each husband had wasted away and died; [Jenny] had been like a squirrel racing a wheel day and night in an endeavor to make them historical; they could not survive it" (65). Jenny Petherbridge makes an attempt to attach significance (history) to each one of her previous husbands, the act of building them up, the transcribing of the ego onto the object, seems to be what actually kills them in the end. Whereas, so far as her relationship with Robin goes, Jenny's attempt at destruction of the object is the means by which she – and her degenerate lesbian partner – are able to create/birth "the child." The problem here is the original instance of symbolic copulation and birth does not allow "the child" the way out which she desires; there is no exiting of the womb-like carriage that is the venue of the warring sexual scene. The entrance into the world on the part of the product of the deadly libidinal – and degenerate – partnership requires another "palliative measure" in order to exit the figurative womb.

Unlike Miller, Barnes never exposes herself within *Nightwood*, the writer is not a character, and as such the replacement of the sexual propensity cannot be vocalized in the same way. The literary product as constitutive of life, a "history" that Jenny Petherbridge could never apply to the objects of her ego, is elucidated upon by Deborah Parsons, another reader attuned to the Freudian influence upon Late Modernity. She states that: "Barnes's arcane and figural language, her flamboyantly ornamental use of metaphorical and allegorical techniques … seem far removed from … the disciplinary logic of the modern novel … Through the overstatement of its own artistry, this singularly stylish text exposes the myth of modernism's claim to aesthetic mastery over the chaos of history" (165-166). The narrative alleviation of the sexually degenerate being is transferred to Dr. Matthew O'Connor, a character frequently referred to by critics as both writer and reader of the various narrative strains that intersect throughout the novel. Tyrus Miller notes that O'Connor "plays another role, distinct from being a character among other characters, each with their own 'solutions': he is a reader of the whole" (158), while Miriam Fuchs suggests that O'Connor maintains an all-seeing narrative viewpoint wherein all stories are parlayed through him: "the doctor moves deftly and successfully, presented by an omniscient third-person point of view" (128). O'Connor presents himself in a somewhat similar way to Freud in his authoring of *Beyond the Pleasure Principle*, presenting a unique insight into the corroboration between the life and death instincts, stating that: "Life, [is] the permission to know death. We are created that the earth might be made sensible of her inhuman taste" (830). O'Connor becomes the psychoanalyst, pondering the issue of humanity and its drives, and ultimately suggests to Nora – in the chapter "Watchman, What of the Night?" that he also provides answers through the means of writing: "must [he], perchance, like careful writers, guard [him]self against the conclusion of [his] readers ... [he has] a narrative, but [we] will be put to it to find it" (95-97).

At the very end of the same chapter, as Dr. O'Connor is telling Nora his interpretation of the war/sexual interaction between Robin and Jenny, we see that his role as the "writer" of narratives allows "the child" a way out of the womb. Insofar as the degeneration of sex causes an inability for the subject to consummate and produce life, Barnes presents O'Connor as writer in the way that Miller does so of himself, wherein the writer is able to consummate a "pleasurable" life drive through an alternative palliative measure. The ending of his version of the events has O'Connor "writing" "the child" out of the womblike carriage: "And then at the child – there was terror in it and it was running away from something grown up; I saw that she was sitting still and she was running; it was in her eyes and in her chin, drawn down, and her eyes wide open" (106).

The "new production" that is "the child" is freed by the implacable and rambling narrative strains of Dr. O'Connor; through him she is able to be freed of the symbolic womb and flees from the elder "something grown up" that is the two elder lesbians, Robin and Jenny, as well as their degenerate sexual war. This narrative intricacy, *Nightwood*'s ambivalence towards structural exactitude, is the very thing that scholars have noted as constituting a newly produced body, both in the physical and narrative senses. Speaking to the end of the passage analyzed above, specifically the part where O'Connor eerily sees into the future saying that "one dog will find them both" (89), Elizabeth Blake suggests that, in *Nightwood*, "figuration gives way to physicality, a death of metaphor that is not just a metaphorical death but also a rearticulation of what it means to be alive" (162). The oracular sensibilities of the ever writing, ever reading, Dr. O'Connor, a man whose narratives are impossible to historicize or placate in any way, end up both alleviating the child of the womb embattled by degenerate lesbian sex as well as predicting a future wherein his metaphorical tales have become concrete. By writing in a form that is entirely new, Dr. O'Connor allows for palliative measures to take up a real, substantial, and productive form; through the artfulness of his narratives Dr. O'Connor gives life to the degenerate underworld of *Nightwood*'s interwar Paris.

Conclusion

At this essay's beginning I made the innocuous suggestion that two novels, Henry Miller's *Tropic of Cancer* and Djuna Barnes' *Nightwood*, that seem to occupy opposite ends of the spectrum of sexual proclivities, could be read alongside one another in order to further our understanding of the role of the author as alleviator of the degenerate body. As we made way into the close readings of the texts I turned my gaze towards the individual conceptualizations of degeneration in each work, suggesting that the way in which they mirror each other, so far as the representation and location of degeneration goes, locates and creates similarly degenerate sexual subjects. What was revealed in the close reading of both *Tropic of Cancer* and *Nightwood*, through a lens tinged with the works of Sigmund Freud, is that both texts present the work of literature as reconstitutive palliative measures undoing sexual degeneracy. Through two characters, Miller's textual doppelganger in the case of *Tropic of Cancer* and Dr. Matthew O'Connor in the case of *Nightwood*, the palliative measures mitigated and relinquished by degeneracy are taken up in the form of narrative production, thus positioning the production of art as a means of rebirth, and life-giving, in the case of peoples stifled by a society of which destruction is the defining factor of the interwar zeitgeist. In reading the works tinged with degeneracy through a post-Freudian lens we are enlightened to the possibility art has in undoing some of the negative tendencies precipitated by a degenerate Parisian world marred by war and death.

Works Cited

Barnes, Djuna. "Lament for the Left Bank." *PMLA*, vol. 130, no. 1, 2015, pp. 110-118.
Barnes, Djuna. *Nightwood*. New Directions, 1946.
Blake, Elizabeth. "Obscene Hungers: Eating and Enjoying *Nightwood* and *Ulysses*." *The Comparatist*, vol. 39, 2015, pp. 153-170.

Freud, Sigmund. *Beyond the Pleasure Principle*. Trans. James Strachey. Norton, 1961.

— —. *Civilization and its Discontents*. Trans. James Strachey. Norton, 1961.

Garland, Sarah. "'The dearest of cemeteries': European Intertexts in Henry Miller's *Tropic of Cancer*." *European Journal of American Literature*, vol. 29, no. 3, 2010, pp. 197-225.

Gifford, James. *Personal Modernisms: Anarchist Networks and the Later Avant-Gardes*. University of Alberta P, 2014.

Gutierrez, Donald. "'Hypocrite lecteur': *Tropic of Cancer* as Sexual Comedy." *Mosaic*, vol. 11, no. 2, 1978, pp. 21-33.

Heise, Thomas. "Degenerate Sex and the City: Djuna Barnes' Urban Underworld." *Twentieth Century Literature*, vol. 55, no. 3, 2009, pp. 287-321.

Herring, Phillip. "Djuna Barnes and Thelma Wood: The Vengeance of *Nightwood*." *Journal of Modern Literature*, vol. 18, no.1, 1992, pp. 5-18.

Miller, Henry. "The Angel is My Watermark." *Stand Still Like the Hummingbird*. New Directions, 1962, pp. 38-41.

— —. *Tropic of Cancer*. Grove Press, 1961.

Miller, Tyrus. *Late Modernism*. U of California P, 1999.

Nordau, Max Simon. *Degeneration*. William Heinemann, 1898.

Orwell, George. "Inside the Whale." *Inside the Whale and Other Essays*. Victor Gollancz, 1940, pp. 1-18.

Parsons, Deborah. "Djuna Barnes: Melancholic Modernism." *The Modernist Novel*. Ed. Morag Shiach. Cambridge UP, 2007, pp. 165-177.

Shifreen, Lawrence J. "Henry Miller's Mezzotints: The Undiscovered Roots of *Tropic of Cancer*." *Studies in Short Fiction*, vol. 16, no. 1, 1979, pp. 11-17.

A Romanticist on Crete
Aspects of Henry Miller's Vitalism

Finn Jensen

Henry Miller's vitalism has many sources, and it runs as an undercurrent under almost all of his work. It is closely connected with his eschatological view of Western society. First comes the great destruction, which in the thirties was not difficult to predict, then emerges a new world where the life force will bloom again. Like Nietzsche, Miller was essentially a yea-sayer!

In the Western metaphysical tradition, a direct connection runs from romanticists like Schelling to Emerson, Nietzsche, and Bergson. They all believe in a pervasive spiritual force that runs through nature and civilization. It is a divine force, and it can primarily be perceived via intuition or inspiration, so in periods where rationality and intellect are the primary forces it is repressed, as is very much the case in progressive Western culture, with its emphasis on development and materialism, and the result will always be disastrous. Schelling called nature a poem confined in a secret and mysterious writing that can only be interpreted in a poetic form. The conscious artistic genius, therefore, is the very peak of humanity, but a scientific genius can also reach divine insight if he is tuned into the spiritual levels. A special kind of genius, and one that plays an important role for Miller, is the so-called "natural genius," an individual living in immediate and spontaneous contact with spiritual forces, while the great majority, and especially people living in the big cities, are completely out of touch with this dimension. In great metropolises such as London or Paris in the beginning of the 19th century, the majority lived artificial lives out of touch with nature and the whole spiritual level; they were literally buried in materialism.

In Schelling's philosophy of nature, he sees everything connected organically, as opposed to the neoplatonic dualistic view where the spiritual level is separated from the material world; in his pantheistic view, the divine spirit is present everywhere in nature from rocks to living creatures. It culminates in the genius, and in its pure form it is God, the pure divine spirit. This can only be experienced by the genius in an epiphany, the highest form of religious experience and one that Miller would cultivate especially in Greece. The vitalistic tradition in the 19th and 20th centuries is primarily built upon the pantheistic tradition, which is much older than Schelling, and it can be followed through the centuries in different shapes that all share an anti-materialistic and anti-development attitude, but with Spengler, who was very much inspired by Nietzsche, it became associated with the apocalyptic idea that Western civilization was coming to an end. This view was shared by many associated with the avant-garde and modernism, especially after the disaster of World War I, which definitely proved that Man had no control over technological development. These ideas were important for Miller after he met with Michael Fraenkel and Walter Lowenfels in Paris, but he added on his own a great inspiration from Henri Bergson, who also saw phantasy and intuition as the principle means for comprehension. Like Schelling's, Miller's ideal was the inspired artist able to reach an epiphany or the classical "*unio mystica*." His central notion of the life force the "élan vital" a parallel to Nietzsche's "will to power" became essential to Miller probably early on in New York. He found here the living contrast to the dying society around him, a vital force, a cosmic dimension from which we have been cut off, but it is still there underneath the ruins, and it represents a vital hope for a whole new way of life, a whole new culture.

Like the romanticists Miller was very much a syncretist and like them he could easily combine modern writers with ancient eastern philosophy or mystics from the 16th century; he took his inspiration where he could find it. A typical example of his vitalistic view is this quote from his essay on E. Graham Howe: "The Wisdom of the Heart" (1939) from the collection with the same title. He presents here what he calls "The Doctrine of the Heart," which he distinguish from "The Doctrine of the Eye" representing the field of rational knowledge that brings us farther and farther away from true knowledge. The heart as a symbol was the one he would choose later on when describing his epiphanies in Greece.

> For the awakened individual, however, life begins
> *now*, at any and every moment; it begins at the
> moment when he realizes that he is part of a great

94

whole, and in the realization becomes himself whole. In the knowledge of limits and relationships he discovers the eternal self, thenceforth to move with obedience and discipline in full freedom. *Balance, discipline, illumination* – these are the key words in Howe's doctrine of wholeness, or holiness, for the words mean the same thing. It is not essentially new, but it needs to be rediscovered by each and every one individually. As I said before, one meets it in such poets and thinkers as Emerson, Thoreau, Whitman, to take a few recent examples. It is a philosophy of life which nourished the Chinese for thousands of years, a philosophy which, unfortunately, they have abandoned under Western influence. (39)

A romantic text will always contain structures or stratifications to illustrate the dialectics between the material and the spiritual forces, and very often it will show us an element of movement especially of the main character. And as a general rule we can say that a character can be judged by how far he/she can move about in the romantic landscape: the more you can move about, the more important will you appear to be. A typical movement can be the hero's trying quest for spiritual insight, but on the other hand this insight can also appear spontaneously as lightning or as a part of the natural genius' fundamental nature and something he/she is totally ignorant of.

In Denmark, we had a very strong romantic movement from the beginning of the 19th century, and parts of it were very much under the influence of Schelling and his pantheistic visions. Hans Christian Andersen (1805-1875) was very typical in this respect, and his tales are very useful when it comes to illustrating the structure and dynamics of a romantic text. Miller mentions Andersen in *The Books in my Life*, but I don't think he was a direct inspiration for him; now Andersen's stories can easily be found on the net. In these tales, you can detect the spiritual life forces directly, or on the contrary, when they are missing, everything goes wrong, as in "The Shadow,"

Andersen's contribution to so-called "dark romanticism." I have chosen two of his best-known tales: "The Nightingale" from 1843 and "The Bell" from 1845. They have similar space structures but with very different types of persons, so they complete each other. I will not go into detailed accounts of the texts, you can do that on your own, but will restrain myself to the most important movements. In "The Nightingale," the structures look like this:

We are in China, and the emperor and his court have isolated themselves in a completely artificial palace built of delicate china, cold and rationally calculated. In the other end of the spectrum, we have the deep wood and the sea: pure nature, and it is here the nightingale sings. The poor fishermen hear it and love it, but they are too poor and busy to dwell very much upon it. The tale begins when the emperor discovers that there is a wonderful bird of which he knows nothing. The only person at the court who knows about it is a little kitchen maid who travels every day all the way from the sea to the palace. She helps the court to find the bird, and it agrees to visit the court, where it at once is captured and kept in a cage. As a typical Andersen side-motif at this point, a phony intellectual appears: the music master who is unable to understand the real value of the nightingale and thinks higher of an artificial one decorated with diamonds and precious stones, which is also presented at court. When the artificial bird sings, the real nightingale escapes. After some time the emperor is dying in his china palace, when suddenly the nightingale appears and chases death away from him. Only then he realizes that there are forces beyond his control and that he will have to open up to them.

In this tale we have the typical culture – nature dichotomy, we have the natural geniuses in the fishermen and the kitchen maid, and as the hero we have the emperor who is able to open up to the life forces represented by the nightingale. And then we have the phony intellectuals, a motif often used by Miller.

The second story, "The Bell," uses the following structure:

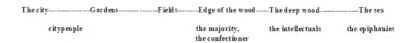

The main dichotomy is exactly the same, but the movements and characters are quite different. The main motif is the sound of a bell, which can scarcely be heard in the city, but as you move out in the fields and near the wood it grows stronger. The characters are a group of young people who have just passed their confirmation and now by definition can be seen as grownups. They decide to walk out towards the wood, but one by one they give up on the walk for a variety of reasons, and a poor boy is unable to participate. They are all attracted by the bell, but the majority ends their journey at the confectioner, where they console themselves with tea and cake. A few move on, but at last only a prince dares to go into the darkest part of the wood, and just as he reaches the sea, the poor boy catches up with him. He had made it all the way on his own, but they move on by different routes and only meet in the end where they share the epiphany, one of the most beautiful in Andersen's writing:

> The forest sang, the sea sang, and the heart of the boy sang too. Nature was a vast, holy church, where the trees and drifting clouds were the pillars; flowers and grass made the velvet carpet, and heaven itself was the great dome. Up there, the red colors faded as the sun sank into the ocean, but then millions of stars sprang out like millions of diamond lamps, and the king's son spread out his arms in joy towards the heavens, the sun and the forest.
>
> At that moment, from the right-hand path, there appeared the poor boy with the short sleeves and the wooden shoes. He had come there as quickly and by following his own path. Joyfully they ran towards each other, and held each other by the hand in the great tabernacle of Nature and Poetry, while above them sounded the invisible, holy bell. The blessed spirits floated around them and lifted up their voices in a joyful hallelujah.
>
> (Translation by Jean Hersholt, H. C. Andersen Center, University of Southern Denmark)

Social differences mean nothing when you are on a romantic quest for the ultimate spiritual experience, but in this text the boys have to pay a heavy price for going all the way.

In *The Colossus of Maroussi*, Henry Miller is also on a romantic journey, and he too had to overcome all sorts of difficulties before he finally could receive his epiphany. But the sources of the spiritual experience could be many other than pure nature; the romanticists could find them, among other places, in ancient history, in faraway exotic cultures, and among "primitive" tribes like the American Indians. All these elements can be found in Miller's writing. When he came to Greece, Miller felt that he had left the nightmare of modern development and capitalism and had come to a culture where the signs of authentic values were still out in the open to be visited and experienced. In the first part of the book, he is like an initiate and is guided around by the masters, especially Georg Katsimbalis and George Seferis,[1] and it is here he experienced one of the most profound of his epiphanies in the ruins of the old theatre in Epidaurus, the ancient healing place and truly holy site:

> At Epidaurus, in the stillness, in the great peace that came over me, I heard the heart of the world beat. I know what the cure is: it is to give up, to relinquish, to surrender, so that our little hearts may beat in unison with the great heart of the world. (70)

Miller seeks his experiences in mythological, religious, and historic places and not often in nature itself. When he travels to Crete, he is on his own for the first time, and he is following an old dream of getting in touch with the Minoan culture, which he sees as the ultimate foundation under the Western culture. As always he is seeking the layers of authenticity to learn from a period from before the great destruction sat in, just as a European romanticist in the 19th century would travel to discover ancient ruins or, indeed, among the common population to extract the wisdom of fairytales and folk songs.

So in Miller's case the horizontal travel from place to place – and on Crete especially the travel from Heraklion to Phaestos – is supplemented by a vertical quest, where he seeks out the traces of ancient culture among the modern elements. He feels that the Minoan culture is close to the ancient Indian cultures and to all other ancient cultures that have blossomed and are now almost forgotten. He calls them "wheels of light":

The vertical life of man was constantly churned by the revolutions of these great gleaming wheels of light. Now it is dark. Nowhere throughout the greatly enlarged world is there the least sign or evidence of the turning of a wheel. The last wheel has fallen apart, the vertical life is done with; man is spreading over the face of the earth in every direction like a fungus growth, blotting out the last gleams of light, and the last hopes. (135)

When he visits Knossus, one of his main reasons to go to Crete, the experience is somewhat overshadowed by his impressions of a group of modern day Greeks. He is satisfied by the profound feeling of peace and joy that he feels connects him to this long forgotten culture, but to the reader it is evident that the spiritual associations are somewhat disappointing, and his day is really ruined when he gets in touch with a group of Greek men in a nearby village:

> The contrast between past and present was tremendous, as though the secret of life had been lost. The men who gathered around me took on the appearance of uncouth savages. They were friendly and hospitable, extraordinarily so, but by comparison with the Minoans they were like neglected domesticated animals. (107)

These people are impressed by meeting an American, some of them have been there themselves, and to Miller's eyes they are totally destroyed by materialism and capitalism; there is no visible sign of any spiritual life among them. And Miller of course provokes them by emphasizing his total poverty, which they simply don't believe, but the most depressing aspect is their enormous enthusiasm for the prospect of war, as one of them expresses: "Me kill everybody – German, Italian, Russian, Turk, French. Greek no 'fraid'" (110). The culture of destruction seems to be embedded in their minds, and to Miller they represent a layer of destruction that has descended even upon this underdeveloped country. Luckily, he will later on meet people who have preserved their spiritual instincts.

In Heraklion, where stays in a little hotel, he has similar confrontations, this time with a group of intellectuals that represents a poor reflection of the real geniuses he met in Athens, but of this group Miller keeps an ironic distance. He is able to provoke them by this profound statement:

> "And what is it about Greece that makes you like it so much?" asked someone.
> I smiled. "The light and the poverty," I said.
> "You're a romantic," said the man.
> "Yes," I said, "I'm crazy enough to believe that the happiest man on earth is the man with the fewest needs. And I also believe that if you have light, such as you have here, all ugliness is obliterated. Since I've come to your country I know that light is holy: Greece is a holy land to me." (116f)

And there is the French woman who owns a little souvenir shop in the town together with her Greek husband and hates every minute she's on Crete. She misses the beautiful trees and gardens of Normandy and gets quite upset when Miller doesn't agree with her and prefers dusty Crete:

> "But it's not civilized," she said, in a sharp, shrill voice which reminded me of the miserly tobacconiste in the Rue de la Tombe-Issoire.
> *"Je m'en fous de la civilisation européenne!"* I blurted out.
> *"Monsieur!"* she said again, her feathers ruffled and her nose turning blue with malice.
> (119)

As a response, Miller allows himself in the text to go off on a surrealistic "Dipsy-Doodle," a fantastic and rambling piece of text where Louis Armstrong is the son of Agamemnon and on his command sets off to trumpet peace and joy everywhere. It is all about how phantasy and creativity triumphs over the narrow minded, white civilized and restricted lives, and in the book it serves as Miller's own revenge and as a demonstration of the artist's supremacy. He can create a text like this, but the French woman in the shop can only dream of nice flowers in pots. Like all people who have seen the light, the romanticists can be very condescending.

It is typical that before he reaches Phaestos, Miller doesn't meet anyone he agrees with. He can't relate to the majority of people, who seem destroyed by the American dream and materialism, and they don't even discover his irony when he makes fun of the buildings in New York or the insanity of the stock exchange. He likes the streets and buildings of Heraklion, he likes the layers of civilization on Crete, but he is unable to connect with the present day social life, so in that respect the city functions to him in a way very similar to that of the typical romanticist. After another failed meeting he is back in his room and dwells upon Crete as the birthplace of the greatest of gods but then destroyed by the endless fighting and finally "shunned by all like a leper and left to expire in its own dung and ashes" (p. 135). That night he has a fantastic nightmare that culminates in a familiar vision in a cave:

> In the shivery depths I saw a great heart bright as a ruby suspended from the vault by a huge web. It was beating and with each beat there fell to the ground a huge gout of blood. It was too large to be the heart of any living creature. It was larger even than the heart of a god. It is like the heart of agony, I said aloud, and as I spoke it vanished and a great darkness fell over me. (136)

Perhaps the tortured heart of the ancient Greek civilization? The next day he is ready to set off for Phaestos. The structures of Miller's journey can be described like this:

102

Miller the traveler, the romantic hero, is of course the only one capable of traversing the whole structure, since he is the only one to see the connection between the ancient layers, the ruins of Phaestos and the vision of the heart. And he doesn't even have to suffer on his quest; he is driven in comfort through the frightening landscape:

> This is nature in a state of dementia, nature having lost its grip, having become the hopeless prey of its own elements. This is the earth beaten, brutalized and humiliated by its own violent treachery. This is one of the spots wherein God abdicated, where He surrendered to the cosmic law of inertia. (137)

They drive through rain on muddy, slippery roads through the mountains, and he has to walk the last climb on foot, "fully aware of being on the brink of a great experience" (139) and thankful for being able to experience it after all his humiliations. On the top he meets the guard of Phaestos, Alexandros, who in this romantic construction is seen playing the role of the natural genius, the only person on Crete with whom Miller feels a true connection. And he recognizes that Miller must be very special to have made this long journey, that there must be a deeper meaning behind it:

> "God has sent you," he said, pointing heavenward and smiling at me as if in ecstasy. Graciously he relieved me of my coat and lunch box, informing me rapturously as he trotted along in front of me what a joy it was to see a human being again. "This war," he said wringing his hands and piously raising his eyes in mute imploration, "this war .... Nobody

comes here any more. Alexandros is all alone. Phaestos is dead. Phaestos is forgotten." (140)

The European crisis is now so deep that no one is seeking enlightenment any more. But Miller and Alexandros communicate wonderfully despite the language barrier, and without the least distance or irony Miller uses an obvious religious language when he describes the situation where he takes in the scenery. Alexandros kisses his hand, and he shows Miller the landscape as if his eyes were saying, "I give you the earth and all the blessings it contains" (140), and then in a fantastic gesture he bends down and cleans Miller's shoes, which Miller finds a bit strange, but he soon realizes the deep meaning of it:

> I send out a benediction in every direction – to old and young, to the neglected savages in the forgotten parts of the earth, to wild as well as domesticated animals, to the birds of the air, to creeping things, to trees and plants and flowers, to rocks and lakes and mountains. This is the first day of my life, said I to myself, that I have included everybody and everything on this earth in one thought. I bless the world, every inch of it, every living atom, and it is all alive, breathing like myself, and conscious through and through. (140).

This is nothing less than the inspired poet in touch with the whole creation, with God, and thereby being like God himself. Schelling would have loved this passage! But this was just the landscape, when he later walks alone in the ruins of Phaestos he has another epiphany:

> At the very gates of Paradise the descendants of Zeus halted here on their way to eternity to cast a last look earthward and saw with the eyes of innocents that the earth is indeed what they have always dreamed it to be: a place of beauty and joy

104

and peace. In his heart man is angelic; in his heart man is united with the whole world. Phaestos contains all the elements of the heart; it is feminine through and through. Everything that man has achieved would be lost were it not for this final stage of contrition which is here incarnated in the abode of the heavenly queens. (141)

This is the culmination, not only of his stay in Crete, not only of his stay in Greece, but in a way of the whole structure of his work. Here he is truly happy. He is alone with a man with whom he can hardly speak, but he is not only on a divine spot, he has the ability to appreciate it fully, and it compensates for all his sufferings. This is not just an empty gesture; it is as genuine as Andersen's interpretation of the nightingale and the bell, both out there where the deep wood meets the ocean. Here we follow Miller alone in a deserted place and without his guides. He then shares a meal with Alexandros and enjoys the local wine as they communicate heart to heart. Then he departs and begins the long journey back through cascades of heavy rain. A few days later he leaves Crete. It may have been disappointing at first, but it kept its promise and delivered the most beautiful of all of Miller's epiphanies. It allowed him to tone down the eschatology for a moment and concentrate on the vitalism of the heart, where he could join the long tradition.

Note

See my article "Miller and Seferis: A Mutual Portrait from One Mythologist to the Other." *Nexus: The International Henry Miller Journal*, vol. 8, 2011, pp. 91-104.

Works Cited

Andersen, Hans Christian. "The Bell" (1845) and "The Nightingale." (1843). Trans. by Jean Hersholt. <www.andersen.sdu.dk>.
Miller, Henry. *The Colossus of Maroussi*. New Directions, 2010.
— —. *The Wisdom of the Heart*. New Directions, 1941.

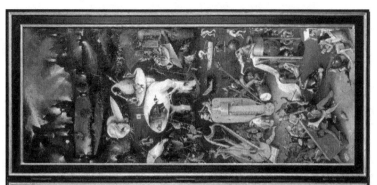

Henry Miller and the Oranges of Hieronymus Bosch

Inez Hollander Lake

Henry Miller mentioned the peace, the quiet and the fog rolling in and out over the velvety hills and blessed it, for here, Miller argued, man could hide from all of the world's ugliness and experience the serene security created by a handful of people who lived in harmony with nature. He was referring to Big Sur, a garden of earthly delights he called home, if not heaven, during the forties and fifties.

While the fifties and sixties in the San Francisco Bay Area were dominated by the noise of the counter culture of Beats, hippies and protesting students, Miller withdrew from what he had once called "the air-conditioned nightmare" of American life, and lived a more quiet life, painting watercolors and eventually moving to Pacific Palisades in the sixties.

In his very own way, Miller had contributed to a counter culture of sorts, or rather he was the eye of his own storm with the publication of his early work which was declared obscene and banned for years, so it could not appear on the bookshelves of American libraries and bookshops.

Miller has remained misunderstood for most of his life and afterwards, and the same goes for the oeuvre of Hieronymus Bosch. This could be the underlying reason for Miller's mention of Bosch in his Big Sur memoir, *Big Sur and the Oranges of Hieronymus Bosch* (1957), a fascinating and Zen kind of read, which, for the record, doesn't have a single sex scene in it.

Here's the passage with the oranges, referring to the middle panel of *The Garden of Earthly Delights* (figure 1) by Bosch:

> Some will say they do not wish to dream their lives away. As if life itself were not a dream, a very real dream from which there is no awakening! We pass from one state of dream to another: from the dream of sleep to the dream of waking, from the dream of life to the dream of death. Whoever has enjoyed a good dream never complains of having wasted his time. On the contrary, he is delighted to have partaken of a reality which serves to heighten and enhance the reality of everyday.

The oranges of Bosch's 'millennium,' [...] exhale this dreamlike reality which constantly eludes us and which is the very substance of life. They are far more delectable, far more potent, than the Sunkist oranges we daily consume [...] The millennial oranges which Bosch created restore the soul; the ambiance in which he suspended them is the everlasting one of spirit become real. (28-29)

Fig. 1 Detail of center panel (lower right) showing oranges

The question is why did Miller pick this particular painting, and more intriguingly, why the oranges and not a particular scene or the entire middle painting of *The Garden of Earthly Delights* triptych?

Or maybe we should backpedal just a bit, and wonder why there are so many oranges in this iconic painting? Please note that most art historians discussing this painting hardly mention oranges at all, but see them as apples, or the forbidden fruit. Oranges, on the other hand, have more interesting connotations here, and ultimately play neatly into Miller's understanding of the painting.

In fact, the symbolic significance of the oranges (or apples) may well depend on one's interpretation of the painting, for is the middle panel, as Miller, together with art historian Wilhelm Fränger, believed, an Epicurean feast of free spirits and a second paradise? More recently, Hans Belting wrote that the middle panel is neither prelapsarian nor postlapsarian but is part of a world where the Fall had not taken place at all: while the Original Sin is absent in the left panel altogether, the middle panel, Belting suggests, is a "paradise that doesn't exist anywhere because it has never become reality. Today it would be called a virtual world" (7). This interpretation does not only align itself with the dreamlike and surreal sensation Miller describes, but it also counters more conventional interpretations that read the panels from left (Paradise) (figure 2) to middle (A Garden of Lust and Excess) (figure 1) to right (a postlapsarian and hellish reality in which sins like gambling, greed, debauchery and gluttony are steeped in a world of darkness and noise) (figure 3).

But there are no absolutes here: the depiction of Paradise shows a Tree of Knowledge next to a rather apathetic Adam with no serpent or the actual moment of the Fall (figure 4), and the last panel, if you take out the imaginary creatures, is remarkably realistic if you look at the top landscape (figure 5). It shows a besieged city and is a scene that Bosch may have witnessed in his own time. Remember this painting was painted at the time of the Inquisition and in 1463, when Bosch was 13 years old, the city of Den Bosch was engulfed in flames in a great fire that Hieronymus must have partly recreated here from memory. The middle panel (figure 1) could be heaven to some, or a prelude to hell to others, which is why I entitled this paper "What Fresh Hell Can This Be?" which is actually a quotation from Dorothy Parker, who used to exclaim this whenever someone rang her doorbell.

But to come back to the oranges: any discussion of the oranges in the painting should include a discussion about provenance: the painting ended up in Madrid, Spain, where it hangs in the Prado, but the piece, though fashioned as an altar piece, never graced an altar but

Fig. 2 Left panel

Fig. 3 Right panel

was on display in the home of Engelbrecht II, of Nassau, who is thought to have commissioned the piece. The Nassaus were a prominent family in the Lowlands and one of its descendants was William the Silent or "William of Orange" who became the founding father of the Dutch Republic. The Nassaus already owned "Orange," a piece of land in the south of France (obviously, where oranges grow) when Engelbrecht commissioned the painting, so Bosch's use of this particular fruit might be a reference to his patron. Orange is still the color of the Dutch royal family, which is why Dutch athletes wear orange in international competition.

But there is more going on here: oranges are not native to Northern Europe, but the first orange probably already arrived in the Netherlands during the Middle Ages, via China — which is why, also, the Dutch word for orange is not "oranje" but "sinaasappel" or "China apple." It's highly likely that Bosch was familiar with these China apples, even though they clearly were an "otherworldly" and expensive fruit: the connotation of wealth and luxury is important here; if you ever wondered why we have salt and pepper on the table, aside from the obvious fact that we use them to season our food, the decorative use of salt and pepper on the dining table goes back to seventeenth-century Holland where it was considered a sign of wealth or status to put it on your table because salt and pepper came from far away and you had to pay a premium for it.

The same applied to exotic fruits like oranges, lemons, and limes. In other words, the oranges in the middle painting could be used to symbolize wealth, decadence, and the kind of otherworldly exotica that one would associate with any garden of Eden, especially from the perspective of the not-so-exotic and perennially overcast Lowlands. Speaking of Eden, the orange is sometimes used as a substitute for the apple in the hand of the infant Christ but also in depictions of the Tree of Knowledge, so in this sense the oranges are a foreshadowing of things to come (see middle panel).

But interestingly, the orange symbolism is as divergent as the different meanings of Bosch's painting or triptych. For example, in Christianity, the color stands for joy with connotations of God's blessing. Conversely, orange is also associated with wrath, one of the seven deadly sins. But there is more, for in Eastern cultures, oranges denote fertility and creativity (which is why, in Vietnamese culture, newlyweds receive oranges for presents). In Buddhism, orange is a manifestation of divine love, which is why Buddhist monks wear saffron robes. But orange is also seen as the color between gold (the color of the spirit) and red (the color of libido or lust). Since the balance between the spirit/the love of god and lust/earthly or human love is hard to maintain, orange is also perceived as a color of lust and infidelity, human traits which could potentially lead to orgies (as portrayed in the middle panel), which explains, perhaps, why Dionysus was commonly dressed in orange.

Fig. 4 Detail left panel

Miller's initial attraction and discussion of the middle painting might have been triggered by his reading of Fränger's book, but the sense of sexual liberation of the middle panel could have been another reason why Miller took it up. The American writer Peter S. Beagle sees Bosch's middle panel as "an erotic derangement that turns us all into voyeurs." As Erica Jong has said most perceptively and succinctly, sex to Miller was about self-liberation, "a way out of the body, through the body" (48). Thus, when Miller looked at Bosch's painting, he probably didn't see a display of lust or sin, but a form of catharsis and vision, acquired through intimacy.

In *Big Sur and the Oranges of Hieronymus Bosch*, Miller's sex scenes have disappeared altogether but the fascination with transcendence, of rising above the self to reach a form of paradise is still there. Interestingly, however, it's not Bosch's orgy or displays of lust, but the beauty of Bosch's oranges that becomes the catalyst and explanation for an enhanced vision.

Fig. 5 Detail right panel

When Miller was pointing out the "hallucinatingly real" quality of the oranges, I first thought that Miller was referring to the sophisticated color palette and mixing of colors by Dutch masters, which makes fruits like lemons in still life paintings equally and "hallucinatingly real" (23). Many an art historian has already written about this. Having never seen the painting in actuality myself, I researched Bosch's technique and found that this could not be what Miller was talking about, as Bosch used a style that is known as "alla prima," in which pigments are not layered (like Rembrandt was an expert in, for example) but put down in one application with no previous layers or underpainting.

What Miller means instead is that Bosch's oranges, as is also evident in his depiction of the painter's animals, have a hyper- or

114

super-reality about them, which borders on the magical and dreamlike. Bosch's creations, whether they be oranges or animals "belong to another age, an age when man was one with all creation [...] Bosch [...] acquired a magic vision. He saw through the phenomenal world, rendered it transparent, and thus revealed its pristine aspect"(23). These words echo interpretations of the painting by Belting, who described the Garden as a place where "humankind lives in nature and is at the same time part of nature [projecting] a vision of humankind living in harmony with nature in a way that defies reality" (7). Most of important of all, "Where there is no sin, the fruit does not signify forbidden sexual desire, but the natural fertility served by the pleasures of the flesh" (Belting 47, 54).

By doing so, Bosch recreated his own virtual paradise and that's exactly what Miller attempts to do in his memoir. For that, he doesn't even need Big Sur (or sex) —all one needs, Miller argues, is an optimal use of the infinite windows of the soul [...] "Vision," Miller tells us,

> is entirely a creative faculty: it uses the body and the mind as the navigator uses his instruments. Open and alert, it matters little whether one finds a supposed shortcut to the Indies — or discovers a new world. Everything is begging to be discovered, not accidentally, but intuitively. Seeking intuitively, one's destination is never in a beyond of time or space but always here and now [...] One's destination is never a place but rather a new way of looking at things." (27)

Unfortunately, many men, according to Miller, make their own prison, finding fault with everything they rest their eyes upon, and eventually remaining unawakened and in the dark, a situation that is made visible in Bosch's third panel. In other words, the third panel, even though Miller doesn't refer to it per se, would not be an actual, Christian or pagan hell, but man's own creation, too, if he goes through life blindly and is unwilling to "open more windows" when he finds flaws in his own paradise or reality.[1]

What's so interesting about all of this is that if Bosch were in fact, as Fränger seemed to have believed, part of a hedonistic underground sect (a theory that many have refuted since), it would make him a kind of Dutch Henry Miller of the fifteenth century. As such, the two artists, with their sprawling, undisciplined, and obscure imaginations, could both be regarded as the poètes maudits or rather artistes maudites of their time. One could easily see how in different periods, both Bosch's and Miller's visions subverted a baseline of morality, while their art may have been considered shocking, scandalous and hard to appreciate. This shock value, however, has a function of its own: "Without salt," Erica Jong writes, "we are unpreserved. Without obscenity, there is no divinity. Henry embraces dung so he can have angels" (128).

At the same time, the reader of *Big Sur and the Oranges of Hieronymus Bosch* can't escape the impression that Miller doesn't need the dung anymore, as he is extremely adept at revealing the immanence of Nature, or God in Nature, if you will, and lives a pious, frugal, humble, charitable, selfless, and graceful life that the best Christians among us would want to emulate. But I also see in Miller, as Miller saw it in Bosch, the artistic ability to be a conduit for the divine element that is all around us. In his Big Sur memoir, the divine catharsis of the sexual element of his early work is replaced with the divine catharsis of an inspired reality that reminds one of Spinoza who basically said that God, Nature and the infinity of matter and thought that surround us are all integrated.

Spinoza was excommunicated and considered an atheist, just as Miller was outcast for obscenity and considered a writer of filth, but both men don't deserve those labels. In fact, Spinoza never even disavowed God or his faith in God but defined the presence of God in a more enlightened and rational fashion, and this is exactly what Miller does, and does very effectively in his memoir. In this context, Bosch's oranges come to represent the spirit or God's blessing or what Buddhists see as a manifestation of divine love, while, to Miller personally, they became an artistic portal to connect with what Miller described and actively embraced: a contemplative life that is aware and in awe of the divine that surrounds us, if only we are willing to engage with it. Or, as Miller, wrote in the last pages of his memoir:

> [...] an author hopes that in giving himself to the world he will enrich and augment life, not deny or denigrate it. If he believed in direct intervention, he would be a healer and not a writer. If he believed that he had the power to eliminate evil and sorrow, he would be a saint, not a spinner of words. Art is the healing process, as Nietzsche pointed out. A man writes in order to know himself, and thus get rid of himself eventually. That is the divine purpose of art. (400)

116

Fig. 6 Detail of center panel

117

Miller also said, "A true artist throws the reader back upon himself," which is what Bosch does with the viewer. While critics and scholars agree that the Christian viewer in the 15th and 16th centuries must have experienced *The Garden of Earthly Delights* as more of an open book, the painting has become more hermetically closed over the years. Painting outlandish da Vinci-like and surrealistic structures (figure 6), and a scene that seems to enact part of the evolution as described by Darwin (figure 2) four centuries later, the painting proves Bosch was endowed with a vision above and beyond himself.[2] According to Miller's definition, he enriched and augmented life, and his artistic vision created a new world and a new way of looking at things. Living on the cusp of the Reformation and the modern world that the Dutch Republic helped create, Hieronymus Bosch somehow embodied the sensibility of the modern artist who didn't use Scripture for merely didactic reasons but also used it to disrupt and confuse. "Once art is really accepted," Henry Miller wrote, "it will cease to be. It is only a substitute, a symbol-language, for something which can be seized directly. But for that to become possible man must become thoroughly religious, not a believer, but a prime mover, a god in fact and deed" (*Nothing* 41). Even though Miller was commenting on his own writing here, the quote takes us right back to the enhanced vision of the divine oranges of Hieronymus Bosch. Miller understood Bosch, as Bosch would have understood and enjoyed Miller.

Notes

[1] "Seeing the world through [Bosch's] eyes it appears to once again as a world of indestructible order, beauty, harmony, which it is our privilege to accept as a paradise or convert into a purgatory" (23).

[2] Hieronymus Bosch (1450-1516) was an almost exact contemporary of Leonardo da Vinci (1452-1519)

Works Cited

Belting, Hans. *Garden of Earthy Delights*. Prestel, 2002.

Jong, Erica. *Henry Miller, or the Devil at Large*. Grove, 1993.

Miller, Henry. *Big Sur and the Oranges of Hieronymus Bosch*. New Directions, 1957.

— —. *Nothing But the Marvelous: Wisdom of Henry Miller*. Ed. Blair Fielding. Capra, 1991.

A Letter from June
Inspired by *Femme Fatale: The Life of June Mansfield Miller*

Ida Therén

Arizona, January 1979

The thought, I couldn't let go of. Had I really been ill?

Or, just a woman.

An artist that never was.

Sometimes, at night, the thoughts come over me until I can't fend
them off. Suddenly I'm wide-awake, head buzzing as if invaded by
killer bees. It's just me and all the memories and this damn room
with all its dust and cheap old furniture. All the things I could have
said, done.

The phone calls to lost friends I should make to clear up certain
things. The *thank you*s, the *I'm sorry*s. The unspoken apologies, the
unpaid debt. The revenges not yet acted out.

Then I finally fall asleep and the morning after the to-do list from
last night seems invisible again, soaked up by the world of dreams.
Quiet, lost in the depths of memory until the next sleepless night.

The thoughts of Hannah, Florrie, Ossie. Anaïs, Jean.

Henry.

It was during a moment like that that I wrote him, in the middle of
the night, sending it off in a morning blurry. I was staying in dirty
hotel rooms, living off handouts from friends and strangers. I had
just gotten out of Pilgrim State and had nowhere to go after all those
years at the hospital, lost in the world I had been thrown back into,
like a child with nothing more than a faint memory from rein-
carnated pasts on how to live.

It was the first time I had written him in years.

I was constantly sick, in and out of the hospital, barely able to pay the bills that lined up after each visit. And then there were the ghosts in my head, the blurred thinking, paranoia. I didn't know what was worse: the physical pain or the one of not being able to think clearly. It took me five years to gain the weight I had lost at the hospital.

It was that year that I found out that Stratford had died. I had just gotten out of the hospital when his lawyer wrote: "Stratford died in Los Angeles January 7th, 1956." There seemed to be no money in it for me. He had already remarried to that actress. I didn't cry a single tear.

I had cried enough.

One of the few people from my old life that I was still in touch with was Emil. He helped me out with small things, medical help and money for medicine. Still, to this day I swear that I would not be here if it wasn't for him.

Kind, old Emil, who wrote bestselling cook books about salt free diets. Still, fat and unhealthy himself.

He was always a man of extremes.

What was it Henry wrote:

"A good work is always one of extremes"?

I was surprised, thrilled, when a letter came one day. I immediately recognized Henry's handwriting, even though it was shaky from old age.

"June, I wonder how you're doing–"

In the late fifties I stayed at Hotel Continental on 95th street. It was worse than anything at the Bowery. Barely any lamps, rooms lit mostly by candlelights. No heat. A true hellhole, with rat shit all over the place. All around you were murders and violence.

I wanted to work with helping people and I started volunteering at the welfare department. To get to do an entry test to get into civil service I had to volunteer for six and a half years. I decided to do it. I was sick and the arthritis made the pain constant. I had a hard time walking after the ECT accident but I was convinced I should go through with the process. So I did.

Something had hit me there, at the hospital. How I wanted to help. How that what my life had always been about, even though I hadn't quite figured it out until then.

Living to help others.

People said I dressed "severely," like a nun. But I had always dressed in black, perhaps it looked more dramatic as I lost weight and became thinner, and started looking a lot older than I was. I will never forget what that man Dick wrote, that I looked "cadaverous and ill." But I did feel like a nun. In a way, I lived like one as well.

I was broke, starving and could never afford to eat anything fancy, not even meat. The only way I survived was through social security, which I got during those last years of the 1950s. Once, I had a sinusitus and needed penicillin but couldn't pay for the medicine, my teeth were all gone and my eyes bad. I needed money to go to the doctor and have it all looked after. It had gone awry, and gotten infected and possibly chronic. It could even affect my personality, he said.

Apparently Elkus was also in touch with Emil, and he had in turn told Henry how I was doing. Henry wrote me, and I wrote him back, asking a friend for help to put everything down on paper. I told him I needed help, unable to afford being proud. I told him anything would be fine, books, money, pictures of him and his family. His beautiful watercolor paintings.

That time, Henry's wife Lepska sent me fifteen dollars, saying that was all they could spare. She said they would send more money whenever they had it, with Henry adding that he could give me anything, but not money. During those years I rarely had a set address, and I told Henry to send me letters care of Gotham Book Mart.

I send out letters to friends and managed to scrape together two dollars here, fifteen dollars there, until I got enough money to buy the penicillin I needed to stay alive until Emil came to my rescue. He treated me for free every day for nine months. I will never forget what he did for me.

It still pains me to think how he left so early. Emil, with that heart of gold.

In 1956 Henry wrote me and told me to speak to Annette Kar Baxter, this young feminist academic, who was writing a doctoral dissertation about Henry, the "expatriate writer," at Brown University. She wrote me, and after careful consideration I decided to reply. I was hesitant at first, but when she told me she wouldn't write anything about me in the book, she just wanted some references, I finally agreed to meet with her. We met a few times at the end of 1956, and in 1957. She was such a sweet person. Sensitive, a careful listener. Right away I felt I could trust her. I knew it, the gut feeling I had always listened to. The one that had always been right. I remember how Annette looked at me, terrified.

"What happened to you?"

I tried smiling, even though it hurt me even to move my mouth. My arthritis had gotten worse, and I my body shrunk, like an old tree twisting into itself.

"Just some shocks."

I guess she told Henry how I was doing because later on I found out that Henry had asked her and her husband, especially when he heard that he was a physician, to keep an eye on me. Since we all lived in New York, and all. Sometimes they would invite me over for the holidays. I guess they felt bad for me, all alone in my cold flat. They were such a loving, sweet family, two small kids that ran around and made the spirit of the room lighter. They smiled at me, wanted me to play. Adrienne, who was around ten or so, called me Aunt June. The way they ran around and sang made the room feel alive. If I closed my eyes I could pretend it was my own family, this beautiful, intellectual, healthy bunch. And me, sick and fragile, in the middle of it all, as a great aunt who had shown up from nowhere.

In 1957 I read about Henry in a newspaper someone had left at Gotham. I was friends of the owner, who was also a fan of Henry, and they let me get my mail there. There was a big picture of Henry in the paper and fine print below. I had to lean close to read it, my eyes were getting worse and I couldn't afford new glasses. "Henry Miller, chosen to be a part of The National Institute of Arts and Letters."

Henry was already becoming something of a cult figure in the Village. Everywhere I went I would see Beat kids dressed in black turtlenecks talking about *Tropic of Cancer*.

Of *Mona*.

I started getting letters from Big Sur every week or so, in the late 1950s. Usually it was Henry's wives, especially Eve and Lepska, that wrote the actual letter, telling me how Henry and the kids were doing. It pleased me to hear from them, even if I couldn't help a pang of jealousy as I thought of Henry and all those children. The second shot he got, the one I never had after our child, that we never got to see.

I replied sometimes, telling him how I was getting better thanks to Emil and the Baxter family. It made him happy.

Once in a while Henry sent me money, but never a lot. A ten, a twenty. I guess he didn't have much, despite all the fame. But you can't eat notoriety.

If anyone, I would know.

"There are many mouths to feed", he said. Henry seemed to have changed. He had gotten back in touch with his daughter, Barbara, "the little one." He started taking care of his sister. It made me happy. I always knew he was kind. Some people just mature slower and take some time to find their heart.

Say what you want of Henry, but he always valued human relationships. The integrity of it. That's why I could never be mad at him; he was an artist, that's all.

The books that Henry had written in the 1930s started coming out, starting in 1959, printed in Paris. Annette's book came out in 1961. She sent me a signed copy in the mail, with a thank you note on the first page. It was called "Henry Miller: Expatriate", her doctoral thesis that finally came out as a book. Calls me "fabulous." Inside the book I'm referred to as "Mona", but in the introduction she writes my real name. In the introduction, Annette thanks "June Edith Smith Corbett," and in the footnotes she marks my name, referring to interviews with me in 1956 and 1957.

I remember thinking that it was as if history repeated itself: just like Anaïs had written a book taking DH Lawrence seriously in a time when he was still censored, Annette wrote about Henry, still unable to publish his work in America.

There was one thing in the book that stuck with me. She wrote something about how Henry, in a way, never left for Europe. He was always still in America, trying to understand what Americanness was all about. The ugly, hard, rough. Everything he loved, somewhere deep inside, but didn't want to admit loving.

I couldn't help but think, that there was some truth to it. Perhaps I was the only one, whoever left.

Annette moved on to research "American Studies" at Barnard College, and we didn't see each other so often. She became a front figure in the new field of "Women's Studies." I still see her in the paper sometimes.

It was around those years that my mother's basement got flooded. I had put almost all the things I owned in there. All my papers, little souvenirs, newspaper clippings. Memories. I had to throw away most of it, but we managed to save some of Henry's original manuscripts. His first novels, some short stories with his notes in them. I'm sure he wouldn't have minded them getting lost, after all not all of them were his greatest work.

Gone in a flood. How poetic.

But more importantly, there was the love letters he wrote me, the ones when he called me *Rebecca*. The Jewish name he had given me those first few years.

Henry told me I could do whatever I wanted with the scripts. I decided to save them, and they are still here, in the box below the bookshelf with my special books.

The beautiful, loving, sympathetic love letters.

I will take them with me as I leave this place. To the grave.

1961 was one of those years when everything seemed upside down. Even the numbers. Everything seemed to be bending backwards.

It was thirty years ago since I last saw him, when Henry and I met that spring.

It was the same year that Annette's book had come out (1961), and he had written me, last minute, saying he was in town. Could he come over? I thought about it for a while.

"Yes."

So strange, but exciting. I wanted everything to be perfect.

I took all the money I had and went to the market, to make sure he would be met with all the things he loved. Bacon, eggs, chocolate cake, brandy. A very expensive Anjou that I knew he would love.

Before he arrived, just around 2 'o'clock, I spent the whole morning getting ready. Painted my face, put on my best velvet dress, a brassiere that would make my sagging chest look fuller.

I was sixty years old, and Henry was seventy. We were both old, but it didn't feel like it when I saw him there, by the door in my flat in Forest Hills, in Queens. It was the only place I had been able to afford with my meager social security. Henry, tall and smelling of damp tweed. Round glasses, a hat covering the bald spot on his head.

The first time we saw each other since we said goodbye, that stormy farewell in Paris.

A flashback to the past. I looked at him, an admiring look. He looked healthy, handsome, full of energy and enthusiasm. Just like he had always done. Some people just stay the same, and Henry was one of them.

I was not feeling good. The shock treatments and the joint pain still kept me up at night, and made me walk like a cripple. I could only imagine how I looked. An old, worn woman.

Our meeting lasted for about three hours. Henry was uncomfortable. I don't know what bothered him, but I had a feeling it was me. My body, so different from the one he had known. The one he had loved.

Such a disappointment. The mystery he had written all those novels about, shattered into pieces.

He told me that his mother had just died. That his children were doing well. That he was hoping his books were coming out in the States soon. That he was excited about Annette's book, that the fact that a serious academic wrote about him could be a good thing to show to the censors.

Henry, already a celebrity, even in his own country.

He had a ton of lawsuits hanging around him, he told me that was why he hadn't told me earlier he was coming to New York. That he was about to leave the country.

Later I found out that he was about to ask another young woman to marry him. That's the reason he was in New York. But I didn't know that then.

Some things never change. Some people, that is.

I told him about what I had gone through since we said goodbye. About Stratford, about the hospital years, the shock treatments, poverty. He turned pale, seemed taken aback by it all. After the hours we spent together he suddenly stood up, his hand shaking as he held on to the chair to stand straight.

"I can't take hearing anymore of this. If that would have been me I would have killed myself."

Maybe they were right, my friends who kept telling me I was the strong one between Henry and I. Even when I didn't believe it. Maybe I was stronger. But maybe life just beat me up harder.

I am not proud of it, but the truth was I was hoping he would stay, like that good old days. I gestured towards the bed, but it made him uncomfortable. He stood up.

The way he looked at me. A fragment of the woman I once was. Drained. Barren. Dry.

Empty.

I knew the second that the door slammed.

My power was gone.

I thought I saw a tear in his eye as he rushed towards the door. A quick farewell, that was all. He had barely touched all the food on the table, my money for the week left there, waiting to get spoiled.

That power struggle we started the first night at the dance hall at Times Square.

Henry's eyes were blank when he looked at me, just as he exited the door.

I wanted to yell, as he left: How does it feel to be a winner?

His letting go. His triumph.

Henry Miller's

BOOK OF
FRIENDS

A TRILOGY

Including
"My Bike & Other Friends"
and "Joey"

Book of Friends: A Trilogy,, 1987 (Santa Barbara, CA: Capra Press)

A Commentary on Errors: On Book Three of Henry Miller's *Book of Friends: A Trilogy*

Akiyoshi Suzuki

I. Commentary

Commentary is a traditional method of studying literature. Commentary is a set of explanatory or critical notes for the definition and interpretation of meanings of words, phrases, sentences, and their synthesis, or the text. Commentators investigate not only form, figuration, syntax, style, and other linguistic phenomena, but also the background of the text, such as culture, social reality, law, religion, way of thinking, nature, and others. Commentary is, in a sense, a challenge against the essential configuration of a text, or the deconstruction that Paul de Man insisted on.[1]

Both the East and the West have traditions of commentary. As the West has a tradition of exegesis, or interpretation of the Bible, and annotations on representatives of the literary canon, such as Chaucer, Shakespeare, and so on, the East also has similar traditions, including commentaries on the *Book of Poetry* in China and the kochū (ancient commentary), kyūchū (old commentary), and shinchū (new commentary) on *The Tale of Genji* in Japan.[2] New commentaries, whether in the East or in the West, always renew former commentaries with new and newer interpretations. If commentary is a challenge to deconstruction as the essential configuration of a text and the renewal of interpretation, the history of commentary is in a way the history of interpretation.

Incidentally, as long as commentary is an approach to the "true" meaning of words, phrases, and sentences in a text, the practicability of commentary is assumed by the reliance on the correctness of letters written or printed in a text. In spite of the best efforts of the publisher and the author, however, texts have errors in spelling, errors of fact, and errors of memory that go beyond the list of corrigenda or emendations even after a second printing is published. This is true, for instance, of Henry Miller's *Book of Friends: A Trilogy* (Capra Press, 1987), which was written in Miller's last years. At that time, Miller's eyesight was failing. We may reasonably surmise, hence, that Miller was barely able to polish the galleys of that book. Still, the author of a literary work sometimes uses license for special effects, and hence I withheld judgment with the words "may reasonably surmise." In fact, in the text, there are grammatical and spelling errors, some with "[sic]" and some without it, which means that some of these errors may be licensed. As for misunderstandings and lapses of memory, some of Miller's statements are a kind of excuse for error: "I had no use for fiction, though many of my readers regard my work as being largely fictive. I myself am at a loss to give it a name";[3] "I may not use their right names, nor do I promise to be totally truthful or accurate in what I shall say about them."[4] It is a little hard to judge what is truly an error.

Even if we find a true error, however, we should not cross it out just because it is an error. We should remember the Freudian slip; in an error we may find what a person really feels and thinks. We cannot deny a probability that Miller made a slip but he could not correct errors in the galleys because his eyesight was failing. Comments on errors can, hence, potentially expand the horizon of interpretation and study of Miller's texts, though such work may amount to discovering alluvial gold, both in value and in difficulty. I shall nevertheless make commentary on errors with the expectation of contributing to a reading of Miller's texts with a new approach.

The text I cover here is "Joey" and "Other Women in My Life," or Book Three in the *Book of friends: A Trilogy*. I have chosen Book Three for the simple fact that I translated it into Japanese as a co-translator of the Japanese version of *Book of Friends: A Trilogy*.[5] I must mention that I do not have the slightest intention of throwing cold water on the author, the editor, or the publisher by pointing out errors left in the text. As mentioned earlier, I am only attempting to contribute a fresh eye and a new idea for the study of Henry Miller. This essay is, hence, a short essay, a commentary on the errors in Book Three, an example of a new type of commentary, and simultaneously a trial for expanding the horizon of Henry Miller Studies.

II. Commentary on Errors

There are 22 potential errors in Book Three of Henry Miller's *Book of Friends: A Trilogy*, as far as I could tell. I would appreciate it if you would point out other potential errors in case you find them.

(1) [p. 235, ll. 26-27] I've experienced this feeling many times, But you've got to stick it out.

There is a comma after "times," and "But" is capitalized. These might be simple errors in punctuation or capitalization. A period, instead of a comma, should be put after "times" or "But" should be lowercased. We can find other potential errors of punctuation and capitalization in the text. Sometimes an author of a literary work, as mentioned earlier, takes license in order to create special effects, and hence we should not always regard ungrammatical punctuation and capitalization as a mere error. In Miller's Book Three, however, ungrammatical punctuation and capitalization, instances of which I point out here, have a high probability of being simple errors in spelling, not special effects.

(2) [p. 241, ll. 7-8] In addition to being a clown, a buffoon, a wit and a *bon compain* ...

Miller is referring to his friend Fred here, and hence "compain" may be Miller's spelling error and, for its original spelling in his mind, be "copain." "Bon compain," written in italics for emphasis, may be Miller's slip as well, showing his hidden real thought, that he wanted to complain to Fred, or the image of Fred he may have had as someone who always complained. The French word "copain" appears several times in the text, including "mon copain" on p. 252.

(3) [pp. 241-242, ll. 34-1] When the accident occurred he was a first unaware that the floor was covered with broken glass.

"A first" would be Miller's simple error in spelling or the omission of the final "t" in "at" because the pronunciation of the next word begins with the consonant "f."

(4) [p. 243, ll. 18-20] One evening he announces in his usual grave manner that his grandfather had just died and that he would be leaving in the morning to attend the funeral ceremonies.

A spelling error. Judging from the consistency of the tense of the verbs and the meaning of the sentence, the tense of "announces" should be the past. "announces" must have intended to be "announced" by Miller.

(5) [p. 248, ll. 25-26] It washere at the that I imagine him to have done his greatest reading.

First, "washere" needs a space between "was" and "here." As for "at the" before the "that" clause, it is ungrammatical, though now that postmodern, experimental literary works have come on the scene, we cannot easily judge the "at the" to be ungrammatical. There are cases of no noun after a definite article in American literature, especially in works by writers who doubt the existence of the world in recognition in language. For instance, in his novel *Agapē Agape*, William Gaddis sometimes places no noun after a definite article, as in the following example: "we don't know how much time there is left and I have to work on the, to finish this work of mine while I, why I've brought in this whole pile of books notes pages clipping...."[6] Another famous postmodern writer, Donald Barthelme, also intentionally broke syntax, for instance in *Snow White*, to show that the agency "I" cannot be recognized or appear with ungrammatical and thus meaningless sentences, following Judith Butler's theory of gender performance.[7] Certainly, Miller mentions "I must confess there's a great joy, for me, in cutting a thing down, in taking an ax to my words and destroying what was so wonderful in the heat of the first writing" for "editing."[8] But nonetheless, his "ax-wielding" does not involve intentionally breaking syntax to show a linguistic philosophy. In fact, as we realize in reading, he did not write texts for the purpose of their being impossible for the reader to read them. Rather, Miller, who seemed to dislike the artificial and freely wrote, just following his memory and imagination in his notes, elaborated his style and dwelled on syntax. For instance, Leon Lewis points out—showing examples of stanzas made by arranging some original prose from

132

Tropic of Cancer—that Miller set passages from this text as a poem.[9] The poetic elements in Miller's prose are true to his essay about Brenda Venus in "Other Women in My Life" in Book Three as well. Part of this essay reads like beautiful verses. For instance, "What's more, our *souls* meet. They meet at will or haphazardly, but surely, truly, sublimely. We sustain one another. I keep her from falling apart; she keeps me from bursting at the seams. We mollify and jollify one another. We appreciate one another."[10] Miller was not interested in writing for writing's sake. He criticizes Nabokov because "he's too literary a man, too engrossed in the art of writing—all that display of virtuosity."[11] If we find something grammatically wrong in Miller's text, it is due to his carelessness, as Bernard Wolfe mentioned to Miller in the *Playboy* interview that "It's also been said that you suffer from 'verbal diarrhea,' that your 'billowing, undisciplined, rough-hewn prose urgently requires the attention of a sharp blue pencil'."[12] "At the" before the "that" clause, therefore, must not be according to Miller's intention.

(6) [p. 248, ll. 28-34] I feel almost positive it was there he got to know his Goethe—*Conversations with Eckermann, Dichtung und Wahrheit, The Italian Journey*: perhaps Faust too and Wilhelm Meister. When tipsy and acting the buffoon the line which often came to his lips; "*Das ewige Weibliche zieht uns immer hinein.*" He would mouth this famous phrase with the same mock solemnity that a Jesus freak might quote the Golden Rule.

"Das ewige Weibliche zieht uns immer hinein" must be a garbling of "Das Ewig-Weibliche zieht uns hinan" in the second part of Goethe's *Faust*,[13] judging from its similarity and its context in the passage quoted earlier. "Das Ewig-Weibliche zieht uns hinan" in *Faust* means "The eternal feminine draws us upwards." By the guidance of the eternal feminine Faust ascends to heaven. The phrase "das ewige weibliche" (the eternal feminine) appears on page 307 as well in Miller's text.

The sentence Miller wrote, however, is different from its original at three points. First, Miller changed "ewig" to "ewige," an adjective for the nominative case of a neuter noun. This is probably a simple error of grammar on Miller's part. Second, Miller added "immer," which means "always," to emphasize the usual state of guidance of the eternal feminine. Finally, he changed "hinan" (upward, upwards, up) to "hinein" (inward, into). In short, Miller says "The eternal feminine always draws us inward." In the original sentence, heaven is placed on high. If this is so, where "inward" does the eternal feminine always draw us?

Did Miller misunderstand the sentence in *Faust*, make a slip of the tongue, or intentionally change some words? Judging from Miller's words "this famous phrase" after the German sentence, it seems he made a slip. In addition, Miller states "He [Fred] would mouth this famous phrase" and that Fred is very popular among women and is a philanderer. The German sentence Miller wrote may imply a popular image (the eternal feminine always draws men into women, and he is in heaven) or a sexual image (the eternal feminine always draws men into a woman, and he is in heaven), which Miller had of Fred.

(7) [pp. 251-252, ll. 34-1] This man, who had lost his good right arm as a *Legionnaire* was the same man ...

A simple punctuation error. There is only one comma for the relative pronoun clause after "This man." So, one more comma is needed after "Legionnaire" to be "Legionnaire, was."

(8) [p. 252, l. 8] Towardfour in the morning ...

A simple error in spelling. "Towardfour" needs a space between "Toward" and "four" to be "toward four."

(9) [pp. 252-253, ll. 33-2] *Les Degourds du Onzieme*, by Courteline. A book I often wanted to talk to Fred about but never did. There were certain authors both French and English.

"Courteline" is Georges Courteline (1858-1929), a French prose writer and playwright strong in comedy. Miller explains that *Les Dégourdis du onzième* (accent and spelling corrections and decapitalization mine) "by Courteline" includes "certain authors both French and English." The list of Courteline's works does not include the title *Les Dégourdis du onzième*.

However, another French author, André Mouëzy-Éon (1880-1967), who was also good at writing comedy, published a play with a very similar title to *Les Dégourdis du onzième*. The play is *Les Dégourdis de la onzième*. It has a military setting. It was made into a very popular film, directed by Christian-Jaque, in 1937, and Fernandel played the leading part.[14] "Les dégourdis" means "the shrewd ones" and "onzième" means "the eleventh," but that information alone is not enough to understand the title. The title, *Les Dégourdis de la onzième*, is reminiscent of a similar, idiomatic expression "les ouvriers de la onzième heure" in chapter 20 of the Gospel according to St. Matthew in the French version of the Bible. The literal meaning of that expression is "the laborers of the eleventh hour," but the expression signifies to "reap what others have sown," or "reap the benefits without any of the effort."[15] It may be that *Les Dégourdis de la onzième* is a play on the French idiomatic expression from the Bible, and the title also means to "reap what others have sown."

The analysis above is, however, relevant to the drama written by Mouëzy-Éon, not to a work by Courteline, which Miller refers to as a book that refers to "certain authors both French and English." Besides, according to Miller, Courteline's book is *Les Dégourds du Onzième* (*Les Dégourdis du onzième*), but not *Les Dégourdis de la onzième*. The difference between the two titles lies in the grammatical gender of "du onzième," in the masculine gender, and "de la onzième," in the feminine gender. Thought of in the context of France, "du onzième" may, in Miller's mind, have been suggestive of "the eleventh district of Paris" or "the eleventh regiment." If so, *Les Dégourdis du onzième* may mean "shrewd ones in the eleventh district of Paris" or "in the eleventh regiment."

Still, as mentioned before, Courteline did not write a book entitled *Les Dégourdis du onzième* or even a book of a similar title. Is it possible that only a few people, including Miller, knew of such a book? Or, did Miller just misremember the title of the book or its author? Inasmuch as Miller concretely remembered and mentioned that the subject of the book was "certain authors both French and English," it is probable that he misremembered the title, thinking he was referring to some other book by Courteline, not the work by Mouëzy-Éon that has a military setting. Did the reason why "les dégourdis," or "shrewd," came from Miller's pen lie in a Freudian slip, or Miller's real thought about Fred, that he always "reap[s] what others have sown?" Or is the reason Miller's suppressed feeling of "shrewdness" with regards to himself, that he had been waiting for a chance to stand in a position of advantage over Fred, who was encyclopedic in his knowledge of literary authors and works, by telling him about a book on "certain authors?"

(10) [p. 257, l. 14] asamara

This word, "asamara," appears in a sentence that speaks of the poetry created by a woman from the U.K.: "She in turn quoted from her own work, which was excellent and extremely modern. Not crazy either. Rather a mixture of coolth and passion, restraint and abandon, immanence and permanence, nightly emissions, *asamara, fragile jonquils*." Analyzed in context, the word "asamara" may be a spelling error for "samara" or "a samara," or a key fruit.

There is another possibility, that "asamara" is a Japanese word. "Asamara" is vulgar slang in Japanese for "morning wood" or "morning erection." Miller, who was erudite and very interested in the East, especially in China and Japan, may have known this. The poet "in turn quoted from her own work," as Fred recited from French and German poets, and after that, they went into Miller's bedroom and made love. Remembering this episode, Miller writes about her poem as an "excellent and extremely modern" one and "a mixture" of "nightly emissions, *asamara, fragile jonquils*." As scholars of literature like William Empson would say, the word "asamara" is ambiguous and might have the meaning of both a key fruit and morning erection because of the shape of the fruit, and hence Miller might have made a slip of the tongue, combining his appreciation of her poem with his sexual imagination, from his memory of the female poet and Fred using Miller's own bedroom.

(11) [p. 260, l. 13] They acted as if they had just been released fromprison.

A simple error in spelling. "Fromprison" needs a space between "from" and "prison," to be "from prison."

(12) [p. 277, l. 4] ...at the kitchen table. my mother ...

An error in capitalization. "My" is the first word of the sentence, and hence "My," instead of "my," should have been typed there.

(13) [p. 293, ll. 1-2] Her full name was Camilla Euphrosnia Fedrant.

"Euphrosnia" might be "Euphrasmia." In a letter to Erica Jong on July 7, 1974, Miller spelled it another way, namely, "Camilla Euphrasmia Fedrant."[16]

(14) [p. 299, ll. 28-29] The others who passed me by never game me so much as a tumble.

Regarding "game," did Miller make a slip of the tongue or an error in spelling? We know the idiomatic expression "give someone a tumble," which means "to show a sign of recognition or approval" or "acknowledge,"[17] but not "game someone a tumble." In addition, the quoted sentence is in a scene where Miller tries to hitch a ride to go back to his house as he has no money and is tired after a long walk but nobody stopped for him. "Gave me so much as a tumble" is, therefore, suitable, but not "game me." Still, "game" has a meaning of "trick" in slang. So, does the word "game" here connote Miller's feeling that somebody tricks so much because everybody ignores him? Miller often said in public that he accepted everything as it was, but in fact sometimes he could not do this. So he suppressed his true feelings and hence may have made a slip. Or is this overthought? Is "game me" just a result of the process of, first, the abbreviation of "ve" in "gave" by omitting the final sound [v] because the pronunciation of the next word begins with the consonant "m," and second, an incorrect description of "me" as an object for "game" [gei(v) mi] for grammatical correction?

(15) [p. 304, l. 11] …he had shoved nopropaganda on me.

A simple error in spelling. "Nopropaganda" needs a space between "no" and "propaganda," to be "no propaganda."

(16) [p. 315, ll. 16-17] I immediately gave chase./Now Alice didn't hold….

A formatting error. "Chase" is the last word of the paragraph and "Now" is the first word of another paragraph. So, an indent is needed before "Now."

(17) [p. 320, ll. 25-26] But then I added that that was no reason to choose it forher work.

An error in spelling. "Forher" needs a space between "for" and "her," to be "for her."

(18) [p. 321, l. 18] ...same time an idealist. for example, in my ...

A capitalization error. "For" is the first word of the sentence, and hence "For" is correct.

(19) [p. 327, ll. 23-24] I stood on the subway steps reflecting what do do.

An error in spelling. "What do do" must be "what to do."

(20) [p. 331, l. 5] They they were all in a state of disrepair....

This duplication of "they" must be an error. One instance of "they" must be deleted.

(21) [p. 333, ll. 3-4] ...even the hundreth time around.

"Hundreth" is also a simple error in spelling. In Miller's mind, the word must have the "d" between the "e" and the "t," to be "hundredth."

(22) [p. 334, ll. 28-29] ... there is always lurking somewhere the shades of Dixie Friganza.

On page 334, the reader suddenly sees the woman's name "Dixie Friganza," without any information about who she may be, where Miller refers to Brenda Venus, whom he loved at the time. The name "Dixie Friganza" appears only there in Book Three of *Book of Friends: A Trilogy*. Miller often adds a description of friends and acquaintances who are not well-known to readers, but he did not do so for "Dixie Friganza." This means that "Dixie Friganza" is a well-known woman, at least among people in the U.S.A. Nonetheless, neither encyclopedias nor websites refer to "Dixie Friganza."

Instead, we find a woman whose name is similar to Dixie Friganza. The woman is Trixie Friganza (1870-1955), an actress famous in the U.S.A. Miller, who was familiar with film, probably intended to write "Trixie," in spite of the fact that he wrote "Dixie." Trixie appeared in many films. In one of the films, *A Star Is Born* (1937), the female protagonist aspires to be a Hollywood actress. [18] As mentioned before, the name "Dixie Friganza" appears in a context where Miller is referring to Brenda Venus. Brenda also wanted to be an actress at that time, and hence Miller may have written the name "Dixie Friganza," associating Trixie Friganza in *A Star Is Born* with Brenda. As for "Dixie," we cannot clearly say whether Miller intentionally or unconsciously wrote the name instead of "Trixie," but it is hard to state confidently that Miller just made an error in spelling. "Dixie" is the historical nickname for the Southern United States, where Brenda was born. In fact, Brenda's identity as an American Southerner impressed and fascinated Miller, and he points out certain Southern characteristics that he then relates to Brenda, writing "the Southerners were better soldiers, nobler, more courageous more daring and inventive. All this apropos the south long before the intervention of Brenda."[19] Brenda is a woman from "Dixie." We cannot put aside the probability, therefore, that when Miller referred to Brenda, he intentionally or unconsciously wrote the name "Dixie Friganza," imagining and hoping that Brenda could make her dream of becoming an actress come true without being discouraged by adversity, superimposing Trixie Friganza in the film *A Star Is Born* on Brenda, or a woman of "Dixie."

III. Agenda: For Close Reading in the Time of World Literature

So far, I have made a commentary on the errors in Book Three of *Book of Friends: A Trilogy*, pointing out potential errors and annotating and interpreting them. Many errors can be regarded as simple spelling errors, but others deserve careful and thoughtful consideration. Miller wrote on various people he related to in his life, even if only in Book Three. The errors worth considering are mainly in the passages about Fred. If the errors are slips of the tongue in a Freudian psychoanalytic sense, Miller may have skewed his sense and view of Fred, even though he said that Fred was his best friend.

After reflection, we may realize that there is no collection of commentary on Miller's texts in spite of the fact that there are many words, phrases, and sentences that have complicated meanings, connotations, usages, and backgrounds. As a trial, let me annotate the word "planturous" in "Joey." It goes something like this:

[p. 252, ll. 21-22] ... he opened the blouse of the girl standing next to him, pulled out her planturous teat and turning to me said ...

"Planturous" is synonymous to the French adjective "plantureux," which means "copious" or "abundant" in English. We can see the word "planturous," for instance, in Episode 6 in *Finnegans Wake* as follows: "ex-gardener (Riesengebirger), fitted up with planturous existencies would make Roseoogreedy (mite's) little hose" (p. 133). Miller himself uses the adjective in *Tropic of Capricorn*, in this way: "there are planturous, seismographic cunts which register the rise and fall of sap" (p. 194). A quick conclusion from the two examples would be dangerous, but the adjective "planturous" may have been tied with the voluptuous female body in Miller's mind.

We are not in a time of world literature, which requires close reading at the first step in the procedure of approaching a text, instead of reading it using a theory as a framework to the text, as world literature as an approach to texts is predicated on translatability.[20] For the response to the requirements of close reading, too, collections of commentary on Miller's texts, as well as commentary on the errors in his texts, are anticipated.

Notes

---

[1]As for issues of interpretation, commentary and exegesis, and deconstruction, see Longxi Zhang's brilliant landmark study, *Allegoresis*, especially chapter 3.

[2]The Japanese tradition of commentary started with *kochū*, or ancient commentary. *Kochū* was used from the end of the Heian period (794-around 1185) to the beginning of the Kamakura period (around 1185-1333 or 1338). Comemntators of *kochū* put stress on the interpretation of a word and focused on a word's origin because they believed that a word originates from only one source. Therefore, commentators of *kochū* denied the variety of word

meanings used in different passages but insisted that all words only have one meaning. Besides, in commentary of *kochū*, mysterious ideas, like inspiration from gods, were often used for defining a word. Following this, a new method of commentary, *kyūchū*, or old commentary, was used in the middle of the Edo period (1603-1868). *Kyūchū* is characterized by the rational interpretation of a text in its context. Later, the old commentary was replaced by *shinchū*, or new commentary, which is the practical study of a text in its social context under the influence of *kokugaku*, or study of Japanese classical literature. After the Edo period, as Japanese government propelled the policy of *datsua-nyuo* (leave Asia and join Europe), Japanese commentary moved away from *shinchū* to a new method made using the learning and knowledge procured from the West. This method of commentary was applied to the study of foreign literature in Japan.

[3]Miller, *Book of Friends*, pp. 271-2

[4]*Ibid.*, p. 272

[5]*Tomodachi no Hon*, translated by Tōro Nakamura, Yasunori Honda, Akiyoshi Suzuki. Suisēsha, 2014.

[6]Gaddis, p. 1

[7]See Miura, *Postmodern Barthelme*, pp. 79-137.

[8]Wolfe, "*Playboy* Interview," p. 86.

[9]Lewis, *Henry Miller*, p. 100.

[10]Miller, *book of Friends*, p. 335.

[11]*Ibid.*, p. 87.

[12]*Ibid.*, p. 86.

[13]Goethe, *Faust*, p. 206.

[14]Cf. All Movie and IMDb.

[15]Lamy, *The Cambridge French-English Thesaurus*, p. 33.

[16]Jong, *The Devil at Large*, p. 271.

[17]To "give someone a tumble" also has a sexual connotation.

[18]Cf. All Movie and IMDb.

[19]Miller, *Book of Friends*, p. 334.

[20]World literature does not include studying only translated texts prevailing in the world; a close reading of an original text and interpretations and arguments from multidimensional viewpoints are also important. As for the method of approaching a text in world literature, see Zhang's *From Comparison to World Literature* and

Suzuki's "How Should We Read Literature from a Certain Area from the Viewpoints of Other Language-speaking Areas?"

Works Cited

All Movie. <http:www.allmovie.com>. Sep. 2014.

Gaddis, William. *Agapē, Agape*. Viking, 2002.

Goethe, Johann, Wolfgang von. *Faust II*. Philipp reclam Jun VerlagGmbH, 1991.

IMDb. <http://www.imdb.com>. 14 Sep. 2014.

Jong, Erica. *The Devil at Large: Erica Jong on Henry Miller*. Grove, 1994.

Joyce, James. *Finnegans Wake*. Oxford UP, 2012.

Lamy, Marie-Noklle. *The Cambridge French-English Thesaurus*. Cambridge UP, 1997.

Lewis, Leon. *Henry Miller: The Major Writings*. Schocken, 1986.

Miller, Henry. *Book of Friends: A Trilogy*. Capra, 1987.

— —. *Tropic of Capricorn*. Grove, 1961.

Miura, Reiichi. *Postmodern Barthelme: On the Magic of a "Novel" [Posutomodan Bāserumi: "Shōsetsu" to iu Mono no Mahō nit suite]*. Sairvusha, 2005.

Suzuki, Akiyoshi. "How Should We Read Literature from a Certain Area from the Viewpoints of Other Language-speaking Areas? *The IAFOR Journal of Literature and Librarianship*, vol. 3, no. 1, 2014, pp. 9-39.

Wolfe, Bernard. "*Playboy* Interview: Henry Miller." [*Playboy*, Sep. 1964]. *Conversations with Henry Miller*. Eds. Frank L. Kersnowski and Alice Hughes. UP of Mississippi, 1994, pp. 79-98.

Zhang, Longxi. *Allegoresis: Reading Canonical Literature East and West*. Cornell UP, 2005.

— —. *From Comparison to World Literature*. SUNY UP, 2015.

The Henry Miller Memorial Library

Katy Masuga

On the side of Highway One as you wind along a narrow two-lane road through the rugged cliff side terrain known as Big Sur, California, 100 miles north of Hearst Castle in San Simeon and 30 miles south of Monterey Bay, you'll find the large canopy of a redwood grove has created a bowl butted up with its shoulders against the mountainside, and here sits the Henry Miller Memorial Library, welcome to all and sundry.

The Library is the former home of Galician-born, Austrian-raised Emil White, staunch Marxist, seaman, jack-of-all-trades, and latter-day painter, whose two brothers perished in the Holocaust (of nine total siblings).[1] Emil left his family and Europe as a very young man for New York where he worked odd jobs before settling for a time in Chicago as a bookseller and eventually becoming a transplant in Big Sur, like Henry Miller himself, but for the rest of his life at the behest of this selfsame pal, who claimed in 1944 to have found "Paradise." Emil joined him within months.

History indicates Emil and Henry first rubbed shoulders in 1923 when Emil was hired for a brief time at Western Union in New York, where Henry was hiring manager, although no connection or friendship came of it then. Two decades later, Emil's first foray into

Henry's writing was *The Cosmological Eye* (1939), which he picked up while working at the Argus Bookshop in Chicago.[2] Giving his own lectures on socialism, hosting debates between Stalinists and Trotskyites, and passionate by what he read in Henry's writing, Emil took up a hat collection of the bookstore patrons once in a while, which was sent to Henry via Ben Abramson, owner of Argus in Chicago (whom Henry had also met while on the "air-conditioned nightmare" research tour of America in 1942). As fate would have it, according to the most recent biography and Emil and Henry themselves, Emil and Henry randomly met one day on the streets of Chicago during this period, and the rest is history.[3] (Emil notes he was actively seeking to cross paths with the great writer Henry, having known he was in town.[4]) Emil embraced Henry "like a brother," and for the rest of their lives, Henry considered Emil one of the greatest if not greatest — or at least most reliable — friend he ever had.

After the Chicago meeting, the two aspiring men of letters remained in correspondence. Henry finished up his American tour and returned to New York, but he soon left for greener pastures in Beverley Glen, California in 1942 when Gilbert Neiman, writer and professor whom Henry met on a previous Los Angeles visit, offered him a free room next to his own home. Henry found some success with his watercolors in southern California but nothing to write home about, so in 1944 he readily accepted an offer on a room from a new writerly friend, Lynda Sargent, first introduced to Henry by Greek artist Jean Varda.[5] Not long after, Henry took up residence in a ramshackle one-room cabin on Partington Ridge in Big Sur, belonging to Lynda's ex-boyfriend and Carmel's ex-mayor, Keith Evans, then away in the Army.[6] Thus began Henry's "new way of life,"[7] without electricity, sewer, phone, or any other modern convenience.[8] He received supplies and mail up to three times a week after descending the one-mile dirt path to meet the courier.

At the same time that Henry was making his way into rustic but invigorating Big Sur living, Emil had left Chicago for the Yukon for a nine-month hard labor gig (that luckily turned into a desk job), taken up in order to avoid a possible draft into WWII. In recalling his trajectory, Emil writes of the forceful impact the Canadian frontier had upon him.

> Remember, I was born and grew up right in the midst of the Carpathian Mountains. In Austria I've climbed most of the mountains surrounding Vienna.

From vantage points in Innsbruck and Salzburg, I've gazed upon the famed Tyrolean Alps. I've taken sunbaths atop the much discussed Brenner Pass and passed through the snow topped mountains of Switzerland on my way to France. I've seen the Catskills and the Adirondacks. I've hitch-hiked across the Green Mountains of Vermont and have spent half a summer in the cool White Mountains of New Hampshire. But *never, never* in all my life have I ever seen anything to compare with the mountains of the Canadian Northwest![9]

It was there that Henry wrote Emil some months later with news of his California paradise asking Emil to join him, which he promptly did. His appreciation of the Yukon, and general love of unbridled nature, may have added to his eagerness to embrace the wild splendor of Big Sur as presented to him by Henry in his letters.

Henry and Emil

145

Over the roughly next two decades Emil and Henry would be inseparable pals in Big Sur, with Emil serving for a time as Henry's secretary when he first arrived. However, this latter arrangement lasted apparently only until Henry inadvertently taught Emil to paint, likely near the end of 1944, at which point Emil gave up his sidekick role to pursue more seriously his new found passion and for which, along with his Big Sur guidebooks, he would become known in his own right.

While sharing stories with Elayne Wareing Fitzpatrick in the late 1970s, who at the time was writing for the *Big Sur Gazette* and teaching Humanities and English at Monterey Peninsula College, Emil recalls the moment he first picked up a paintbrush after sharing in a couple bottles of French wine that had unexpectedly arrived as a gift to Henry in the mail. Stimulated by the wine, Henry first started painting. Emil says:

> He was so excited. He'd say, "Look at this! Look at that!" He was dancing and jumping all the time. Then he looked at me. "Why don't you do one too?" He was afraid I'd get bored while he was enjoying himself. I said, "What could I do? I don't know anything about painting. I never held a brush

in my hand." He said, "Well, try it anyway!" So I did. He really liked what I did, but he had to finish the painting for me because I didn't know how to put in a sky or a foreground. A French artist came the next day and, to my amazement, he liked my painting better than Henry's. That encouraged me to paint more. Two years later, I was having a one-man show in San Francisco![10]

Henry remembers the event a little differently: "Emil used to watch me work very attentively. After a time he got the notion that he too could paint, if he tried." Henry goes on to explain that they occasionally worked on a "joint endeavor" together, which usually turned out as a "monstrosity," although it gave Emil "courage." Eventually, Emil developed his own style and did very well with the public.[11]

By 1962, now divorced a fourth time (from Eve McClure), Henry left Big Sur for southern California again, Pacific Palisades to be exact, to be near his children from his third wife, Janina Martha Lepska, who in 1951 had left Big Sur to settle in Los Angeles and remarry a good-looking adventurer, artist, musician, athlete, decorated paratrooper, French Resistance fighter, and UCLA researcher in biophysics.[12] While in Pacific Palisades, Henry married and divorced again and died some two decades later in 1980.

During Henry's Big Sur period, Emil too had married twice and divorced, having two children himself, both sons with his second wife Pat, who was, " 'a mail order bride' who had worked as a secretary in an office of Frank Lloyd Wright before coming out to Big Sur."[13] Pat moved with the children to Monterey before remarrying and immigrating with the entire family to Australia in 1962 in an effort to "get as far away from Emil as possible."[14] Pat and her new husband Marco chose Australia as "a better place than California for raising three boys" in response to the nuclear scare of the Cuban Missile Crisis after the failed Bay of Pigs Invasion, and, at the time, the Australian government was offering incentives as a gesture to increase its skilled population.[15]

Within a year of Henry's death, Emil, still in Big Sur, created the Henry Miller Memorial Library in 1981 (then without a name) in homage of his pal, right in his own home while he was still living there, with the support of the Big Sur Land Trust. One article at the time reports how Emil was finishing up his breakfast while talking to several tourists who were asking questions about various Henry Miller pictures hanging about.[16]

When Emil died in 1989, he bequeathed the Library completely to the Big Sur Land Trust. Its first official director was Beat writer and artist Jerry Kamstra, followed by a new director, Carmel journalist Chris Counts (1992-1994), and since 1994 it has been directed by the multi-talented, Swedish-born sailor and Renaissance man Magnus Toren.[17] In 1998, Magnus established the Henry Miller Library as a nonprofit corporation, and in 2012 the Big Sur Land Trust donated its holdings as landowner to the Library itself, finally making the Henry Miller Memorial Library, Inc. an independent nonprofit and sole proprietor of both the land and Library.[18]

"The Henry Miller Memorial Library is not a mausoleum," Magnus Toren said to me during a chat. A resident of Big Sur since 1984, after literally sailing around the world and hitchhiking his way up the California coast, Magnus eventually followed an unlikely path to his current home: he caught the eye of a local woman who invited him to her home on Partington Ridge, where he has remained ever since. Equally serendipitous, he has been the director of the Henry Miller Memorial Library since he stumbled upon the preceding director vacating the role one random day in 1994.

> I asked how he was doing. "I'm leaving," he said. I applied for the job immediately. I had three qualities going for me: 1) my cultural background (I'm a French-speaking, well-traveled Swede), 2) I had already been living in Big Sur for nearly a decade (and was the caretaker of a well-known family), and 3) I had sailed around the world, a marker of self-sufficiency and reliance. They knew I could do everything from fix the bathroom to do the accounting to organize the archives. I was a jack-of-all-trades.

Like Emil himself, Magnus saw an opportunity and, after competition from a selection of qualified candidates, managed to land the role that he still holds with gratitude and hard work along with a lot of patience, creative thinking and perseverance.

The Library was of course created in the name of Henry Miller through the name of Emil White, but it sustains itself by taking an active role in art and cultural events in the community. It can be a conflicted experience maintaining a "memorial" library: do you focus solely on the writer to whom it is dedicated? If so, in what capacity? To include nothing beyond the memorabilia constitutes a museum. Do you add what you interpret to be the writer's philosophy of life and art? How about what you imagine the writer would have wanted? And any presence for those artists, writers, musicians and figures who themselves admired or were influenced by the writer? Anyone who has visited the Library since 1994 will see that Magnus has been doing all of those things.

The following then is an exploration of a few stories, or as Henry would say *histoires*,[19] of the Henry Miller Memorial Library through a cross section of some of the people who have known it best and who were kind enough to share their snapshots of Big Sur as relates to Emil and Henry and the Library. When I first asked for contributions, everyone included here instantly accepted and with such a joyful disposition. They have been extremely warm-hearted and open to my desire in hearing from them and graciously agreed to include their thoughts and memories. I am enormously grateful for their support but even more so simply for their generous spirit.[20]

Consequently, what follows is a small collection of reflections, anecdotes, photographs, letters and a song from those willing and wanting to share their part in the *histoires* of the Henry Miller Memorial Library for *Nexus: The International Henry Miller Journal*.

Stefan White, one of Emil's two children, was born in Salinas and spent time in Big Sur and environs as a young child until 1962, returning several times as an adult, most notably many years later in 1989 while assisting his father at the end of his life. Several of the old photographs that illuminate these pages were provided by him as well as many details of the life of Emil and family. The other images kindly come from Terry Way Photography, which regularly documents Library events. Alisa Fineman, who offers a song, came to Big Sur to write her university thesis in Environmental Studies in the early 1980s and was a close friend of Emil until this death and continues to have a presence at the Henry Miller Memorial Library through her musicianship. Mike Scutari offers insight on his role of assistant to the Library since 2010. Heidi Hopkins grew up in Big Sur along with her four siblings (her oldest sister was a playmate of Henry's son Tony) and shares several letters between Henry and her mother, Nancy Hopkins, first president of the Big Sur Land Trust, some of which come from the volume Heidi published in 2007 of Nancy's 1950s-60s correspondences with family and friends.[21] There are of course many more contemporary voices to be heard from in Big Sur and neighboring communities regarding the Library, and in 2015 Magnus began an oral history project, which includes both the storyteller evening at the Library and a podcast series entitled "Big Sur Stories" that documents as many of the *histoires* of the region, as generations continue to come and go. An excerpt from "Big Sur Stories" here includes reflections by Tasha Doner on her childhood as the daughter of the artist Ephraim Doner, also a Big Sur transplant whom Henry first knew in Paris in the 1930s. Author, professor, and journalist, Elayne Wareing Fitzpatrick, an old friend of the Hopkins family, Emil and many others, moved to coastal central California in the 1970s and wrote, among many other publications, *Doing It with the Cosmos: Henry Miller's Big Sur Struggle for Love beyond Sex* in 2001. Chris Counts, longtime news and arts writer for *The Carmel Pine Cone*, was first assistant and then director at the Library before Magnus. The last section of this article focuses on Magnus and the Library, the development of its events, and its future as it confronts the increasing difficulties in the region of preservation and overpopulation.

STEFAN White was born in Salinas but grew up in Big Sur, Pacific Grove, and Australia, returning to Big Sur several times between 1980 and 1989. In 1989 he stayed the full year after his father called him in New Mexico, asking for his help, as he was dying of Parkinson's (having been diagnosed in the 1970s). It was both an opportunity to patch up a fraught relationship and for a young man to experience life in California after having left it as a small child. In good humor, Stefan said, "The library was to me what Emil claimed painting was for him: a wonderful way to meet women." He immediately added, "Looking back, I could kick myself for my immaturity at the time, although I sincerely did my best to fulfill Emil's wants and needs and make his life with Parkinson's as comfortable as possible. Spending the last seven months of his life with him was a gift. Sharing special moments and coming to accept the few insurmountable differences between us."[22] Stefan spent all of 1989 with Emil in Big Sur until his death in July, staying on as a caretaker in the "library" before returning to his home in New Mexico.

Emil had been estranged from his children since before their departure for Australia in 1962, when they first left Big Sur for Pacific Grove on the Monterey Peninsula where Pat met and married her car mechanic, Marco McClintock (the very same "Marco" in Dr. Seuss's *And to Think I Saw it on Mulberry Street*, whose father was Seuss's editor).[23] Pat and Marco had another son, Bruce, before leaving for Australia where the family permanently remained to raise the children. Pat died in the mid-1970s.

Stefan and Dan were in touch with Emil by letter while growing up, although, as Stefan stated, "there were plenty of times with long gaps."[24] Emil visited Australia at one point, two or three years after the family had emigrated. Stefan recalled the peculiarity of his arrival.

> We went out to recess at primary school and kids came running while screaming: "There's a man sleeping on the oval!"[25] We went over to check it out, and it was Emil who'd been waiting for us to get out of school... Emil hated Australia, saying it was "the asshole of the Earth," too unsophisticated, too raw, too primitive for him and probably too hot and dry, too. The doctor he went to see because of diarrhea there offended him. Emil asked him if the medicine he'd given him would work, and the doctor replied, "If it doesn't, you can try a cork."[26]

Emil's impressions of Australia are somewhat ironic in light of his own living arrangements in coarse and rural Big Sur. His sentiments may have had not a little to do with his disappointment at having lost his children to their stepfather on another continent, even if he was also responsible for it. After caring for Emil on his deathbed, Stefan met an Austrian woman named Gerti shortly thereafter, who instilled in Stefan an interest in Austria, where he would eventually emigrate in 1994 — but not before trying out California and Australia again. Eventually he was "homesick" for Austria after his visits in the early 90s, thus permanently returning.[27]

During our exchanges, Stefan noted that it had just occurred to him then that he was unexpectedly living "the perfect sequel" to his father's life. He explained: "Emil always wanted me to learn German and visit Austria. I hated the sound of the language and vowed I'd never learn it. A few days after he died, in came the lady who would enable me to fulfill two of Emil's unfulfilled expectations of me."[28] After passing through dramatically distinct incarnations of the meaning of home across his childhood, Stefan declared, "I feel much more European than either American or Australian. I love the natural beauty of the States and Australia, but feel much more at home here in Europe."[29] In that way, Stefan has returned to the childhood home of Emil and in a manner has also returned Emil home through himself, having reconnected with him in Big Sur, playing a significant and welcomed role in the end of Emil's life.

ALISA Fineman came to Big Sur to co-care for Big Creek Reserve, managed by her university UC Santa Cruz, and to work on her senior thesis in Environmental Studies, "Where Extremes Meet." She met Emil in 1984 while conducting interviews with Big Sur residents about a controversial land bill that divided the community for a time.[30] Some of her subjects included Ansel Adams, Zad Leavy, Nathaniel Owings, and of course Emil White. Many of the 50 interviews she took began unexpectedly when her subjects often said, "I won't do an interview, but would you like to take a walk?"[31] During one such visit, Alisa arrived at the Henry Miller Memorial Library—which also happened to be Emil's home (still without a name)—and he invited her in for a cup a tea, eager to talk about his friend Henry, showing her the tiles in the bathroom by Ephraim Doner and chatting about painting, literature and music. (Soon thereafter, when Alisa started playing gigs at Cafe Amphora, on the deck below the historic Nepenthe,[32] she met Ephraim Doner herself sometime around 1984, who eagerly told her, "By the way, I'm also the one who taught Henry how to play ping-pong!"[33])
    Emil chose to speak about Big Sur values like kindness rather than conflict, sharing with Alisa the tradition of toasting to kindness which later inspired the song "Cup of Kindness" that she dedicated to him on his 84th birthday. Alisa said, "Though the song was initially inspired and written for Emil, it took on its own life as songs will do, with a universal message that continues to speak to everyone."[34] A great hit (Alisa went on to name her 1989 album *Cup of Kindness*), she has since played it "a million times" including in 2009 at the memorial for Billy Post, great grandson of one of Big Sur's first homesteaders.[35]

I saw a shining light
Warm and childlike in your eyes.

Before I really knew you
I had a feeling down inside
that your soul was made to feel and share
Life's pleasures pure and fine.
You're some one who knows friendship
        the way colors know their wine.

Here's to a cup of kindness
A medicine so strong.
From you I learn that love and friends
        forever keep us young.
Here is to a cup of kindness on the coast
May it always be the time
        for friends to make a toast.[36]

Emil in late life with "Chinatown" (1947) from the series *I'm a Stranger Here Myself*.

"People toast to kindness here," Emil explained to Alisa upon one of their first meetings, "at any party or gathering. No matter who you are, if you live in a mansion or under a bridge or on a bus." It was a phrase, Emil said, that he in turn had learned from Henry, "this toast to kindness," which was a catchphrase for the spirit of the age in which Emil and Henry first met in the 1940s and that pervaded—and still pervades—the Big Sur coastal community. Indeed, Elayne Wareing Fitzpatrick also confirmed this supposition, when she writes, "the Big Sur motto then was 'kindness'."[37] Thus for Alisa, as she shared with me, it was signature Emil, representing his value of friendship.

Emil regularly asked about Alisa's family any time they met, though he had never even met them. It was a personal gesture. "As a matter of fact," Alisa explained, "I would ask him questions because of his Austrian Jewish background and ask how he got to where he was. And I'd say, 'My grandfather doesn't seem as happy as you. How can that be? How can you be so different?' But Emil wanted to talk about what he valued, and friendship is what he valued, particularly in Big Sur." Henry had a related thought reflecting on Ephraim Doner: "Only the gay dog knows how to be tough, how to butter his bread with caviar, so to say, when there's nothing but mustard to be had."[38]

Alisa was inspired by what she witnessed as Emil's genuine conviviality. "People who keep each other whole. Have different opinions and still sit down and have tea and see each other's humanity and celebrate that and honor their disagreement."[39] Not everyone would agree, however. Emil was known to have a mean streak and had a difficult relationship with many around him including his family and friends. A long-time and prominent community member once asked Alisa, "I love the song, but why the hell did you have to write it for Emil White? He was a mean son-of-a-bitch." She laughed and replied, "Because it's a universal song."[40] If Emil's positive relationship with Alisa was exceptional, she was aware of that. Henry also counted Emil as one of his best and most reliable pals, dedicating *Big Sur and the Oranges of Hieronymus Bosch* to him. "We have to honor our own relationships with each individual," Alisa reflected in our talk, pointing out Emil's own responsibility for his individual relationships including with his sons and his caretakers, to both of whom Emil was known to have been unkind.[41] According to his son Stefan, Emil was "an odd mix of personality traits: authoritarian and compassionate, generous and miserly, uninhibited and restrained, promiscuous and moralistic."[42]

Alisa explained, "Emil had that magical child inside that informs our creativity." She connected to that artistic view of his, particularly as she began to develop her career as a musician while finishing up her work in environmental studies. "When you get us altogether, musicians and artists, we transcend. Art is the unifying force. Art and wonder and awe and beauty and ugliness and Mother

Nature. Her power reigns far more supreme than anyone's bank account. If you decide to live in Big Sur, you have to go with the flow. If Mother Nature decides the road is going to be closed for a month, that's it! We're all just trying to find ourselves and make sense of what it means to be a human being."[43]

Alisa described how the Library embodies that spirit: "That space holds friendship passed down as a value. Magnus has worked really hard to help preserve that value. Not just with literature, but in general the values of times passed. When we come to play music, for example, people want that thing, that thing that calms and revives us."[44] In dedicating his role to preserving and cultivating those values through cultural events, Magnus, Alisa said, is also "reviving, renewing, reaffirming that they exist, that it's different than it was, but that it's got that vibe from the past."[45] I asked Alisa about the role of the Henry Miller Memorial Library today as directed by Magnus from when she was first introduced to it when it was still Emil's home.

> Magnus' work at the Library tells me that ultimately no matter how things change, everybody wants something genuine. But we have to work hard to create that genuine thing and, as Emil said, that people invest in friendships. Magnus is goodness. And he thinks out of the box. It takes a Magnus. He is forever reinventing and getting excited. Thinking in broad strokes.[46]

HELPING Magnus with that not-insignificant task is Mike Scutari, who has been his assistant at the Library since 2010. Mike was first introduced to the Henry Miller Memorial Library after a volunteering gig with (((folkYEAH!))) physically brought him down the lighted pathway on some still, redwood evening into "a seriously enchanted forest environment."[47] He was lucky enough to land a role soon thereafter as Magnus' only employee and assistant, where he has been now for eight years. Here he responds to a few questions.[48]

– What is your relationship to Henry Miller?
Arm's-length. His isn't my favorite author but I believe larger influence is incalculable in terms of self-expression and his honest, confessional style. If anything, from my vantage point it seems as if history is finally catching up to Miller; I've seen more and more

writers and commentators call attention to this legacy than I did 10 years ago.

– What are your thoughts on the incarnation, role, purpose, use of the Henry Miller Memorial Library?
As an oasis for the arts, it's a refreshing and needed thing in our current political and social climate. People want to stop and slow down; often they can't, but at the Library they can. Their sense of relief and gratitude is palatable.

– What is the Henry Miller Memorial Library to Henry Miller, in your opinion?
Henry was clearly a controversial figure during his life, and the Library has been integral in keeping his legacy alive; this, of course, was Emil's primary intention, and I think he would be rather pleased.

– What is the Henry Miller Memorial Library to the current community?
It's your classic community art space—theater, fashion shows, music, classes, you name it. It's something none of us should take for granted.

– What role has the Henry Miller Memorial Library served in relation to your own life?
I've been here 8 years. Got the job after my predecessor quit. I fervently believe that the gig is one of the top 10 jobs in the country. Beyond being privy to the amazing programming, it's very stimulating to engage with visitors from all over the world. Why, just yesterday, I talked to guests about: a) the contrast between Eastern and Western conceptions of "suffering," b) Roberto Bolano's novel 2666, which is set to become a play, and c) the nightlife in Brazil.

SPEAKING of "Eastern and Western" philosophy, near to the Henry Miller Memorial Library are two spiritual centers: the Tassajara Zen Center, the first Zen monastery outside of Asia, created in 1967 by the San Francisco Zen Center, and the Esalen Institute with its infamous cliff-side hot springs, known to have been used by Esselen Indians as far back as 6,000 years ago. It became a westernized tourist locale as early as the 1880s and is currently a full-service retreat offering workshops in meditation, yoga, self-awareness, practices in the "Human Potential Movement," Gestalt therapy, massage therapy, and other forms of healing arts and contemplative exploration. When Henry lived in Big Sur, he spent time at the hot springs with his family and friends, including Ephraim and Rosa Doner and their daughter Tasha, as did Emil who actually lived on the grounds for nine years.

Tasha Doner is the featured child painter in *Big Sur and the Oranges of Hieronymus Bosch*, where Henry several times refers to admiring her skill. Reflecting on his sources of inspiration, he says, "Studying, with intent to imitate, one of Tasha Doner's 'masterpieces'—she was then a child of seven!—I made one of the best bridges ever. At that, it was not nearly as good as the bridge which Tasha had dashed off in my presence."[49] Several pages later, he goes into detail in similar ekphrastic form as he had in "The Angel Is My Watermark" from *Black Spring*:

> I want to come back to Tasha Doner for a moment. Whenever I get desperate over my inability to paint what I see or feel, I always summon Tasha to mind. When it comes to horses, for example, Tasha can start at the front or the rear end—it makes no difference—and always turn out a horse. If she tackles a tree, same thing. She'll begin either with the leaves and branches or with the trunk—but it always makes a tree, not a whisk broom or a bouquet of tin foil. If she happens to begin at the left-hand side of the paper, she moves straight across until she reaches the right-hand margin. Or vice versa. If she starts in the middle, with a house, let us say, she first puts in all the doors, windows, chimney and roof, the steps too, and then proceeds to landscape the grounds. The sky she usually puts in last, if there's room for a sky. If not, what matter? We don't always need a sky, do we? The point is that between her thoughts and her very busy fingers there's never a gap. She goes straight to the mark, filling every inch of space yet leaving air to breathe and perfume to inhale. There are crayon compositions on her walls which I prefer to any Picasso, as I said before, and even to a Paul Klee, which is saying more. Every time I visit the Doners I walk reverently up to her pictures and study them

anew. And every time I study them I find something new in them.[50]

Henry's admiration for Tasha's painting is not ironic. He was deeply "drawn to the work of children and of the insane," he claims, believing in a purity of form therein that runs deep and true — in the manner in which Big Sur itself as an unhinged, potent force of exuberant nature may be thought to have appealed to Henry in general. The power of its raw, untethered landscape was staggering, producing a sublime beauty, unfound in anything "civilized".[51]

In her chat with Magnus for "Big Sur Stories," Tasha Doner talked about enjoying the hot springs at Esalen as a kid with her parents and with Henry and his family, her one-room school in Carmel, and her parents' words of wisdom that she carries with her.[52] Henry speaks highly of the Doners in *Oranges*, here with a passage on Ephraim:

> What is it about the man that moves me so at times? The fact, or the realization of the fact, that he neglects absolutely nothing. Or, to put it positively, that he shows concern, genuine concern, for everybody and everything. Every time I take leave of him the word ritual comes to my mind. For there is something about this loving concern which he manifests, something of awareness in it, perhaps, which lends to all his actions the flavor of ritual observance. As soon as I think in this wise I perceive why it is I am always so happy in his company. I know then that every act of Doner's is a demonstration of the truth, as Eric Gutkind puts it, that the supreme gift which life offers us is the chance to know eternal life. To put it more mundanely, when Doner adds a little seasoning to the food he serves he is putting another touch of God in it, nothing less.[53]

Henry believed that Ephraim epitomized the life of the artist, "to become an artist one must first *be* an artist. No one is born an artist. One elects for it!"[54] And through that election, all stories become one's own stories, and nothing is either strange or revolting or taken with any more gravity than a gentle wind through the trees. "For, of all the friends and acquaintances I have had," says, Henry,

"[Ephraim] is the only one with a predominant soul."[55] As for his painting, Henry says, "He admired, nay loved his own work. And rightly so. They all contained some part of him—heart, liver, kidneys, no matter what. And all were imbued with soul."[56]

In her interview with Magnus, Tasha noted how one of the last things her father said to her before he died was that she was a "Mensch," indicating he found her "a lot stronger and more capable in the world than he had thought."[57] In the Jewish tradition, it is a term of honor and reverence, indicating some one who is dignified, admirable and, of course, a noble force in and of the world.

ANOTHER of the children of the community during Henry's sojourn was Heidi Hopkins, whose mother Nancy Hopkins was co-founder of the Big Sur Land Trust and who played a role in helping Emil set up the Library in 1981. Nancy met her husband Sam on a Sierra Club backpacking trip in 1947 and moved into the home they self-built on Partington Ridge shortly thereafter, becoming neighbors with the Miller family. Nancy died in 2001 and Sam in 2003. In 2007, Heidi published a collection of her mother's correspondence of the 1950s and 60s that includes much information about the various figures she knew in Big Sur, naturally including Henry and his family.

In *Doing It with the Cosmos*, Elayne writes that Nancy first discovered Henry's books when she was a student at Berkeley in the 1940s. A musician friend asked her to check out *Tropic of Cancer* from the library for him, which required a professor's signed approval. Not knowing what it was, she realized flipping through it later why her professor had an awkward, hidden smile as he signed on her behalf.[58] After Nancy and Henry became neighbors and friends, their children played together and some of Nancy's letters include descriptions of Henry's children's parties, including one for the sixth birthday of his daughter, Valentine. There are two more letters here below: one concerning Henry's relationship to his children as Nancy saw it, and a final, satirical letter she wrote directed to another friend regarding a party invitation at the Hopkins' that, in good faith, references both Henry's "bad boy" reputation as well as the equally inaccurate reputation of Big Sur as the nexus for anarchist orgies that circulated at the time.

November 15, 1951
    We are going to Val Miller's birthday party on Sunday. She will be six, and Henry is going around in circles

160

trying to plan the thing. Shanagolden has listed all the things he needs such as prizes and favors and colored hats, Maud is bringing the cake and ice cream, and I think the affair will be the tremendous success that it has been every year so far. Sam is the most excited of the three of us. We attended it last year and he had the most wonderful time. He's even looking forward already to the Easter Egg Hunt at Post's Ranch...when it came around last April he stayed home because he thought only mothers and children would go. He was so disappointed when I came home and told him that everyone in the countryside was there, including all the roughest and toughest of his cronies!

[Some days following]

Sunday was also a big day for her, for Valentine's party was a most roaring success. Jory got away with a fantastic amount of ice cream and cake...everyone kept feeding her. But she has a cast-iron stomach and had no evil effects. There were 19 or 20 children there, ranging from 14 down to 8 months, and even more adults, and the Miller ménage was really a delightful madhouse. Such games and popping of favors and exploding of balloons and prizes and more prizes and ice cream for the children and wine flowing like water for the grown-ups and the most beautiful birthday cake with real little wooden horses prancing around the top on a carousel that spun around under a striped canopy...that cake was the most beautiful I've ever seen. We finally carried Jory home about six o'clock and plopped her right in to bed minus her supper...I felt that oatmeal on top of about seven pieces of cake would be a superfluity, to put it mildly...and such was her fatigue that she slept until 9 o'clock the next morning!

December 17, 1952

We had a farewell dinner for Henry last night...he and Eve leave for Europe next Monday. The Rosses and Tolertons and Maud Oakes also graced our board, and I had made a huge venison meat loaf which was delicious (everyone said...better still, they showed it by all coming back for seconds and thirds). It was the first time that Henry and Eve had ever had venison, so they were properly amazed. Dear Henry brought a bottle of whiskey, and I had to think "how true to life" for whiskey costs six or seven

161

dollars a bottle and yet it will always be the poorest person...the person least able to afford it...who will *always* show up at the party bearing such a gift for the host and hostess. He was full of talk about Val and Tony...nothing so delights my heart as a person who really loves his children as Henry does...he will go into endless little details about the imaginative games that Val dreams up and can recite her letter word for word...how she writes to him "Dear Daddy, Last night we played trick or treat. Do you know what is trick or treat? Trick or treat is when you go to someone's house and say trick or treat and they give you something." The way Henry tells this little episode makes it seem like something not quite of this world, but of a sweeter, finer world which is childhood. And, also very Henry-like, he described his horror when someone...some progressive-school teacher friend of his... approached him to purchase for Val a book on sex-instruction for six-and-seven-year-olds and this book had "all the scientific terms for EVERYTHING...no euphemisms...just SCIENTIFIC WORDS! I WAS APPALLED!! Teaching those words to *children*!!!" The rest of us had to chuckle gently, remembering that after all Henry has written books any paragraph of which would be enough to curl your hair, and yet cannot bear the thought that his daughter should even be able to call the parts of the body by their correct names!

April 1958

Of course we want you to ask all the friends you want! The wilder the parties, the better. Fill the pool with champagne and have a moonlight orgy. Big Sur will be very disappointed in you if you don't do something just a little bit insane. This is the land of laissez-faire, you know. You can't dream up anything that hasn't already been done. Actually, Big Sur is beginning to get rather respectable, for as it has gotten more "chic" the prices have risen accordingly and fewer and fewer of the Bohemian element can afford to buy or rent homes here...so the beards and sandals (complete with dirty feet) have moved south to Gorda where a new colony flourishes. And Henry Miller has two cars (one a Cadillac) and plays ping-pong and has become positively bourgeois...his son reads nothing but comic books and his

162

daughter pin-curls her hair at a pink-satin-and-tulle vanity table. Quel malheur! Whither the Left Bank?

SPEAKING of the Left Bank, over the course of our numerous exchanges for this article, Elayne Wareing Fitzpatrick shared with me a talk she gave at Shakespeare and Company in Paris on Henry Miller and Robert Louis Stevenson in 2005 entitled "Strange Bedfellows," in which she discusses their mutual admiration of the American Transcendentalist poet Walt Whitman whose perennial philosophy — or what Elayne calls "Whitman's all-encompassing outlook"[59] — she sees as the root of both writers' attraction to the contemplative life.[60] Herself seduced by a similar calling, Elayne moved from her native Utah in 1974 to Carmel Valley to live closer to nature and build a home she dubbed "Capricorn Brae" on wild acreage with sheep, goats, Shelties and some chickens.

"I didn't know about Miller's intellectual/philosophical side until I read *Big Sur and the Oranges of Hieronymus Bosch*. Much later, prompted by some relationship stuff in my own life, I decided to learn more about *his* personal life. Then I delved into the essays he really liked to write."[61] (Elayne admitted she had at first written him off because of his public image but came back around after *Oranges*.) She added, "And when I read his book paying tribute to D. H. Lawrence, I was astounded because he had disliked the man early on."[62] Henry's popular negative image related to his "banned books" still rings true. To this day, he is infrequently included in university course syllabi. He's mostly discovered outside the classroom — from friends, aspiring writers and artists, at parties, poetry readings, and so on. Elayne explained her own experience.

> I was a child during Henry's time — the Great Depression years. When I was a teenager, Miller's 'Tropics' books etc. were read by flashlight 'under the covers'. And books/films like *Quiet Days at Clichy*, which he wrote only to make money, were how they continued to judge the man — and still do? When I finished writing *Doing It with the Cosmos*, there were (and still are) plenty who knew only the 'banned book' part of Miller. I wanted people to see that he was much deeper, intellectually and philosophically, than they suspected.[63]

I strongly agree with Elayne. I chose to do my Ph.D. research on Henry because he made me laugh out loud—not exactly how dissertation topics are chosen, but it was due to his incredibly singular, "philosophical" language coupled with his brazen experimental form that I found compelling and original.

Elayne, now 93, never met Henry in person. She moved to coastal central California after Henry was already in Pacific Palisades. She did, however, know Emil "all-too-well" for many years as the self-described "Mayor of Big Sur."[64] "My friendship with Emil dates back to the 60s when I began coming to Monterey summers to teach Philosophy and English at Monterey Peninsula College and revive interest in Robinson Jeffers."[65] Elayne also knew Harry Dick and Lillian Bos Ross ("Shanagolden"), pioneer artists of Big Sur. Harry Dick Ross had been tutored by a famous Utah artist, and Elayne wrote an article on him for the *Big Sur Gazette* and *The Salt Lake Tribune Home Magazine* in 1979. Valentine Miller sent her father the article, and he responded enthusiastically.

> Dear Harry Dick—Congratulations! That was a wonderful, warm, alive portrait of you that Val sent me. Should have been in the *N.Y. Times*. Couldn't figure out what paper it was in – perhaps the local Big Sur one? Anyway, the lady who wrote it did a masterful job.

Needless to say, Elayne cherishes that letter. She of course also knew other Big Sur residents of the era including Rosa and Bob Nash, about whom she also wrote a feature for the *Big Sur Gazette* in 1979, describing the couple's intensely rural lifestyle (their open air bedroom under the stars), and Rob's fascinating linear art that Henry intricately describes in the essay "Journey to an Antique Land," calling it, among other things, "pictographic messages, rendered in ideolinear code," an interpretation that Nash casually dismissed as Henry's "projections."[66]

Today, Elayne still cultivates her acre in Carmel Valley, still writes and still offers workshops on Carmel's original "Nature Bohemians."[67] She has traveled the world, including numerous visits to Henry's favorite – Greece. Elayne considers her main legacy to be the full-color coffee table book *Nature Wisdom: Mystical Writers of the Big Sur-Monterey Coast* (2012).

A generation came and went, and another followed. Elyane was still there. "I also knew the 'keepers' of the 'library' after Emil died, including the ill-fated Jerry Kamstra who vowed he would become the 'new Henry Miller' until the Big Sur Land Trust decided differently."[68] Jerry Kamstra was hired to direct the Library after Emil's death and did so for about two years until his then-assistant Chris Counts took over as director in 1992.

AFTER giving up his position as director in 1994, Chris awaited the new director, Magnus, to take over. However, in a message to me, Chris recalled that when Magnus was slated to begin in 1994, "he announced he was leaving on a sailing trip around the world," before taking up his post.[69] Therefore, during that leave of absence, Chris explained, "a very resourceful local woman named Leslie Nowinski ran the library for seven months until Magnus returned, and later, she worked for many years as his assistant."[70] As an important component in the history of the Library, Chris reiterated, "she did play a role in the evolution of the library that's worth remembering."[71] He also recounted his own first engagement with the Henry Miller Memorial Library:

> I first visited the library in 1986, and the very first interview I did for *The Carmel Pine Cone* newspaper was about "the library," which didn't have a name then. It was simply Emil White's house. About a year later, *Life Magazine* did a colorful spread about Emil and the library. After Emil died, Zad Leavy and Nancy Hopkins led the effort to create the library and find a director.

Chris noted that during his time as director, "Many of Henry's old friends showed up in those days, including his last wife, Hoki, and his last girlfriend, Brenda Venus."[72] He also provided a tale concerning a moment of serendipity during the 100th anniversary of Henry's birth, where Erica Jong was invited as the guest of honor but cancelled at the last minute and with much fanfare. Naturally, Chris and Jerry had already made her required elaborate arrangements and booked her suite at the incomparable Ventana Inn. When Brenda Venus coincidentally inquired if the Library might have a place for her to throw her sleeping bag for the festivities, Chris and Jerry knew exactly who their replacement guest of honor was going to be. "Besides being beautiful, she was gracious and down-to-earth, and the attendees were thrilled to meet her. She was truly the star of the show."[73]

165

THERE are several articles and interviews that tell of Magnus Toren's globetrotting story of getting to Big Sur and becoming Library director, including in a 2016 interview for Richard Dion's *Soul of California* podcast series.[74] Magnus has enacted enormous change at the Henry Miller Memorial Library since his arrival in 1994, and we have had several conversations about his relationship to the space.[75]

> I came in 1984 thanks to my wife. She took me up on Partington Ridge very close to Henry's house. I had no idea in those days. I did know Emil White and had been to the Library for various smaller literary events that he had, but I had identified the region with Robinson Jeffers. I had no dream of taking over the Library. There was very little in the Library in those days. There was very little activity. It had a small kind of low-key display of Emil's paintings and a few remnants here and there. I was eventually hired by Big Sur Land Trust. I had everything to gain and nothing to lose. I was starting from scratch.

At the time of Magnus' arrival, there was only one events venue in town, and so he brought in music—the singer/songwriter element, "and it kind of mushroomed," he explained. "Along with Henry's name and the location of Big Sur, those two things were so appealing to so many artists." Patti Smith, Neil Young, Philip Glass, Lucinda Williams, Arcade Fire, Fleet Foxes, Marianne Faithful, Rufus Wainright ... the list goes on.[76] The Library hosts poetry slams and readings and other literary events and caters to community and private events, including weddings and memorials.

Of course, the musicians mentioned above and all of these contemporary elements do not have a direct link to Henry Miller per se. The musicians were influenced by him to some extent, and the events themselves are part of what Magnus and the Library freely interpret as part of the Henry spirit. "Henry inspires us and these others, musicians, artists, what have you, to express themselves, to try and to fail, to write, forget the audience, pursue your own voice, do your own thing." I ask Magnus if he can then explain in what way the Henry Miller Memorial Library embodies but also "disembodies" the figure of "Henry Miller" —what the space is in relation to Henry but also not at all in relation to him, in terms of the purpose it serves for current and future visitors.

It has been a beacon for Henry Miller as an artist and a writer. It exposes people to his name and is a place of pilgrimage. People come from far away and pay homage. They read out of his books with a passion. That's what the purpose is: celebrating Henry's complete embrace for the humanities. There is no one more suitable to have a center for the arts. Henry believed memorials defeat the purpose of man's life. The Henry Miller Memorial Library is not a mausoleum! I think Henry would really enjoy and appreciate it. It's a place for young people to hang out, and old people too. Henry would totally love it.

We have to talk about the mission of the Library then as it relates to the impact these events have on the community and on the landscape, the magnitude of the ever-increasing influx of visitors.

> Adding the shows at the Library has always felt very right, but, yes, there's also been—especially in last 6 or 7 years—a little bit of a sense of contradiction. It has to do with the quantity of people clogging up the highway and almost overwhelming it. How do we protect it? But it's not just about the biological health of the region but also the health of the quality of the experience of the visitors.

This is a topic that not only comes up frequently but also comes up historically. In *Emil White of Big Sur*, Emil mentioned the last concert Joan Baez gave at Esalen, where Emil lived for nine years and she one or two. He wrote, "It turned out that Joan's was the last major concert ever to be held at Esalen because too many people were showing up for such events by 1972. The hordes of people caused too much damage to the beautiful grounds, too much garbage, too big a disruption."[77] Emil painted a guitar case memorializing the concert, "Joan Baez Concert," which was his final ever painting. Imagining that a concert in 1972 was ultimately too destructive, one must attempt to fathom the level of damage that humans could cause now and therefore respond positively to the importance of monitoring and treating that.

I asked Magnus if he could share a particular experience that relates to the Library, and he mentioned an unexpected encounter with Victor Villaseñor, Mexican-American author, whose family came to America from Mexico shortly before he was born, to where he grew up, in Carlsbad, California. He spoke only Spanish until he started school and was bullied for not speaking English. Years of discrimination and difficulty led Victor to drop out of school as a teenager and run away to Mexico where he found solace in the wealth of colorful arts around him. With a new sense of his identity and heritage, Victor returned to America, crossing the Rio Grande when he was barely 20. He discovered his passion for literature but continued to have a problematic relationship with the physically written word. He was later diagnosed as dyslexic, persistently struggling with reading and writing. Magnus shared Victor's experience at the Library recently:

> Victor told me, somewhere along the path when he was young and back in America, how he encountered *Tropic of Capricorn* and sat down on a southern California beach and started from Page One. He learned it like that, from Page One from reading *Tropic of Capricorn* and moved all the way through it til the end, page by page. That's how he learned how to read. When he came to the Library not long ago, and I met him, he was humble with no flare or presence of any kind, and he picked up a copy of *Capricorn* lying on the table... and began to read from it. He started reading out of the book aloud. It was amazing. Soft, quiet at first, humble. Everyone started listening, in perfect silence and in the moment, until, I think, all the hair on our arms were standing on end.

The episode exemplifies the subtlety and yet powerful significance of the Library itself. I asked Magnus if the Library is the vision of what he thinks Henry and Emil would have wanted, and also what he wanted to do when he took over in 1994.

> Yes! To see the Library continuing to be this modest place on the side of road that harkens back to time gone by remains vitally important. There is a timelessness that the Library embodies. To keep the

energy unassuming and noncommercial—we're not trying to sell you a bunch of things. The focus is on the literary and cultural heritage of Big Sur, which I think is well served by the Library, a place that feels like it's a little bit frozen in time. The kinds of symbolic attributes that I would support in the future. And, also, we are grateful that we can afford to keep it low key here. It's really nice to have a place that is so lowdown. We are consciously plunky, and people really enjoy that. It appeals to the nostalgia.

This idea connects to what Alisa said about "that thing," that thing that people want when they come to Big Sur. "They don't need to be hit over the head because they've already been over-stimulated all elsewhere in the world, in their lives."[78] The Library serves that purpose too, like the music and art itself. It's a retreat in its own way, to come away from city life or simply from one's everyday life whatever it may entail, and engage in a peaceful moment surrounded by redwoods, the sound of the sea and maybe a good book or a poetry slam or a concert on the lawn. Magnus continued:

I'm hoping in the last years of me being there that I can set it up to leave something that makes its low-key yet meaningful impact. I have to think about our significant archives: where to place them, for example? The Library is also a source of good information about the coast. In the long term, we want to serve the cause of the supportive and fine-tuned visitor experience that, also long term, is about not cramming this place with people.

There's an interesting problem about the appeal of Big Sur, even before Henry arrived. In *The Soul of California* interview, Magnus mentioned that the people of the region were not necessarily too happy about Henry's arrival because of the attention he brought to "their hideaway" and how it "threatened" that status according to some of the residents. Curiously, Henry had the same criticism of Emil, suggesting that his successful guidebooks were bringing in more people than he personally was comfortable with, as befitting the region. Magnus also mentioned himself feeling "guilty of doing the same thing," although, as he put it, "the cat has long been out of the bag."[79] Nevertheless, the challenge exists as how best to manage the large number of visitors in relation to the fragile and diverse eco-system. Magnus identified the paradox when he said, "It's at risk for being loved to death."[80] A strong advocate for equal access and a supporter of the tourist or "visitor" industry at large, Magnus envisioned the next 5 to 10 years must produce a viable solution for Big Sur to retain a state of balance between nature and humankind. "Big Sur symbolizes, and should continue to nurture, the idea of peace and the contemplative life more than the highly active life that we live outside an oasis like this."[81]

Gentrification has been unavoidable (or, in any case, thus far has not been avoided: the cost of housing in the area, for example, is on par with the staggering costs in mid-northern California as a whole, i.e., the San Francisco Bay Area), and the "battle for the wilderness" is as old as "the white man's" civilization has been present in the region. Magnus constantly referenced the importance of preserving Big Sur for posterity, for its "cultural and natural value" and suggested that the success of one may come at the detriment of the other, though hopefully not and not necessarily if we play our cards right. The position of the Library in that mix remains to serve as a beacon for forging ahead with creativity, inclusivity, conservation but also human expression and a perpetual reminder to remember and honor the past and integrate it with respect and appreciation—and Big Sur "kindness."

The author at the Henry Miller Memorial Library

171

[1]According to Emil's son Stefan White, Emil was able to assist his sister Toni and her husband Edi escape to the USA after the *Anschluß*. Edi had been sent to Buchenwald, and Toni was able to free him. Another of Emil's sisters, Malka Weinmann-Wieselmann, survived the Holocaust from within Holland, where she extraordinarily rescued nearly 50 children from extermination. See "'Poor devils' of the Camps: Dutch Jews in the Terezín Ghetto, 1943-1945." *Yad Vashem Studies*, 2015.

[2]In *Emil White of Big Sur* (material taken from interviews of the 1980s), Emil claimed it was 30 years later in Big Sur, after finally reading *Tropic of Capricorn*, that he learned his best pal, the writer Henry Miller whom he had admired since reading *The Cosmological Eye* in 1939, had been his hiring manager at Western Union back in 1923. (Fenton Humphrey, Joanne. *Emil White of Big Sur*. Windjammer Adventure Publishing, 1997. P. 10) However, in an interview with Elayne Wareing Fitzpatrick around 1979 or 1980, Emil stated it was "that same day" in 1942 he learned this bit of personal information. Either way, the connection came as a surprise. (Wareing Fitzpatrick, Elayne. *Doing It with the Cosmos: Henry Miller's Big Sur Struggle for Love beyond Sex*. Xlibris, 2001. P. 91.)

[3] Hoyle, Arthur. *The Unknown Henry Miller: A Seeker in Big Sur*. Arcade Publishing, 2014. P. 80, Miller, Henry. *My Bike and Other Friends*. Capra Press, 1978. P. 45, and *Emil White of Big Sur*, P. 10.

[4] *Emil White of Big Sur*, P. 10.

[5] Henry first met Jean "Janko/Yanko" Varda at an art opening in Pacific Palisades, and it was Jean who introduced Henry to Big Sur on a trip to visit his studio in Monterey in February 1944.

[6] *Unknown Henry Miller*, P. 69-70.

[7] Miller, Henry. *Big Sur and the Oranges of Hieronymus Bosch*. Pocket Books, 1975. P. 3.

[8] After he married Lepska and they had their two children, Henry eventually was able to buy the cabin and acreage of his neighbor Jean Wharton in 1946 on credit until his French royalties arrived, a home which remained in the family until 2000, although Henry only visited Big Sur once more before his death, after having permanently departed in 1962.

[9] *Emil White of Big Sur*, p. 12.

[10] *Cosmos*, p. 93.

[11] *My Bike*, P. 47.

[12] *Unknown Henry Miller*, P. 177.

[13] Stefan White in discussion with the author, May 2018.

[14] *Ibid.*

[15] *Ibid.*

[16] Corwin, Miles. "Henry Miller's Big Sur Pal Made Cabin a Memorial." *LA Times* 5 Sept. 1988. <http://articles.latimes.com/1988-09-05/news/mn-1078_1_big-sur>.

[17] "The Happiest Man Alive: Magnus Toren Keeps Henry Miller's Memory and Spirit Alive in Big Sur. The Happiest Man Alive." *Monterey County Weekly*, 2 Mar 2000. http://www.montereycountyweekly.com/news/local_news/magnus-toren-keeps-henry-miller-s-memory-and-spirit-alive/article_faf336ab-0a9e-5e9d-9105-1e52a7b7c198.html. Accessed 13 May 2018.

[18] Abraham, Kera. "Henry Miller Library Comes of Age." *Monterey County Weekly*, 7 Feb. 2012. <http://www.montereycountyweekly.com/blogs/news_blog/article_688a07d4-da54-5f6b-b67a-daff1d24f340.html?TNNoMobile>.

[19] In *Sexus*, Henry wrote that "*histoire* should be story, lie, and history all in one was of a significance not to be despised. And that a story, given out as the invention of a creative artist, should be regarded as the most effective material for getting at the truth about its author was also significant. Lies can only be embedded in truth." (Miller, Henry. *Sexus. Part I, The Rosy Crucifixion*. Panther Books, 1970. P. 246.)

[20] Additional thanks also go to Ondrej Skovajsa for sharing endless pages of two Henry Miller biographies when I was unable to get my hands on my own copies during the writing of this article.

[21] Hopkins, Nancy. *These Are My Flowers: Raising a Family on the Big Sur Coast / Letters of Nancy Hopkins*. Ed. Heidi Hopkins. Heidi Hopkins, 2007.

[22] Stefan White in discussion with the author, May 2018.

[23] Another chance meeting in the street between old friends brought together college buddies Ted Geisel (Dr. Seuss), who, after almost thirty rejections, had just given up on the possibility of his first children's book ever being published, and Mike McClintock, who had just become children's editor at Vanguard Press. The rest is history. See Claire Bicker's article "Albany resident Marco McClintock, 87, namesake of Dr. Seuss character." *PerthNow*, 20 Feb. 2016. <https://www.perthnow.com.au/news/wa/albany-resident-

marco-mcclintock-87-namesake-of-dr-seuss-character-ng-80b864b88c0dbc16c4b9a17a8eb56da4>.

[24] Stefan.

[25] In Australian English, an "oval" is a ground for Australian rules football and is also generally the name for the grassy playing field on school grounds.

[26] Stefan.

[27] Stefan added, "Although I'm married to another Austrian, Gerti and I are still friends."

[28] Stefan.

[29] *Ibid*.

[30] In the 1980s, Big Sur was at the heart of a historic engagement on the level of social structures and conservationism, called "a battle for the wilderness."

[31] Alisa Fineman in discussion with the author, May 2018.

[32] Nepenthe is a historic restaurant in Big Sur built in 1949 that incorporates the former cabin of Orson Welles and Rita Hayworth into its structure, a cabin originally built in 1925 by Christian Scientists. It is the same cabin in which Lynda Sargent, tenant of Welles and Hayworth, offered Henry Miller a room when he first arrived in Big Sur in 1944. See "Stories and Folktales." *Nepenthe.com* <https://www.nepenthe.com/stories-and-folktales-1>.

[33] Alisa.

[34] *Ibid*.

[35] Alisa played "Cup of Kindness" at Emil's memorial in 1989 as well. Stefan also recalled agreeing to Alisa and her fellow musician friends playing, whom he called "a wonderful group of extremely talented musicians, profound songwriters and thoughtful human beings." In addition to Alisa, they were a troupe called "City Folk," an ironic name that Stefan noted in our exchange reminds him of a series of paintings by Emil called "I Am a Stranger Here Myself," which were based on the endless replies he received when asking for directions in San Francisco or Los Angeles. No one seemed to know because they were strangers too. Stefan shared this anecdote with me, which Emil shared himself in *Emil White of Big Sur*, P. 39. Stefan added, "Both Henry and Emil were city folk, although obviously Emil found a way for the world to come to his door in the country."

[36] Fineman, Alisa. "Cup of Kindness." *Cup of Kindness*, Alisa Fineman, 1989.

[37] *Cosmos*, P. 38.

[38] *Oranges,* P. 193.

[39] Alisa.

[40] *Ibid.*

[41] *Ibid.*

[42] *Emil White of Big Sur,* P. 108.

[43] Alisa.

[44] *Ibid.*

[45] *Ibid.*

[46] *Ibid.*

[47] Mike Scutari in discussion with the author, May 2018.

[48] *Ibid.*

[49] *Ibid.,* P. 90.

[50] *Oranges,* P. 96.

[51] In conversation with Elayne, included in her book on Henry, Emil said something directly to this point in response to visitors' comments about Big Sur's appeal: "'It must be wonderful to live in such a place forever.' It is. But think twice about it before you try it. Or read Robinson Jeffers first. He described it all before it ever happened. He saw it as a poet would see it. Jeffers didn't make it attractive. He made it dramatic, violent, awesome. And that's what Big Sur is even today. But you won't discover that until you live there awhile." *Cosmos,* P. 94.

[52] Toren, Magnus. "Tasha Doner." *Big Sur Stories,* 19 Dec. 2015. <https://bigsurstories.wordpress.com/2015/12/19/tascha-doner/>.

[53] Tasha Doner.

[54] *Oranges,* P. 193.

[55] *My Bike,* P. 57.

[56] *Ibid.,* P. 65.

[57] Tasha Doner.

[58] *Cosmos,* P. 67-68.

[59] Wareing Fitzpatrick, Elayne. "Strange Bedfellows: RLS and Henry Miller." Spring 2005, Shakespeare and Company, Paris, France.

[60] She has also called it Whitman's "all-encompassing love of Nature" in conversation with the author.

[61] Elayne Wareing Fitzpatrick in discussion with the author, May 2018.

[62] *Ibid.*

[63] *Ibid.*

[64] Elayne also called Emil a "playful 'pincher' of young female college students" whom she'd take to Big Sur on tours. This moniker provokes many concerns and questions, particularly in light of *#metoo*, not least of which is whether or not those "young female college students" found the pinching as "playful" as Emil did.

[65] *Ibid.*

[66] Wareing Fitzpatrick, Elayne. "Bob Nash Celebrates Life in Delicate Line Drawings." *Big Sur Gazette*, March 1979.

[67] Elayne is currently working on a book on "transforming despair 'organically' in this age of meds and algorithms, with the help of William James as the 'father of American Psychology'."

[68] Elayne.

[69] Chris Counts in discussion with the author, May 2018.

[70] *Ibid.*

[71] *Ibid.*

[72] *Ibid.*

[73] *Ibid.*

[74] Dion, Richard. "Henry Miller's Big Sur." *The Soul of California.* 21 Sept. 2016. <http://thesoulofcalifornia.libsyn.com/big-sur-and-henry-miller-it-doesnt-get-any-more-mythic>.

[75] Magnus Toren in discussion with the author, May 2018.

[76] It is not insignificant to also mention the events of a smaller scale showcased at the Library including California folk musician, Ed Masuga, my little brother! See edmasuga.com.

[77] *Emil White of Big Sur*, P. 84.

[78] Alisa.

[79] *The Soul of California.*

[80] *Ibid.*

[81] *Ibid.*

Miller Notes

Editors' note: This feature seeks to alert readers to current scholarship on Miller, as well as to significant popular references to Miller or his work. Reviews have not been included. If you would like us to acknowledge a new item (or an omitted item from the following list), please contact the editors at <jdecker@icc.edu>.

2016-2018

New Works by Miller

Miller, Henry. "Glittering Pie." *Romp*, vol. 1, no. 5, 1969, pp. 22-25, 66.

This essay, which is a re-titling of the opening pages of Miller's *Aller Retour New York,* is illustrated with four action photos of strippers dancing in a club.

> At the burlesk Sunday afternoon I heard Gypsy Rose Lee sing "Give Me a Lei!" She had a Hawaiian lei in her hand and she was telling how it felt to get a good lei, how even mother would be grateful for a lei once in a while. She said she'd take a lei on the piano or on the floor. An old-fashioned lei, too, if needs be. The funny part of it is the house was almost empty. After the first half-hour everyone gets up nonchalantly and moves down front to the good seats. The strippers talk to their customers as they do their stunt. The coup de grace comes when, after having divested themselves of every stitch of clothing, there is left only a spangled girdle with a fig lead dangling in front—sometimes a little monkey beard, which is quite ravishing . . .

Curiously, dashes were substituted for the following words and phrases in the 1969 *Romp* printing, but printed in full in Ben Abramson's 1945 edition of *Aller Retour New York*: testicles; shit; one of his testicles; piss in; holding their boobies, especially when said boobies are full of milk; and laying her except he had a golden wand.

Submitted by Roger Jackson

Miller, Henry. *Quiet Days in Clichy*. Translated by Farid Qadimi. Ejazz, 2018. [Persian]

Published in Tehran, this is the first Persian translation of *Quiet Days in Clichy*. In fact, Roger Jackson's bibliographies list no other Persian translations. In his introduction, Qadimi contends that "Miller is a perfectly modern writer in search of an easy-going, flowing modernity which lacks identity since he knows well that whatever is hard and stable is doomed to vanish in a puff of smoke. Modernity is imperfect, and Miller is fascinated with such imperfection."

Miller, Henry. "Reading in the Toilet." *The Writer's Reader: Vocation, Preparation,* Creation. Ed. Robert Cohen and Jay Parini. Bloomsbury Academic, 2017, pp. 151-173.

Reprints chapter XIII from Miller's 1952 *The Books in My Life*. Cohen and Parini include the excerpt in the "preparation" section along with selections such as Walter Benjamin's "Unpacking My Library" and Ha Jin's "Deciding to Write in English."

Miller, Henry. *Tropic of Cancer*. Martino Fine Books, 2015.

Possibly pirated facsimile version of the 1961 Grove Press edition. Amazon description reads "not produced with Optical Recognition Software." The website for Martino Fine Books provides no information other than a Connecticut post office box, an email address, and a telephone number.

Submitted by Karl Orend.

Miller, Henry. Tropic of Capricorn. Midwest Tape, 2009.

This audiobook on CD consists of ten discs with a total running time of twelve hours and thirty minutes. Narrated by Campbell Scott, it was first released in 2008 with the current set repackaged by Midwest Tape, a library supplier, and released on May 5, 2009.

Miller, Henry. *The World of Sex.* **Penguin Modern Classics, 2015.**

This addition to Penguin's Modern Classics series presents what may be the "cutest" edition of the work—the book is smaller than usual and features a bright read cover. This version, however, is simply a reprint of the revised 1957 edition. The original 1940 edition of this book-length essay is still waiting to be reprinted for twenty-first-century readers.

Penguin is certainly making an effort to keep Miller's major works in print, especially in Britain. As noted by James Campbell in his 2016 article for the TLS, however, these editions are generally lacking introductions that would provide new readers with appropriate context to Miller's books.

Submitted by D.A. Pratt

Miller, Henry, and Blaise Cendrars. Se scopro un bel libro devo condividerlo con il mondo intero. Translated by Federica Cremaschi, with Introduction by Jonny Costantino. Lamantica Edizioni, 2016.

The title of this Italian edition of the Miller – Cendrars correspondence loosely translates as "If I Discover a Good Book, I Must Share it with the World." It was published in a limited edition of 120 numbered copies, on light blue paper, in a small format measuring 4 x 6 inches.

Submitted by Ernst Richter

Books

John Burnside. *On Henry Miller; Or, How to Be an Anarchist* **Princeton UP, 2018.**

John Burnside (b. 1955), a Scottish writer whose poetry has won the Whitbread (2000) and T.S. Eliot (2011) prizes, and whose bibliography includes many fiction and memoir titles, intertwines episodes from his youth, teenage years, and as an adult with his interpretation of Henry Miller's bucking "The System" (161) in *On Henry Miller*. The two main purposes seem to be to show that anyone can be an anarchist and "to recover and reimagine a seriously playful condition..." (161). According to his account there is much to overcome to awake the average person's rebellious streak:

> Had our education been different (had we been raised by wolves, say, or anarchists in the woods), we might feel ready for such a task. But from the age of around eighteen months onward, the Western child is conditioned to live by the clock, to be hungry when he is supposed to be hungry, to sleep, or at least lie down, when Mommy wants her to sleep, to learn this skill and not that, to go to law school when she really wanted to be a dancer—the list goes on and on. We are taught to be creatures of habit; though more often than not, they are somebody else's habits, and not our own. Those habits include voting for people who have no intention whatsoever of representing us in government..., listening to what a man says because he has (or says he has) money, and believing, after decades of evidence to the contrary, that we can trust what we read in the papers or see on the evening news. They are reprehensible habits all, but when we look around, there isn't a political equivalent to Weight Watchers or A.A. to offer help (it's an appealing thought, though: Voters Anonymous). (74-75)

The chapter titles clearly state Burnside's approach: "By Way of a Preface"; "In Praise of Flight"; "Like a Fluid (The False Pornographer)"; "On Love and Property"; "Henry Miller as Anarchist"; "Like a Fluid (The Great Romantic)"; "The Air-Conditioned Nightmare"; "The Time of the Assassins"; and "The Creature World," followed by endnotes. Such bright signposts signaling his intentions are needed due to the murky, gaseous writing that befogs most of the terrain.

"By Way of a Preface" contains the drabbest writing I've encountered in a while from a garlanded author. The first paragraph, like the long quote above, illustrates what readers have to contend with:

I was stuck. The book was almost finished, and I was trying to make a decent fist of liking it (though only to myself, for I had yet to summon up the chutzpah to show it to anyone else), but I was failing miserably. From beginning to end (though with a great big hole where the sex should be), the book I had privately titled *Henry Miller; Or, How to Be an Anarchist* was a perfectly honorable, if rather lopsided, homage to the work I most loved by a writer I mostly admired, but the whole thing was dull as ditch water. At the same time, apart from a grudging admission that Kate Millett's critique of *Sexus* in her groundbreaking study of misogyny in literature, was more or less fair, most of my "appreciation" of Miller was based, like a house built on sand, on a plucky attempt to pretend that a handful of cringe-worthy passages (though by no means all) about sex were no longer relevant and could be passed over quickly. Or rather, that they were somewhat relevant, but they had already been given enough attention, to the detriment of other, more interesting and, even (in my view), more rewarding books. (ix-x)

The best place to start—where a Princeton editor might have, particularly since this title appears under the press's Writers on Writers series — is with the over-reliance on *was*. In the five-sentence paragraph this verb is used eight times. It might be thought that Burnside meant that repetition to indicate the "stuck" mindset he speaks of, but then you have to consider that he composed the Preface *after* the draft he isn't fond of when he had time to think about the journey taken, a journey that includes, to name a few stops, armchair psychologizing about Miller's parents, the influence of Frank Harris and "soft pornographic" (31) titles (*The Pearl* and *Man with a Maid* recur throughout) on Miller's approach to and characterization of women—specifically Ida Verlaine from *Sexus* (1949), in a passage Millett made much of—Thoreau, Whitman, and Rimbaud, the cost of marriage and the cost of divorce, Miller's campaign for the Nobel, and world over-population. Some of these features could have provoked Burnside into providing a lively opening. Apart from the listless verb use, there is a reliance on clichés—"decent fist," "dull as ditch water," and "house built on sand"—and an overabundance of commas and parentheses that prevent sentences from generating momentum. From his poetic works Burnside knows about the importance of rhythm, so its frequent absence is puzzling. The book is an exasperating read.

Apart from how things are expressed (though not much apart) stand Burnside's ideas, which are often broad generalizations. While he is clear that this book is not "lit-crit" (161) but a response, in a personal vein, to what Miller makes him think about, he does owe readers more evidence than he provides. The unfortunate result is that what he says comes across as undifferentiated from the unsubstantiated opinions that issue from the most mediocre blogs. Burnside twice refers to a study that says women prefer chocolate to sex (28-29, 39) yet, despite its importance, never gives a citation for it; uses the term *"The Tropics"* (xi), a deplorably inaccurate shorthand error; repeats himself and smothers his attempts at humor (as with the dead remark on Voters Anonymous above that would have been better left for a reader to work out); and confuses a constellation of impressions about how society works, "an anarchic knowing" (80), with "the basic principles of a science... whose main purpose would be to align human behavior as closely as possible to the natural world" (80). Is anarchy a science? Is something else meant? It's hard to tell since the science goes unnamed.

Burnside proffers certain ideas. The first of note is that he detects in Miller's work *la fuite*, a term taken from Henri Laborit, that can be translated as "'flight'" (2) or, more comprehensively, "a leap of the imagination, a total renewal, a commitment to the soul's logic..." (2) This escape can "have the feel of a game..." (3) Miller defies societal expectations by abandoning them so that he can rebuild and relocate elsewhere without, to put it one way, obeying claims upon his life force. This brought to mind George Orwell's "Inside the Whale" and his terming Miller's practice *quietism*. Burnside brings in citizen of the world George Dibbern's memoir *Quest* and Miller's favorable 1946 review of it (later reprinted in *Stand Still Like the Hummingbird* [1962]) to underline that for Miller, as for "any other follower of the Daoist-Anarchist path, what matters is to live according to one's inherent nature" (20).

Such a path is hard to take, even for Miller, given the negative molding of a personality that, from the first long quote above, looks to be inescapable, and considering the times in which he grew up, when the only models of masculinity were, Burnside argues, his weak father, the Theodore Roosevelt "iron man" (64), and the Frank Harris "self-regarding braggart" (64). To accommodate Miller's case, Burnside devises a fourth ideal: the "'adept'—a term drawn from magic and alchemy... This figure, part-trickster, part-secular saint..." (64), is found in folk tales and medieval ballads. This attempt at sociology disdains discussion of whether children are shaped more by their friends, their kin, and their environment than by remote public figures that, in later life, erratically impinge on their senses (Miller's childhood exposure to Teddy Roosevelt would have been much less than a child now to Beyoncé in this media-saturated era) and strikes me as a gross oversimplification of affairs. Burnside also makes a misstep when he writes that "[f]or Miller, his mother was a template for the loveless, judgmental, joyless wife whose entire view of her husband, and of the quality and potential of married life, is based on property" (44). That may reflect a portion of Miller's views, but *it isn't his mother*, for we don't know her life outside of what her son presented.

For me, it's impossible to read Burnside's digressions and not compare his paltry word-hoard with Miller's fireworks. Apparently, this is not a shared complaint. On the Princeton University Press website, there's a page devoted to this book, and it contains a blurb from Jay Martin, author of the Miller biography *Always Merry and Bright*, who states: "Paralleling Miller's style, Burnside is impressionistic, digressive, hyperbolic, and sometimes outrageous... Burnside and Miller make a good match."[1] No one should be taken in by that commendation. Miller in full flight didn't allow his sentences to sag so heavily, to be devoid of memorable imagery and word explosions, and to be so free of associational jumps.

On Henry Miller flickers into life fitfully. One example is in the chapter "The Great Romantic" where Burnside mulls over how we, as readers, "allow our hearts to be broken, now and then, by a shred of fiction..." (97). He brings in *The Colossus of Maroussi* (1941) where Miller chances across a young girl of indeterminate age, but not above 14. Burnside breathlessly italicizes this line: "If Fate were to put her in my path again I know not what folly I might commit" (102). (Some readers may think of Conrad Moricand in *A Devil in Paradise* [1956].) As Burnside says, this is "unsettling to read. But why? Beatrice was only twelve years old when Dante first saw her, so whatever evil motive we might ascribe to Miller we must also ascribe to Dante. Either that, or we have to concede that there is no such thing as 'spiritual love.'" (103) His argument shifts to how "forbidden love" (103) is an abstract as well as an actual occurrence, and ends up at a safe distance from Miller's remark on this real young girl: "but is it not possible that this passage finally blows Miller's cover and reveals him, not as the sly pornographer, or as the Frank Harris wannabe, but as one of the great romantics?" (105) That's going to be, as Burnside admits, a decision left to every reader. If he had spent more time on this provocative passage he might have come up with something disturbing or profound, or both. Instead, his digressive nature gets the better of him and is coddled by his editor.

Much of Burnside's energy goes towards touting key texts to understanding Miller's rebelliousness: *The Colossus of Maroussi, The Air-Conditioned Nightmare* (1945), and *The Time of the Assassins* (1946), for him, embody Miller's anarchism, a newly found concern for the natural world (linking him with the works of Rachel Carson), and a quasi-philosophical approach to life expounded more fully, though by no means systematically, than in the works of the 1930s. John Burnside, in "The Creature World," draws material from those works that he can use to critique *mainstream* ecology/environmental methods..." (161) (He may want to consult Curtis White's *The Barbaric Heart* [2009] since it addresses this issue, but without reference to Miller. While that may be a rich topic, it is brought up on the book's dying pages, and arrives too late to rescue *On Henry Miller* from its severe defects.

[1]Martin, Jay. Blurb for *On Henry Miller*. Princeton UP, <https://press.princeton.edu/titles/11246.html>.

Reviewed by Jeff Bursey

Fraenkel, Michael. *Death in a Room (Poems, 1927-1930),* **edited with a Preface by Karl Orend, Alyscamps Press, 2018.**

This is a limited edition chapbook, featuring fifteen poems by a significant contemporary of Henry Miller while he was in Paris. This edition is the first in a series intended to introduce Fraenkel to twenty-first century readers. Orend's preface begins dramatically: "Michael Fraenkel is remembered by almost no one today." Orend's general effort to change this situation will be a worthy project—especially since Fraenkel wrote one of the best essays on Miller's writing.

Submitted by D.A. Pratt

Nash, Noreeen. *Titans of the Muses: When Henry Miller Met Jean Renoir.* **CreateSpace, 2015.**

Rejaunier, Jeanne. *My Sundays With Henry Miller.* **CreateSpace, 2013.**

Memoirs can divulge an intriguing peek into the everyday life of an individual, often revealing an untold perspective of the subject's sentiments. For a literary figure such as Henry Miller—whose most famous novels are semi-autobiographical—it is not surprising that memoirs would arise in an effort to reveal a more intimate impression of the man. Remembrances of Miller range from the memoir-esque, "intimate biography," *My Friend, Henry Miller* (1956), by Alfred Perlès, as well as Brassaï's *Henry Miller: The Paris Years* (1975) and *The Happy Rock* (2002), to those emerging after his death, most notably by Barbara Kraft and the published sections of an anticipated memoir by Harry Kiakis. Added to this growing list of memory writers are Jeanne Rejaunier and Noreen Nash, two friends who knew Miller during his early Pacific Palisades years, in the latter 1960s. Read together, Rejaunier and Nash portray Miller in his ultimate domain: conversation.

Pacific Palisades was a playground of sorts for Miller. After struggling financially most of his life, his windfall came with the American publication of his numerous banned books. Moving to Los

Angeles to be closer to both his children and proper medical care, he promptly came in touch with the outskirts of the Hollywood scene. In his house on 444 Ocampo Drive and at various afternoon gatherings and dinner parties, Miller was introduced to a diverse array of people in the entertainment world, such as Lucille Ball, Rita Hayworth, Jack Nicholson, and Warren Beatty. First invited through a mutual friend, Miller began attending and became a regular at the Sunday afternoon parties hosted by physician Lee Siegel and his wife, Noreen Nash. The Siegel's residence served as a significant social gathering place for Miller. It was here that he met young ladies seeking careers in Hollywood, including Jeanne Rejaunier, and he would later invite his soon-to-be 5th wife, Hoki Tokuda, to the Siegel's—eventually marrying her in their home in 1968. It is the Siegel residence that forms the backdrop for *My Sundays With Henry Miller* as Rejaunier, one of Dr. Seigel's patients, quickly formed an intellectual attachment with Miller.

An important signpost for approaching this memoir appears in the preface, which contains reprints of undated emails sent between Rejaunier and friend, Lee Merrin. In an effort to assemble materials and recollections related to her friendship with Miller and useful for composing the memoir, Rejaunier tells Merrin, "I'm trying to piece it all together; I do have some scattered notes, photos, memories...ah, yes, definitely lots of those, some of it a blur, some strong, despite passage of time" (7). To be certain, most memoirs contain the element of indistinct memory, but since a significant portion of Rejaunier's memoir is comprised of presumed conversation between Miller and his companions it is of particular import to bear in mind that the conversations are indeed more in line with recollections rather than factually recorded dialogue. That being said, the memoir moves through a series of topics that, in all likelihood, did take place in some form or another—but not precisely as the memoir parenthetically relates. Factually, therefore, it cannot be assumed that Miller voiced all of the opinions or knowledge attributed him within Rejaunier's abundant and lengthy quotations.

The bond between Rejaunier and Miller was shaped through their varied but relatable life travels and a shared, diverse reading and music background. The book seems organized by thematic content, so one Sunday's conversation is made distinct from another based on the topic, or topics, of the day. As recounted in the memoir, discussions concerning mutually admired authors created the initial connection between the Rejaunier and Miller. As with Barbara Kraft, Rejaunier had met Anaïs Nin before meeting Miller, and not surprisingly, as with Kraft, knowing Nin did not help form the attachment between Rejaunier and Miller. While both Nin and Miller were living in Los Angeles, there was very little interaction between the two in their later years, and the old friendship apparently failed to be a conduit through which to gain Miller's respect. Instead, it was distant writers and like-minded opinions that lured Miller's interest to a person. Marie Corelli, D. H. Lawrence, Lawrence Durrell, Artur Rimbaud, and Blaise Cendrars are discussed to some degree—pretty standard names in the Miller canon—but there are a handful of other authors not often mentioned in relation with Miller, including Irving Wallace. In this capacity, the memoir serves as a reminder that Miller had been a voracious reader throughout his lifetime and retained much of the knowledge he gleaned from these texts.

As Miller aged, he became increasingly dependent on astrological signs, and Rejaunier and her friends shared a similar predilection. Occult and metaphysical topics, consequently, appear throughout the conversations, as Rejaunier's knowledge was significant enough to assist in writing *Astrology and Your Sex Life* (1965), by Dr. Maria Graciette. Having introduced Graciette to Miller, the memoir recounts conversations on topics revolving around sexual fulfillment, out of body travel, flying saucers and often touches on the teachings of Theosophy. Along with astrology, Miller's interest in Theosophy became more intense as he aged; he was known to give friends a copy of *Boyhood with Gurdjieff* (1964), by Fritz Peters, for which Miller had written the introduction. A leading mind in the Theosophy movement in Europe and the United States, Gurdjieff became a popular figure among a segment of the Hollywood scene, and the memoir highlights the prevalence of his philosophy throughout several conversations.

A final theme in the memoir worth touching on is Miller's interest in film and the film industry. Always an avid film buff, Miller often went to see films more than once. At the Siegel residence (Dr. Siegel was dubbed the "physician to the stars"), there were ample opportunities for Miller to meet aspiring actors, discuss films and directors, and, as recorded by Noreen Nash, occasionally meet such greats as director Jean Renoir, director of the highly extolled *The Rules of the Game* (1939). Miller's actor friend, Joe Gray, has a minor presence in most of the chapters, and he too added a personal depth to Miller's interaction with the Hollywood scene. One unique film discussed is Andy Warhol's *The Life of Juanita Castro* (1965), which starred Mercedes Ospina, who briefly knew Rejaunier and became infatuated with Miller before she tragically died from unknown causes in the fall of 1965. Along with Warhol's film, various other films are mentioned, including *Cleopatra* and *The Seven Minutes*, based on an Irving Wallace novel.

While it is stimulating to get an intimate glimpse of Miller during his later years, there are definite critiques to be made about this memoir. In the afterword, one of the praises that Rejaunier bestows on Miller is his ability to tell engaging stories. Yet, if there is one thing missing from this memoir it may very well be the voice of the primary subject: Henry Miller. All of the conversations have been "embellished" with so many facts that, at times, they read like what might be termed a "Wikipedia conversation." As a personified impression of Miller, the conversations fall flat and scarcely bring him to life; even a brief comparison alongside *Face to Face with Henry Miller* (1970) and *Conversations with Henry Miller* (1994) reveal the difference between the voice of the real Miller and the Miller that Rejaunier has portrayed. Indeed, the extensive conversations throughout the memoir often become tedious, as they make Miller, and those in conversation with him, sound pedantic and full of facts and historical events. Poor Joe Gray is left looking like an unnecessary punctuation mark, with untimely interjections to steer the memoir chapter onto other topics. The dialogue difficulties become even more pronounced as all the individuals with speaking roles have uniform voices, essentially that of Rejaunier.

Two other concerns are that the memoir lacks momentum and clear direction. Outside of its possible thematic organization, only one section of the memoir carries any real semblance of drive. This particular segment details the brief friendship with Mercedes Ospina and her infatuation with Miller. Engaging for the narrative-like qualities, this part draws attention to the lack of linear progression in the other sections affected directly by the fact that there are an inadequate number of dates given in the memoir. With few concrete time markers, the exact—or even relative—dates of get-togethers and other significant events are left mostly unspecified; additionally, it is unclear exactly how long Rejaunier and Miller were friends or what eventually caused the friendship to lose its intimacy. Overall, the memoir covers four or five years, from 1965 until sometime after the publication of Rejaunier's best-selling novel, *The Beauty Trap*, in 1969. All this is not to say that *My Sundays with Henry Miller* is without interest for Miller enthusiasts or that it lacks aspects of solid writing, but perhaps a different approach to these Sundays with Miller may have proved more engaging. Sadly, due to these deficits, I feel Rejaunier has missed the mark in chronicling "a previously unknown side to Henry Miller" (Book cover).

A Brief Look at *Titan of the Muses*

Titan of the Muses is essentially a short memoir covering the brief acquaintance between Henry Miller and Jean Renoir. Written in the 1980s and then stored for several years, Noreen Nash's memoir specifically focuses on the meeting of the two men. Even though Jeanne Rejaunier is listed as coauthor, the memoir reads very different from her work discussed above. Structurally, the memoir is broken into three small parts: a section on Miller and his personality, a succeeding section on Jean Renoir and his personal traits, and a final part summarizing the handful of meetings between the men. The two foremost sections are short and succinct overviews of both artists, with emphasis highlighting the personal characteristics that Nash observed in each man. The third section arises through a discussion between Nash and her husband, Dr. Lee Siegel, to determine if and when Miller and Renoir should meet. We then read about an initial dinner party and particular topics discussed and films viewed. In general, the memoir gives a concise bird's-eye-view of the party, with no extensive dialogue being reproduced. The portraits of the two men and the dinner event are covered in a mere 36 pages, and it becomes clear that the two old men, while friendly with each other, formed no enduring bond. The rest of the book contains snippets from other works by Nash, as well as Rejaunier. Overall, Nash affords a quaint depiction of the meeting between Miller and Renoir, only showing slight favor toward the "angel" Renoir over "the lecher" (used lightheartedly) Miller.

Reviewed by Wayne E. Arnold

Articles and Book Chapters

Adamson, Judith. Review of *The Works of Graham Greene, Volume 2: A Guide To The Graham Greene Archives,* **by Jon Wise and Mike Hill (Bloomsbury, 2015).** *Graham Greene Studies,* **vol. 1, 2017, pp. 178-180.**

In her review of Wise and Hill's book, Adamson reports that Greene advised The Bodley Head to publish *Tropic of Cancer*: "I personally would be all for publishing Henry Miller." Adamson suggests, however, that Greene's statement stemmed primarily from his desire to "encourage [James] Michie to come to The Bodley Head" as director in 1962.

Submitted by James Gifford

Allen, Dorothy. "Movie Review: *Quiet Days in Clichy."* **Men's** *Digest,* **no. 158, vol. 19, no. 4, Jan. 1974, pp. 13-16.**

This article contains eleven photographs from the film.

When this film by Danish movie producer Jens Jørgen Thornsen arrived in the US, it was promptly impounded by the Los Angeles Customs to await trial on the charge of obscenity. On July 6, 1970, Judge William P. Gray declared the film not obscene:

> Bearing in mind the increasingly frankness in matters pertaining to sex and nudity, and the possible artistic merits of the film, I find the film appeals to the normal interest of sex and nudity which the average person has in such matters . . .

Allen gives special attention to the film's "closing sequence, an orgy to end all orgies, in a bathtub involving Joey, Carl, and three Eurasian girls picked up in a bar, that really made the censors quiver and some critics shake—with laughter. One of the girls pours wine all over her nude body and masturbates with the bottle. The others alternatively drink and bathe with the wine and make all kinds of love. Joey tops off the performance by urinating in the crowded tub."

Allen provides a balanced appraisal of the film, citing its "credible rendition of the Miller work, complete with its prolonged and ribald sex scenes" and an "all-too-brief sequence [when] Ben Webster, one of the greatest living jazz tenor saxophonists . . . plays warm sensual music leading to the movie's ultimate orgy-in-the-bathtub. . . . " On the negative side was the selection of the Henry Miller character, Paul Valjean, who was "unappealing in clothes and plain repulsive without them," and the use of black and white film, which, coming on the heels of the charming and beautiful version of Miller's *Tropic of Cancer,* makes this slice of Miller's life something of an anticlimax."

Submitted by Roger Jackson

Beston, John. "Going into Dreamland: From Lewis Carroll's *Alice in Wonderland* **to Patrick White's** *The Aunt's Story." Antipodes,* **vol. 29, no. 2. 2015, pp. 343-352.**

In tracing the various influences on Patrick White's *The Aunt's Story,* Beston notes that Miller's surrealistic writing in *Black Spring* proved important to the composition of the novel. Miller and the other influences (including Olive Schreiner) Beston discusses are important to White because of "the journey that their characters make into their dreamland in a turning from the world around them." Beston further suggests that *Back Spring* attracted White because of Miller's tendency "to live within his own mind."

Birney, Earl. *Conversations with Trotsky: Earl Birney and the Radical 1930s.* **Ed. Bruce Nesbitt. U of Toronto P, 2017.**

Reprints Birney's 1939 review of *The Cosmological Eye*, "The Mad Sanity of Henry Miller." Birney admits that he has not read Miller's banned books but claims that this allows him to judge *The Cosmological Eye* with "a fair amount of sobriety." Birney laments Miller's lack of systematic thought, pointing out that he positions himself at turns as "an anarchist, a Chinese humanist, a sensual primitivist, or a romantic mystic" and that his influences at times clash with one another. Birney does credit Miller, however, with a "Rabelaisian humor and wealth of language." Despite variously calling Miller boring, conceited, and masochistic, Birney finally suggests that Miller "may be one of the great writers of our generation."

Campbell, James. "Miller's Fail." *Time Literary Supplement,* **1 June 2016. <https://www.the-tls-.co.uk/articles/public/millers-fail>.**

Campbell uses the current availability of certain Penguin editions of Miller's works to de facto review Miller's status in 2016 (essentially 125 years after his birth.) He begins with a relatively lengthy quotation from *Quiet Days in Clichy* (it is rather remarkable to see this in the TLS!) to set the stage for how different readers—from George Orwell to Germaine Greer and Kate Millett—have reacted to Miller's writing and how some of Miller's subjects will be problematic at this time. While noting that readers "are no longer shocked by the sex; it's the sexism they shrink from now," Campbell suggests that the "Modern Classics" (the Penguin series) would benefit from contextual explanation. Campbell also notes that Nin's preface to *Tropic of Cancer* is missing from the Penguin edition, as is the epigraph from Emerson.

Submitted by D.A. Pratt

"Celluloins: The 10 Finest Full Frontal Scenes." *Celebrity Sleuth,* **vol. 12, no. 2, 1999, pp. 30-31.**

The editors identify in tenth place Ellen Burstyn's appearance in Miller's *Tropic of Cancer*.

"In 1969, Joseph Strick called me from Paris and asked me to come do *Tropic of Cancer*," elegant Ellen Burstyn recalls. "I didn't think *Tropic* came out very well. But it was the first time that I did a film where there was even a minute in it when I was doing the kind of work that I had been doing at the Actors Studio but somehow never was able to get on screen."

Tropic contained a scene of full-frontal nudity [just two minutes into the film], highly unusual for its time! ... The book was banned in the U.S. for 30 years, and 'filmmakers didn't give it a ghost of a chance to make its way onto film, so explicitly erotic was the content of the novel.'"

Henry Miller later commented, "Physically and in other ways, I discovered that there were some striking resemblances between Ellen and the real Mona."

Note: Seventeen pictures of Burstyn appear with the text. In ascending order the editor's other picks are: No. 9, Hunter Tylo *(The Invitation)*; No. 8, Tara Fitzgerald *(Sirens)*; No. 7, Sean Young *(Love Crimes)*; No. 6, Fionnula Flanagan *(James Joyces' Women)*; No. 5, Dana Delany *(Exit to Eden)*; No. 4, Nicole Kidman *(Billy Bathgate)*; No. 3, Suzanna Hamilton *(1984)*; No. 2, Julianne Moore *(Short Cuts)*; and in first place, Sharon Stone *(Basic Instinct)*.

Submitted by Roger Jackson

"A China Review." *The North-China Herald and Supreme Court & Consular Gazette,* **19 Oct. 1938: 124.**

A monthly review column of the Shanghai *T'ien Hsia Monthly*. In the October edition, the reviewer writes that Alred Perlès's "Letter to Henry Miller on Goethe" is considered "very readable."

Submitted by Wayne E. Arnold

"A China Review." *The North-China Herald and Supreme Court & Consular Gazette,* **30 Nov. 1938: 388.**

The November review mentions Miller's "Tribute to Blaise Cendrars" as being part of the contents in the newest issue.

Submitted by Wayne E. Arnold

Collier, James L. "Portrait of a Fetish Publisher." *Peek-a-Boo* **Winter 1964, pp. 53-54, 58.**

Publisher: "… We advertised [the fetish book] in papers like the book section of the Sunday *Times*.

Collier: *"The New York Times?"*

Publisher: "Sure. The *Times* carries a lot of this kind of advertising. If you take a look through an issue you'll see what I mean. I mean stuff like the magazine *Sexology* and *Fanny Hill* and Frank Harris' *My Life and Loves*. The Harris book is about as rough as you can get. A few years back the *Times* wouldn't have taken an ad for it, but in the past oh, say, five years everything has changed. The big thing was when *Lady Chatterley's Lover* was approved by the courts. That opened the flood gates. If you could print *Lady Chatterley* you could print Henry Miller, and if you could print Henry Miller you could print anything."

Submitted by Roger Jackson

Cowe, Jennifer. Sex and the City: A Situationist Reading of Jens Jorgen Thorsen's Film Adaptation of Henry Miller's *Quiet Days in Clichy*. *European Journal of American Studies*, vol. 11, no. 2, 2016, n.p.

Cowe positions Thorsen as sympathetic to Miller's rejection of cultural norms and their underpinning ideologies. Mentioning that the filmmaker "was hardly a doctrinalist member" of the Danish movement, Cowe contextualizes Thorsen's relationship to the Situationist International and also examines the centrality of several of its (and Debord's) theories to the adaptation's use of psychogeography. Cowe locates the concept of *Détournement* ("the turning of an image against itself") as particularly important to Thorsen's aesthetic in general and to his adaptation of Miller's work in particular. Cowe also critiques the film (and the book's) sexual commodification of women, finding it ironic that both artists rail against capitalism's mystification of sex yet only attempt to naturalize the act for men (women still being treated as objects of exchange). Cowe ultimately claims that the adaptation is the "most successful ... of any of Henry Miller's novels to date."

Crews, Michael Lynn. *Books Are Made Out of Books: A Guide to Cormac McCarthy's Literary Influences.* **U of Texas P, 2017.**

Crews's book examines scores of Cormac McCarthy's key literary influences, including Miller. Crews moves book-by-book through McCarthy's oeuvre and locates Miller's most significant influence on *Suttree.* Crews points out that "excised early drafts and fragments suggest that Miller loomed large in McCarthy's imagination when he first conceived the idea for the novel." Crews suggests that Miller's influence was primarily on the book's sexual content and that while "Miller's work also addresses humanity's spiritual condition, McCarthy's novels foreground these in ways that preclude the full adoption of Miller's aesthetics." Crews identifies multiple references to Miller in McCarthy's papers and letters. A letter section on correspondence demonstrates that McCarthy wanted a "complete" collection of Miller and shows his efforts to track down the *Hamlet* letters.

Decker, James M. "'Routes bizarre and absolutely original': Henry Miller on Luis Buñuel." *Café in Space,* **vol. 15, 2018, pp. 16-27.**

Decker compares several of Miller's writings on Buñuel, including the unpublished manuscript of *Tropic of Cancer,* and considers the filmmaker's impact on Miller's aesthetic.

Deutsch, Laura, ed. "Sex in America: The Educated Lover." **Gallery, vol. 12, no. 5, 1984, pp. 76-79.**

Under the subheading "The Literature of Love" are excerpts from five writers who have "paid homage to a man's sexual longings and joys." In addition to quotes from William Shakespeare, Frank Harris, D.H. Lawrence, Pauline Reage, and Philip Roth, is this excerpt from Miller's *Tropic of Cancer:*

> As she stood up to dry herself.... suddenly she dropped the towel and, advancing toward me leisurely, she commenced rubbing her pussy affectionately, stroking it with her two hands, caressing it, patting it, patting it.... Her words imbued it with a peculiar fragrance; it was no longer just her private organ, but a treasure, a magic potent treasure ... and none the less so because she traded it day in and day out for a few pieces of silver. As she flung herself on the bed, with legs spread wide apart, she cupped it with her hands and stroked it some more, murmuring all the while in that hoarse, cracked voice of hers that it was good, beautiful, a treasure, a little treasure. And it was good, that little pussy of hers! That Sunday afternoon, with its poisonous breath of spring in the air, everything clicked again.

Note: A photograph of Miller appears on page 79.

Submitted by Roger Jackson

Dorian Book Quarterly, various articles.

Lawrence Shifreen's *Bibliography of Secondary Sources* makes reference to the *Dorian Book Quarterly* in a listing under the *Henry Miller Literary Society Newsletter* (E1537). There are, however, several other mentions of Miller in the Dorian quarterly including the following (in some cases, issue month is not known): "Literary Society Promotes Henry Miller," 1960: 17; "Scanning the Bookshelf," 1961: 23-25; "Grove Press Has Published Henry Miller's Banned Book...," 1961: 19-20; "Scanning the Bookshelf," October-December 1962: 26-27; "Syracuse Censors Win a Miller Case," January-March 1963: 31.

Digital copies of these texts are available through the Archives of Sexuality & Gender database <https://www.gale.com/uk/c/archives-of-sexuality-and-gender-lgbtq-part-ii>.

Submitted by Wayne E. Arnold

Emre, Merve. "Ironic Institutions: Counterculture Fictions and the American Express Company." *American Literature,* **vol. 87, no. 1, 2015, pp. 107-136.**

Emre traces the representation of the American Express Company in authors such as Fitzgerald, Corso, and Miller.

Gifford, James. "Late Modernism's Migrations: San Francisco Renaissance, Egyptian Anarchists, and English Post-Surrealism." *Textual Practices,* **vol. 29, no. 6, 2015, pp. 1051-1075.**

Citing the key influence of Henry Miller and Herbert Read, Gifford explores the relationship between radical writers in 1930s-1940s Egypt and 1940s San Francisco. Gifford unearths important links between the Villa Seurat Circle's "anarchist revisions to surrealism" and several overlapping networks of writers working in London, Cairo, New York, and San Francisco. Gifford argues that such revisions involved a rejection of "deterministic Marxism and Economism" as well as an emphasis on the individual. Gifford persuasively concludes that the "anarchist revision to Surrealism was rampant and was not "fragmentary … as virtually all previous criticism has contended."

Glass, Loren. "Freedom to Read: Barney Rosset, Henry Miller, and the End of Obscenity." *Censorship and the Limits of the Literary: A Global View.* **Ed. Nicole Moore. Bloomsbury, 2015, pp. 177-188.**

Glass tackles Rosset's efforts to publish *Tropic of Cancer* as well as his desire to "make the freedoms Miller found in art available to everyone." Glass contemplates the context surrounding Rosset's campaign, including Miller's problematic association with Modernism and the critical ambivalence surrounding his work. After summarizing the various trials and their aftermath, Glass devotes time to Miller's refusal to let Kate Millett quote his books in *Sexual Politics* as well as Grove's ultimate decision to consent, which Glass suggests is based on the same principles that allowed the book to be published in the United States.

Granville-Draper, Peter. "'Into the Night-Life...'—An Enlargement of Notes on the Philosophy and Writing of Henry Miller." *Facet* **1.5, Spring 1947: 177-81.**

This short, biographical/philosophical analysis of Miller's work begins with an overview of Miller's childhood, highlighting his rebellious nature and concluding of the young Miller: "he must have been a very successful failure" (177). Granville-Draper mixes biographical information along with some general observations about why Miller evolved into a writer. Concerning Miller's attitude, he notes that Miller's "nihilistic philosophy is a city-claustrophobic product, it could not have come about anywhere but in a city" (179). Overall, the article is filled with generalizations about the '20s and '30s and how the post-War artistic world is at a standstill—except, perhaps, for Miller.

Submitted by Wayne E. Arnold

Harlow, John. "How Henry Dropped Harry. *Palisadian-Post,* **9 March 2017: pp. 9, 12.**

John Harlow, Editor-in-Chief of the Pacific Palisades (CA) newspaper, not only provides a review of Harry Kiakis's book, *Henry Miller in Pacific Palisades: Selections from a Journal,* but also interviews Kiakis in order to get follow-up information and context.

Submitted by Harry Kiakis

Hough, Richard, ed. *Motor Car Lover's Companion.* **George Allen & Unwin, 1965.**

Hough includes the entire chapter of "Automotive Passacaglia" from *The Air-Conditioned Nightmare*. This volume is a collection of car-related passages; in his introduction to Miller's section, Hough states, with a bit of tongue-in-cheek, that "this part of the book is concerned with motoring not literary controversy" (154).

Submitted by Wayne E. Arnold

Humphries, David T. "Going off the Gold Standard in Henry Miller's *Tropic of Cancer." Canadian Review of American Studies*, vol. 47. no. 2, 2017, pp. 239-260.

Humphries investigates Miller's concern with economics in *Tropic of Cancer*. Viewing the book as an "artifact of resistance," Humphries draws a connection between Miller's linguistic flow and his critique of capitalism and its various superstructures. Humphries further contends that Miller presents alternatives to the "gold standard," both at the economic and literary levels. Contra Bryant's political populism, Miller's is a "populism of outrage" born of immediate experience. Humphries concludes that *Tropic of Cancer* "disrupt[s] economic imperatives and abstractions," thereby validating human experience.

Johnson, Marvin. *From Pinups to Pornography*. Eros, 1971.

A history of sex, mores and pornography with sexually explicit black and white photographs and color plates. Miller is discussed on pages 25, 114–117. After quoting two sections from *Sexus* where Miller "carefully paints a stark portrait of sexual passion," Johnson puts Miller's work in perspective:

> Miller glories in his intimate descriptions of the genitals. . . . Yet [his] writing style is rated highly by critics the world over. In spite of the lurid sex, all of his books have become best sellers and finally *Tropic of Cancer*, which the Supreme Court finally allowed to be sold in the United States, is a

frank motion picture. But the storm-clouds of censorship hang heavy over the movie print which has been confiscated in some states. Presently lawsuits are in litigation as the producers are suing for damages. And so the never-ending battle of what is and what is not pornographic goes on.

Mr. Miller isn't afraid to reveal intimate details of his vomiting, bleeding hemorrhoids and constipation. In this author's anxiety to achieve realism he has brought a vital new dimension to writing. And because of his honesty in presenting these personal aspects of life, he has brought total integrity to his work.

"Jimmy ne Fouette Pas Les Femmes Comme L'en Accuse Miller, Le Maudit." *V Magazine* **244, 5 June, 1949.**

A short article about the character "Jimmie" in *Tropic of Cancer* who knew Miller during his Montparnasse days. In *Cancer*, Miller occasionally refers to Jimmie's Bar, retelling various scenes of debauchery; specifically, there is one in which Jimmie whips his half-naked drunk wife. The author claims that the real Jimmy has now been publicly inconvenienced due to the popularity of *Tropic of Cancer*. He maintains that he has never been violent with his wife and complains that now there is seldom a day when American or French customers do not make some reference to his whipping specialty. Jimmy calls Miller a bum who wrote poorly of him because he had Miller kicked out of the bar for being drunk by 10 a.m. Miller's character for Jimmie may be a loosely veiled reference to James "Jimmie" Charters, barman at the popular ex-pat hangout, Dingo Bar. Charters published a book about his experience as barman in the ex-pat heyday of the 1920s, entitled *This Must Be The Place: Memoirs of Montparnasse* (1934, 1937, 1989). In French.

Submitted by Wayne E. Arnold

Kästner, Erich. "Ein ruhiger Nachmittag." *Die Neue Zeitung,* **2 Dec. 1946: A1.**

Kästner brings along Miller's *Tropic of Cancer* as he strolls around Munich, pondering the difference between journalist and editor. He visits various shops, looks in storefront windows and finally has his nails manicured and hair trimmed. While doing so, he reads the Budapest-printed copy of Miller's book and muses that Miller's writing contains despair and cynicism but is full of sincerity. Researcher's note: Erich Kästner (1899-1974) was a well-known German author who wrote across many genres, including poetry, cabaret shows, and children's books. Nominated for the Nobel Prize in Literature on four occasions, his most famous work is likely to be considered *Lottie and Lisa* (1949), made popular by the Disney movie version, *The Parent Trap* (1961). Kästner was acquainted with Heinrich M. Ledig-Rowohlt, who would become Miller's German publisher. On March 11, 1947, Ledig wrote an introductory letter to Miller, explaining his interest in Miller's work. At the end of the letter, he asked Miller if he had seen Kästner's piece in *Die Neue Zeitung*; the article, Ledig informed Miller, resulted from loaning Kästner his personal copy of *Tropic of Cancer*. (See: Ledig to Miller, 11 Mar. 1947. Folder 13 of 81, New Directions Publishing Corp. Records, circa 1932-1997, MS Am 2077 1152, Houghton Library, Harvard University). In German.

Submitted by Wayne E. Arnold

Koehler, Robert. "Henry Miller: 'At the Bottom of Everything is Love.'" *UCLA Daily Bruin* Vol. CII No. 7, 3 Oct. 1977: 14-15.

Koehler's article covers the three consecutive sold-out live discussions Miller gave in September 1977 at the Actors' and Directors' Lab in Beverly Hills. The article mentions some of the questions asked of Miller. There are a few quotes from Miller's talks, including this gem: "'You're the wife of a young artist, and you want my advice? Divorce him'" (15). The title of Koehler's article comes from another Miller nugget: "'I think that creative people, despite their obsessions, can love better than most people. At the bottom of everything is love'" (15).

Submitted by Wayne E. Arnold

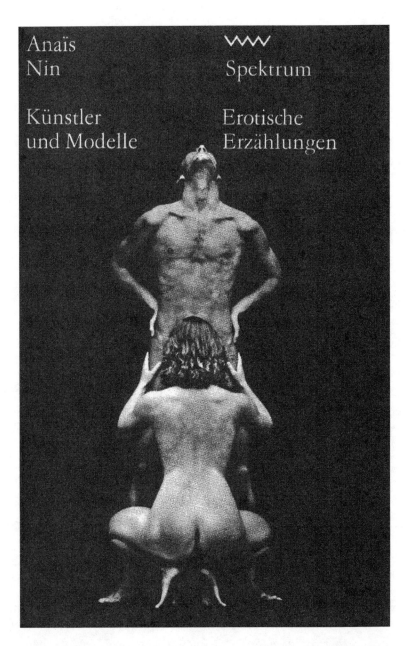

Anaïs Nin

Künstler und Modelle

Spektrum

Erotische Erzählungen

Künstler und Modelle (trans. *Artist and Models*) is Nin's *Delta of Venus* as published by Volk und Welk in the former German Democratic Republic (East Germany) in 1977. This quality paperback has an unattached dust jacket that when removed exposes a front and back cover that is blank. (Submitted by Ernst Richter).

Lambert, Josh. *Unclean Lips: Obscenity, Jews, and American Culture*. New York UP, 2014.

Lambert investigates the role of the Jewish community in defending literature against obscenity. In his introduction, Lambert uses the controversy surrounding *Tropic of Cancer* as a way to frame his broader concerns, pointing out that "As the Chicago trial of Miller's novel illustrates, American Jews played crucial roles in obscenity controversies not just as defendants but as lawyers, judges, and witnesses." Lambert argues that "nativist anti-Semitism" motivated the champions of Miller and other writers deemed obscene.

"Une Lettre Inédite D'Hermann de Keyserling a Henry Miller." *Le Goéland* 83, Sept.-Oct. 1947.

Includes one letter from Keyserling to Miller, dated May 29, 1938. The letter discusses Miller's writing and has a heavy focus on a horoscope created by Conrad Moricand for Keyserling's son, Manfred. There is also a lengthy commentary by publisher-editor, Théophile Briant (1891-1956). Miller replied to Keyserling on June 7, 1938, and this letter, along with three others, was published in *The International Henry Miller Letter* 5, August 1963: 11-20. In French.

Submitted by Wayne E. Arnold

MacNiven, Ian S. "The Road from Delphi: Henry Miller and Greece." *Americans and the Experience of Delphi*. Eds. Paul Lorenz and David Roessel. Somerset Hall, 2013, pp. 281-292.

MacNiven explores Miller's transformative trip to Greece, noting that the writer "arrived prime for a revelation." Glossing both *The Colossus of Maroussi* and "First Impressions of Greece," MacNiven argues that Greece "enabled [Miller] to make [the] transition" to the "wild isolation" he found in Big Sur. He further suggests that the inspiration Miller found in Delphi served as a catalyst for him to tackle *The Rosy Crucifixion*.

Masuga, Katy. "Miller's Henry and Henry's Paris." *Paris in American Literatures: On Distance as a Literary Resource*. Ed.

Jeffrey Herlihy-Mera and Vamsi K. Koneru. Fairleigh Dickinson UP, 2013, pp. 87-104.

In examining the impact of Paris on Miller, Masuga considers both how Miller represents Paris in his narratives and how Miller's physical presence in Paris molded those narratives. Masuga asserts that this doubled vision manifests "the desire to sustain the image of a location as simultaneously actual and abstract." Miller's "imaginative wanderings," Masuga points out, "are usually coupled with deeply physical, sordid, everyday experiences." Masuga views *Tropic of Cancer* as negotiating a series of binaries (e.g., sexuality and purity) that stand for the "unimaginable and contradictory networks" that Miller seeks to depict. She further notes that Paris gave Miller access to "the right kind of resource and inspiration to harness his desire to write." Among these resources are the examples of writers such as Cendrars, Rimbaud, and Proust, who, Masuga contends, grappled with similar struggles over the "limits of writing [and] ... the desire to overcome the impossibility of life in art."

Mayer, Martin. "How to Publish 'Dirty Books' for Fun and Profit." *The Saturday Evening Post*, vol. 242, no. 2, 25 January 1969, pp. 32-35, 72-73, 75.

This extensive article with five photographs is a profile on publisher Barney Rosset and his Grove Press. Rosset also appears in caricature on the front cover surrounded by photographs of his many publications, including the hardbound and paperbound editions of Henry Miller's *Tropic of Cancer* and *Nexus*. The flurry of 60 separate state and local prosecutions surrounding *Tropic of Cancer* almost put Grove Press into bankruptcy.

Neimark, Paul G. "*Tropic of Cancer* – Are its Censors Obscene?" *Men's Digest*, no. 34, March 1962, pp. 14-15.

This article was written following Mr. Neimark's visit with Elmer Gertz, Miller's attorney, who was then in a legal battle defending *Tropic of Cancer* in the Chicago area. Neimark sees the censors as the ones who are guilty of obscenity by "treating a man as if he had no mind or values, and that neither are important, if he does have them."

O'Connell, Shaun. *Remarkable, Unspeakable New York: A Literary History*. Beacon Press, 1997.

In a section covering 1930s literature set in New York City, O'Connell discusses Miller and draws solely from *Aller Retour New York*. O'Connell emphasizes Miller disgust for the city, "a city of the lowest depths" (220), and Miller's dislike of Thomas Wolfe while highlighting their shared anti-Semitic overtones. There is a major blunder by O'Connell in noting that *Aller Retour* was a letter intended for "a French friend, Emil Schnellock" (219), especially considering Miller's letter begins with: "Dear Fred [Perlès]."

Submitted by Wayne E. Arnold

Potter, Kelly. "Naughty Books That Defied the Censor." *Tab*, vol. 7, no. 3, 1957, pp. 98-103.

Potter asks, "How far should an author go in telling how his heroes and heroines make love?" and then lists a variety of books that pressed the boundaries:

> Here are but a few of the titles that caused angry gum-beating in the past: *God's Little Acre* by Erskine Caldwell, *The Postman Always Rings Twice* by James M. Cain, *Lady Chatterley's Lover* by D. H. Lawrence, *Studs Lonigan* by James T. Farrell, *The Black Mass* by J. K. Huysmans, *From Here to Eternity* by James Jones, *Butterfield 8* by John O'Hara, *The Wayward Bus* by John Steinbeck, *Strange Fruit* by Lillian Smith, *For Whom the Bell Tolls* by Ernest Hemingway, *Tropic of Capricorn* by Henry Miller, *Ulysses* by James Joyce, and *Sanctuary* by William Faulkner.

Potter then observes that

> All of these books survived the initial clamor and have finally been acclaimed as not only good, but in some cases

even great works. Only one of them—*Tropic of Capricorn*—was actually banned from the nation's bookshelves. But a few copies are occasionally smuggled in from France, a land where *Capricorn* was and still is widely hailed as a work of art. The book has been described as utterly pagan because nowhere do sinners feel guilty or sins get punished. In fact, it deals so frankly with sex for sex' sake, it violates Christian and Jewish morality, the basis of Western civilization."

Note: Article also contains a photograph of Miller taken in 1947.

Submitted by Roger Jackson

Potter, Rachel. *Obscene Modernism: Literary Censorship and Experiment, 1900-1940.* **Oxford UP, 2013.**

Potter argues that modernist writers created a "confrontational dynamic" that self-consciously pushed against traditional social mores while also "develop[ed] aestheticized explorations of the obscene." Potter also maintains that censorship efforts were "fragmented, widespread, and beyond the reach of the nation state." Among many other texts, *Tropic of Cancer* appears as an example of the aestheticized obscene, particularly in its "use of an illicit sexual lexicon of pricks and cunts, as well as a gendered theory of violent agency" (a phenomenon that to Potter "seems deliberately absurd.") Potter claims that Miller's aesthetic explicitly "invite[s] a visceral response to his linguistic combination of sex and violence."

Rosset, Barney. "Profiles in Censorship: Henry Miller and *Tropic of Cancer".* *My Life in Publishing and How I Fought Censorship.* OR Books, 2016, pp. 179-206.

Chapter 12 of Rosset's posthumous memoir provides a useful summary for younger Miller scholars of the challenges of getting Miller's major books into print in the United States (this story has been given book-length treatment elsewhere when the matter was much more current). The opening passage presents the situation: "It is January 1962. A battle is being waged on multiple fronts. Twenty-one lawyers around the country are fighting in nearly 60 separate legal actions."

In the chapter Rosset described his early attraction to Miller's writing (he wrote a paper about *Tropic of Cancer* in the early 1940s—in this paper he stated: "writers must have a liberal society—or they are stifled."). From his first encounter with Miller's work, Rosset believed that Miller "was a great American writer who said, in his own unique way, exactly what he felt. He expressed himself in an original American idiom" and described him as an embodiment of Walt Whitman. He described his meetings with Miller during the process of getting Miller's major book published. In general his account gets beyond the legalese associated with earlier accounts of these trials and tribulations.

The book also has chapters on other censorship struggles at that time including the publication of D.H. Lawrence's *Lady Chatterley's Lover* and the importation of the Swedish film *I Am Curious (Yellow)*. The chapter on Henry Miller is followed by one on Maurice Girodias of Olympia Press. The book provides readers with an engaging narrative of the period when Miller's works finally became generally available in the United States – this period is difficult to imagine now, in the early twenty-first century.

Submitted by D.A. Pratt

Schmidt, Michael. *The Novel: A Biography*. Belknap, 2014.

Schmidt devotes chapter 32 of his 1200-page study of the novel to "teller and tale." He considers Miller among a host of other writers, including Lawrence, Nin, and Durrell. Schmidt claims that "opencast pornographer" Miller's "focused genital stimulation" sought a largely male audience. Of Miller's non-sexual themes, Schmidt dismisses them as the "toxic residue" of solipsism.

Stan, C.M. "A Passionate Misunderstanding: Orwell's Paris, Miller's China." *English Studies*, vol. 97, no. 3, 2016, pp. 298-316.

Stan remarks on the seeming paradox of the politically engaged Orwell praising Miller for his ostensibly quietist stance in *Tropic of Cancer*. After contextualizing both Miller's work and Orwell's review, Stan argues that Orwell, rather than endorsing Miller's book as a reflection of passive acquiescence, admired Miller's "sincerity" above all. Sincerity, Stan observes, is a fluid concept, and he attempts (via Lionel Trilling) to trace Orwell's conception of it in "Inside the Whale." Stan asserts that Orwell mainly focuses on "a world of surfaces" within Miller's works and ignores Durrell's commendation of Miller's style and form. Stan also examines the significant differences in how the two writers viewed Joyce, with Orwell seeing a character such as Leopold Bloom as a man of the people and Miller viewing Joyce as an elitist. Stan ultimately claims that Orwell presents a limited view of Miller's work based on his own commitment to view of authenticity that Miller did not share.

Stern, Gerald. *Stealing History*. Trinity University Press, 2012.

Stern includes two short chapters on two of Miller's books: *Aller Retour New York* and *The Air-Conditioned Nightmare*. It is Miller's biting and condemning attitude towards the United States that most attracts Stern's critique. While far from being friendly toward Miller, Stern views these two Miller books as being companion pieces: "It's part rage and part *resentment*, and it's about being cheated—of life—and taking revenge, or it's just one long boring sermon" (267). Stern, a native of Pittsburgh, particularly dislikes Miller's treatment of his city, but likes Miller's observations on other areas of the country. In the chapter on *Aller Retour*, Stern does not hold back in his criticism concerning Miller's perceived anti-Semitism, ending his reflections on Miller by considering him "A flawed genius. And a lowlife" (272).

Submitted by Wayne E. Arnold

Stuart, Angus F. "Thomas Merton and Henry Miller: A Correspondence in Vision." *Merton Annual: Studies in Culture, Spirituality, and Social Concerns*, vol. 29, 2016, pp. 180-187.

Stuart focuses on Merton's conception of Miller as a man who, "disenchanted with the world" undertook a spiritual journey. After providing some background about the letters and the men, Stuart writes of *The Colossus of Maroussi* that "it articulates a profound spiritual sensibility, often making use of striking Christian imagery." He then proceeds to examine Miller as a spiritual writer and locates parallels between Miller and Merton's monasticism. Stuart suggests that Miller saw an "outlaw" in Merton and that Merton glimpsed embodying "integration of eternity in the world."

Thompson, Ralph. "Books of the Times." *New York Times,* **13 July 1938: 19.**

Thompson mentions *Tropic of Cancer, Aller Retour New York* and *Black Spring* in a dialogue with a friend who is browsing his personal library. Thompson calls Miller's books "a bit peppery for American tastes." This mention of Miller appears four months prior to the Shifreen reference to Thompson's serial "Book of the Times" (E34).

Submitted by Wayne E. Arnold

"Tropic of Cancer." Best for Men, **Sep. 1970, pp. 44-45.**

This Special Issue on "The New Films on the Spot Marked X" provides a synopsis and review of 17 X-rated films, including *Tropic of Cancer.* This article also contains four photos from the film.

> The intent of the book was, of course, shocking humor, as well as stark reality. Like Terry Southern's work, *Candy,* one has to sift through the "obscenity" with an open mind. The biggest problem in the film is the capturing of the egocentric thoughts of the narrator, Henry Miller. Much of what Miller writes is even today [1970] unfit not only for television viewing, but also film productions.
>
> The sexual fantasies which Miller created in his novel are what gives the true humor to the work. His self-

defined sexual prowess can only make fun of the entire society's view of sex.

The film managed to stick close enough to the book that those who were offended by the Miller method of conveying his thoughts were also offended by the film.

Submitted by Roger Jackson

Woodford, Jack. "The Henry Miller I Knew." *The Men's Digest,* **no. 39, Aug. 1962, pp. 22-26.**

Brief memoir written by American pulp writer notorious for his expose of the publishing industry, *Trial and Error* (1933). A representative passage reads as follows:

> You'd never believe it was Henry Miller if you spent an evening with him at a party, as one can in Hollywood, without being introduced around.

> He's quiet, reserved — says little; but when he does it means something. Dresses very conventionally. Grayish suit which looks as though it belonged on the indivisible man. Nothing of the satyr shows on him. He looks like a bookkeeper about to be retired by his firm with a gold watch in lieu of a decent salary, at the end of a lifetime of endeavor. He indeed held such a job years ago. He was in charge of messengers at the New York Western Union.

Submitted by Roger Jackson

Online Presence

Arnold, Wayne E. "Harry Kiakis, *Henry Miller in Pacific Palisades: Selections from a Journal.* **European Journal of American Studies, Reviews 2017-2, document 9. <http://ejas.revues.org/12176>**

A four-page review that properly identifies Kiakis's unique contribution to Miller studies:

Written in short descriptive bursts that recounts fragments of conversations, social outings and people who popped in and out of Miller's home, Kiakis's memoiresque journal is a play-by-play glimpse back in time to the heyday of Miller's life at 444 Ocampo Drive, Pacific Palisades. The journal avoids many of the hazards that have befallen recent memoirs on Miller, as Kiakis neither retells long stretches of presumed conversation nor adds any post-visit or present day reflections. Instead, his journal comes across with a feeling of fresh recollections, not dulled by 36 years of fading memories.

Crowther, Kenton. "Three Examples of the Higher Balderdash." *Lotus Eater Magazine*, **3, 2015.** **<https://lotuseatermagazine.files.wordpress.com/2015/11/ lotus-eater-mag-issue-3.pdf >**

Crowther groups works by John Lennon and Marc Bolan (of T. Rex fame) with Henry Miller's *Mezzotints*. Crowther alludes to the Jackson edition of the *Mezzotints* before providing some general background on their production. Calling the fragments he has read "a collection of arty, self-conscious pieces that have a tang of the gutter," Crowther claims that Miller juxtaposes "baroque elegance" with "drawling crudity."

Cudenec, Paul. "Henry Miller—Resisting the Virus of Modernity." **5 Aug. 2015. <https://network23.org/paulcudenec/ 2015/08/05/henry-miller-resisting-the-virus-of-modernity/>.**

Cudenec argues that an "alienated" Miller provides an unconditional rejection of modern society. Despite this denunciation, however, Miller, according to Cudenec, avoids a negative perspective by infusing his writing with "some sort of idea of how things *should* be." Cudenec claims that for Miller the ideal is a "free anarchist non-industrial world."

"Henry Miller and Breathtaking Big Sur." *Daily Mail.* **14 May 2018.** **<http://www.dailymail.co.uk/wires/aap/article-5728521/ Henry-Miller-breathtaking-Big-Sur.html >.**

The author briefly considers Miller's time in Big Sur and describes the Henry Miller Memorial Library. Miller is viewed as "anchor[ing] the reader into a place" with his writing.

Shaftel, David. "In Crete, Henry Miller Found His Muse among the Ruins." *New York Times*, **Footsteps, 21 Sep. 2016.** <https://www.nytimes.com/2016/09/25/travel/in-crete-henry-miller-found-his-muse-amid-the-ruins.html>.

Shaftel describes trying to "channel" Miller on his own journey to Crete, particularly his relish for the "rough aspects of travel in Greece." Shaftel contrasts the "formless, sex-soaked" Paris books with the "taut, inspired" *The Colossus of Maroussi* and admires the latter's "lyrical but often unruly prose." Rehearsing Miller's time with Durrell, Sefaris, and Katsimbalis, Shaftel imagines Miller drinking retsina and regaling his companions. Declaring that Miller is his kind of guide, Shaftel discusses Miller's intuitive approach to travel. He then compares Miller's Crete to the overcrowded beaches he encounters, but he soon discovers, Miller-style, a more interesting and less populated Crete filled with tranquility and myth. Shaftel tries to follow Miller's itinerary, and he includes suggested readings for those unfamiliar with the writer.

Wheeler, Steve. "Henry and Me." *Empty Mirror.* **Mar. 2017.** <https://www.emptymirrorbooks.com/literature/henry-miller-and-me>.

Wheeler tells the tale of his first encounter with the name "Henry Miller" as well as his immediate fascination on reading a collection of letters between Miller and Durrell. Inspired by Miller, Wheeler attempted to mimic his style and made a pilgrimage to Paris. First attracted to Miller's style, Wheeler also admires his "rebelliousness" and "subversive ideas."

Wilner, Paul, "Separating the Brand—and the Man and the Writer—from the Myth." *Monterey Country Now.* **10 Aug. 2017.** <http://www.montereycountyweekly.com/news/cover_collections/separating-the-brand-and-the-man-and-the-writer-from/article_a443a53c-7d43-11e7-a071-374fc17cf5fe.html>.

Wilner describes Miller's bad-boy reputation and asks whether many of those who visit the Henry Miller Memorial Library have actually read his works. Calling *Tropic of Cancer* a "great book, earthier and more accessible than more canonical works of the period by Hemingway and Fitzgerald, Wilner also views *Tropic of Capricorn* as "exuberantly lecherous." Wilner considers Miller's work after Paris to be tedious, but he argues that Miller is an "undeniable life force."

Miscellaneous

Allen, Steve, and Marty Rossi. *Hello Dere!* Recorded live at the Sands Hotel/Casino in Las Vegas. ABC Records, Aristocrat Series ABC 2270. [1962]. LP.

For the comedy duo Allen & Rossi, Allen was the handsome, straight-man who fed lines to Rossi, a frazzle-haired, bug-eyed character whose tag-line was "Hello Dere!" The following quote, delivered by Rossi, appears as the opening gag on the first track:

Hello Dere! I'd like to read you page five of the *Tropic of Cancer* [audience bursts into laughter] . . . this book [laughter continues as Rossi introduces another topic].

Page five is the location of the infamous "Tania" passage that prosecutor's high-lighted during court cases as prime evidence for the books pornographic status. The hardcover edition of *Tropic of Cancer* was published on June 24, 1961. Of the 1,600,000 copies of the paperback edition that were distributed nationwide during the early weeks after its October 10, 1961 publication, 600,000 copies were immediately returned. Wholesalers refused to handle the book due to legal action that was under way in their community/state or because of pressure put on them through threats and intimidation by police and political leaders. *Hello Dere!* was available as early as March 1962, a time when there was considerable publicity surrounding the book and a "page five" reference had specific meaning to a general audience.

Berman, Shelley. *The Sex Life of the Primate*. A comedy review performed by Jerry Stiller, Anne Meara, Lovelady Powell and Shelley Berman. Verve, V/V6-15043. [1964]. LP.

The third skit in Act II, "An Expurgated #!?*%," is performed by Lovelady Powell. The reading is from the "Tania" passage of Henry Miller's *Tropic of Cancer*, slightly modified. The asterisks seen below have been added by this writer to denote a "koo-koo" sound that was heard every time a word was censored on the record.

Good Evening. Our society believes that literature should be made available to everyone. Our initial effort is to foster a plan known as "Henry Miller for Children." Now, I have been preparing a children's recording of Henry Miller stories and the following is an excerpt from the recording which I think should convince us all that *Tropic of Cancer* is good clean fun for the entire family:

O Tania, where now is that warm * of yours, those soft, bulging *? Why, there is a * in my *. Oh, I will * out every wrinkle in your *, Tania. I will send you home with an ache in your * and your * turned inside out. He knows how to build a fire, but I know how to inflame a *. I will make your * incandescent. After me, you can * * * * *

Frey, James. *Katerina*. Gallery, 2018.

Similar to Frey himself, the protagonist in this notorious writer's latest novel was inspired by Miller and traveled to Paris to find his muse. The story alternates between 1992 Paris and 2017 Los Angeles—the protagonist is 21 when he moves to Paris to live "the artist's life," and he's middle-aged in California when he receives an anonymous message that draws him back into that life. The American edition was published in September 2018.

Submitted by Karl Orend.

Henry Miller: Prophet of Desire. Dir. Gero von Boehm, Interscience Film, 2017.

Von Boehm's documentary fuses new interviews with Tony Miller, Erica Jong, and Arthur Hoyle, among others, with clips from films, photographs, and new location footage. The film attempts to interrogate the relationship between Miller's fictional persona and his roles as father, friend, and artist. In German.

Submitted by Roger Jackson

Greeting Card. 1968.

A birthday card was marketed in 1968 with a red cover and the words, "Here's a Happy Birthday card with selected [and I do mean *selected!*] passages from the novels *Candy, Fanny Hill, Lolita, Peyton Place, The Carpetbaggers, Lady Chatterley, Tropic of Cancer . . . .*" Inside the card are those passages—"Have" (from *Candy*), "a" (from *Fanny Hill*), "happy" (from *Lolita*), and so on until it reads "Have a happy birthday and many, many more!" This card was not pictured, but only described, in *All Man*, vol. 8, no. 9, June 1968, p. 8.

Submitted by Roger Jackson

Lidchi, Maggi. *Man of Earth*. William Morrow & Company. 1968.

Man of the Earth—so the hero of this highly original novel describes himself. Seeking wisdom and fulfillment, he sets out on a modern pilgrimage to the spiritual heart of India. The hero, Christopher Progroff, goes to an ashram in Ceylon and meets an "Irish Swami" who attempts to browbeat him into the abandonment of self. A break between them occurs soon after Christopher has made an unexpected archaeological discovery, and it is then that he sets off on foot, without destination, possessions or money: the eternal pilgrim.

Two quotes by Miller are used to promote this book. On the front cover: "HENRY MILLER: . . . I really go for it . . . there is the book I would have liked to write."

On the inside front jacket flap is the following: "HENRY MILLER: Look, at the moment I am talking to everyone about one book. You can say it, I really go for it. . . . It fascinates me. Reading it, I was jealous of the author: there is the book I would have liked to write."

The quote came from an interview with Marcia Craipeau in *Le Monde.*

Submitted by Roger Jackson

McCloud, Kathleen. Tropic of Cancer: ***Let's Smuggle.*** **Exhibited at** ***Banned,*** **Santa Fe Community Gallery, Mar.-May 2016.**

Inspired by Miller's time in Paris, McCloud's art installation reimagines a room in the Hôtel Central. McCloud bases her conception on papers and books of Miller's that she inherited from Emil Schnellock. McCloud describes her theme as dealing with the "recurring cycle of transformation played out through war, art, sex, and spiritual seeking."

Kathleen McCloud
www.kathleenmccloud.com

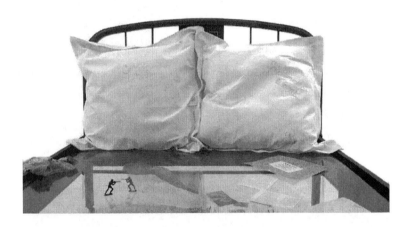

Seeman, Ed. Henry Miller T-Shirt. MANA-T'S, Ocala, FL (no date but contemporary).

Artist Ed Seeman has created a series of montage portraits of the great writers of the past and present and blends a wide variety of their images into a complex, yet pleasing visual impression of the artist. Miller's composite print shows fourteen images of him, two of Brenda Venus and one of Anaïs Nin. There are 36 other writers in this series, among them Allen Ginsberg, Hunter S. Thompson, Jack

Kerouac, Ernest Hemingway and William Burroughs. Available as a print or as an illustrated t-shirt.

Submitted by John Bagnole

Unemployed Philosophers Guild. Banned Books Coffee Mug. Brooklyn, New York (no date but contemporary).

Printed on this coffee mug are the titles of 24 books, all of which have been banned at one time or another. Included on this list is *Tropic of Cancer*.

Contributors' Notes

Wayne E. Arnold is an Associate Professor of American Studies at The University of Kitakyushu, in Japan. He holds a Ph.D. in English from The University of Louisiana at Lafayette and an M.A. in TESOL from the same university. Additionally, he has earned an M.A. in English from Western Kentucky University and an MBA from Wright State University. His research focus is Henry Miller and Japan.

Jeff Bursey is a fiction writer, literary critic, and playwright. His books are *Centring the Margins: Essays and Reviews* (2016), and the novels *Mirrors on which Dust Has Fallen* (2015) and *Verbatim: A Novel* (2015); paperback edition (2018).

John Clegg is a writer currently residing in Vancouver, British Columbia. His creative work has been published previously in *The Warren*, as well as the *Feathertale Review*. The work that appears here is the culmination of John's scholarly efforts as an Honours student in the English Literature program at The University of British Columbia. The author is deeply indebted to the kind and constructive guidance of Dr. Judith Paltin of the University of British Columbia. Without her constant consideration none of what appears here would be possible.

Finn Jensen was born in 1946, and graduated from the University of Copenhagen with an M.A. and Ph.D. in literature. He has written a number of articles and three books about Henry Miller. He hopes the latest, *The Man of the City: Henry Miller and Modernity*, 2017, will be published in the United States this year.

Inez Hollander Lake received her Ph.D. in American Literature from Radboud University Nijmegen in the Netherlands. Her dissertation and biography of Southern novelist Hamilton Basso (1904-1964) was brought out by Louisiana State University Press in 1999. Since then, she published two literary memoirs in the Netherlands and the US (*Ontwaken uit de Amerikaanse droom*, (Amsterdam: Archipel, 2004 and *Silenced Voices*, Athens: Ohio University Press, 2008). As a lifelong aficionado of Henry Miller, she published her first novella

(*Euro Trippy*) on Henry Miller in 2012, but she is now working on a more serious book (and another literary memoir) that she hopes will spark renewed interest in Henry Miller, not as a cult figure or sexist, but as an important voice in American and world literature.

Eric D. Lehman teaches literature and creative writing at the University of Bridgeport and his essays, reviews, poems, and stories have been published in dozens of journals and magazines. His fifteen books include *The Quotable New Englander*, *Literary Connecticut*, *Homegrown Terror*, and *Afoot in Connecticut*, nominated for the Pushcart Prize. *Becoming Tom Thumb: Charles Stratton, P. T. Barnum, and the Dawn of American Celebrity* won the Henry Russell Hitchcock Award from the Victorian Society of America, and was chosen as one of the American Library Association's outstanding university press books of the year. His novel, *Shadows of Paris*, won novella of the year from Next Generation Indie Awards, a silver medal in Romance from Foreword Reviews, and finalist for the Connecticut Book Award.

Katy Masuga, a recent Sorbonne fellow, is a writer drawn to the disruption of conventional forms, influenced by Virginia Woolf, W. G. Sebald and Marilynne Robinson among others. Her research background incorporates comparative modernisms, image and text relations and interdisciplinarity at large in the arts and sciences. Her publications include two monographs: *Henry Miller and How He Got That Way* (Edinburgh UP, 2011) and *The Secret Violence of Henry Miller* (Camden House, 2011), two novels: *The Origin of Vermilion* (Spuyten Duyvil Press, 2016) and *The Blue of Night* Caffeinated Press, *forthcoming*), as well as numerous short stories, and dozens of essays and anthology chapters on subjects ranging from altered books, including the artists Doug Beube and Brian Dettmer, to Blanchot and Wittgenstein in Beckett to Shakespeare and Company in Paris to the vegetarian diet of Shelley's creature in *Frankenstein*. She holds joint doctorates in Comparative Literature and Theory and Criticism and teaches for the University of Washington in Paris.

Akiyoshi Suzuki is Professor of American literature, comparative literature, and East-West Studies at the Graduate School of Global Humanities and Social Sciences and at the Department of

Intercultural Studies of Faculty of Education, Nagasaki University in Japan. He has served in various positions including as a member of the Editorial Committee of the International Association for East-West Studies (U.S.A.). His recent book and articles for international publication are *The Future of English in Asia: Perspectives on Language and Literature* (joint), New York: Routledge, 2015; "Cloaking the Poor: Reading and Representation in American Literature," *The Activist History Review: "Poverty" Issue* (September, 2017): Online; "The East and the West Harmoniously Coexisting as Jacob's Descendants under the Care of Mary of the East and the West: David Mitchell's *The Thousand Autumns of Jacob de Zoet*," *Journal of East-West Thought* 7(4), (December, 2017): 59-82.

Ida Therén works as a freelance writer and book critic for the Swedish daily, *Svenska Dagbladet*. She previously ran the literary journal *CONST Literary (P)review*. Her debut novel, *Mer än en kvinna* (preliminary English title: *More Than a Woman – The Story of June Miller Mansfield*), will be published by her Swedish publisher Natur o Kultur in the fall of 2019. Previously, an excerpt from the novel has been published in *Granta*. In this issue of *Nexus*, we get a taste of the book in the shape of a letter from June. The English translation of the novel will be done by April 2019. For requests, please contact her publisher at <richard.herold@nok.se>. You can find her work at <www. idatheran.com> or follow her at <instagram.com/idatheren>.

The **Nexus** *Award for New Scholars*

First Prize	$500
Second Prize	$250
Third Prize	$100

To encourage such scholarship, we are pleased to announce the *Nexus* Award for New Scholars.

To compete for the award, unpublished writers should submit their essays on any subject pertaining to the Villa Seurat Circle (including but not limited to the following):

Henry Miller

Anaïs Nin

Michael Fraenkel

Lawrence Durrell

June Miller, etc.

All submissions will be reviewed by a panel of Miller experts. Please email submissions to <jdecker@icc.edu>.

Deadline: Submission must be reviewed by 1 June 2019.

Winners will also appear in a subsequent volume of *Nexus: The International Henry Miller Journal.*

Henry Miller in Pacific Palisades:
Selections from a Journal

by Harry Kiakis

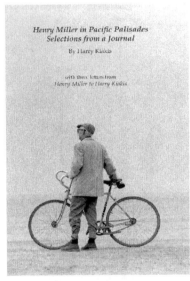

218 pages
31 illustrations

Available at: amazon.com

Includes 3 letters from
Henry Miller to Harry Kiakis

Harry Kiakis met Miller for the first time in May 1968, and for the next 33 months became part of Miller's "inner circle" of friends. This period was a busy one for Miller. His marriage to Hoki was in its first year, two films based on his books were being produced, along with a documentary film *(The Henry Miller Odyssey)*. Miller continued to write; the text for *My Life and Times, Insomnia or the Devil at Large,* and short pieces for magazines, including *Playboy*.

Harry spent time with Miller on 59 separate occasions and at the end of each meeting the events and conversations were dutifully logged in a journal documenting Miller's life during these years. The text reveals Miller's humorous and playful manner, but also his intimate side, his regrets, passions and the relationships he had among friends.

When Miller made a 10-week trip to Paris in the summer of 1969 for the filming of *Tropic of Cancer*, it was Harry and his wife, Connie, he asked to live in his house for the interim. Dealing with a menagerie of Miller's fans and permanent houseguests added another facet to their relationship.

The friendship between Miller and Kiakis came to an abrupt and absolute end, with a phone call made on Miller's behalf, and for the remaining nine years of Miller's life, there was no contact.

Honoring Miller's request—"Harry write your book about me after I'm gone"—the complete story is now told, 36 years later.

About the Author

Harry Kiakis joined the Army at 17 and served in both Korea and Japan. He later graduated from Brown University. He was working as an office manager for Sears when Miller's secretary at the time, Gèrald Robitaille, introduced them. Mr. Kiakis currently resides in Laguna Beach, California.

Reviewer Comments

Written in short descriptive bursts that recounts fragments of conversations, social outings and people who popped in and out of Miller's home, Kiakis's memoiresque journal is a play-by-play glimpse back in time to the heyday of Miller's life at 444 Ocampo Drive, Pacific Palisades. The journal avoids many of the hazards that have befallen recent memoirs on Miller, as Kiakis neither retells long stretches of presumed conversation nor adds any post-visit or present day reflections. Instead, his journal comes across with a feeling of fresh recollections, not dulled by 36 years of fading memories.

—Wayne W. Arnold
European Journal of American Studies, Reviews 2017-2

Thanks to this journal, the lively parties and conversations, as well as some of the drama unfolding under Miller's roof, are depicted

—Wayne W. Arnold
European Journal of American Studies, Reviews 2017-2

Available from amazon.com

"... *a tour de force of verbal dexterity...*"
—Review of Contemporary Fiction

Jeff Bursey

VERBATIM:

A NOVEL

Verbatim: A Novel

By Jeff Bursey

The present state of politics across the globe is both unsettled and unsettling. There could be no better time for a reissue of Jeff Bursey's terrific 2010 novel "Verbatim." In this documentary novel, Bursey portrays both political paralysis and bitter backstabbing. He uses an imaginary transcription of parliamentary proceedings to demonstrate both the petty and the nasty dealings of elected officials and bureaucrats alike. "Verbatim" is simultaneously topflight satire and emotionally affecting, deploying an experimental form that propels the story forward and keeps the reader turning the pages. "Verbatim" is an outstanding novel and a timely read.

> —Larry Fondation, author of the novels *Fish, Soap and Bonds* and *Time is the Longest Distance*

"...through his spirited gift for mimicry, [Bursey] illuminates how the procedures and protocols of governing are perverted to hinder action and fuel the ongoing fractures that only assist the powerful. [*Verbatim: A Novel*] is that quintessential chronicle that captures a time so deftly, as a reader, it's like reading your own memories of it."

> —Christopher WunderLee, author of the novels *The Loony* and *Moore's Mythopoeia*

American Book Review: "Let the record show that this is probably about the funniest intelligent book on politics you can get your hands on these days."

Jeff Bursey is a fiction writer, literary critic, and playwright. His books are *Centring the Margins: Essays and Reviews* (2016), and the novels *Mirrors on which Dust Has Fallen* (2015) and *Verbatim: A Novel* (2015); paperback edition (2018).

THE "NEW" HENRY MILLER MEMORIAL CAFÉ
TROPIC OF CANCER

Hoki Tokuda, Henry Miller's 5th wife, has recently moved locations to a new café in Tokyo. The café has a full bar and Hoki performs her jazz specialties almost every night of the week. The café is overflowing with Miller memorabilia, including books, photographs, and posters.

Hours: 8:00 PM ~ 12:00 AM; Tuesday ~ Sunday

Address: Tokyo, Minato-ku, Roppongi, 2 Chome 3-9, Union Roppongi Building, 1F

〒106-0032 東京都港区六本木２丁目３−９ユニオン六本木ビル１F

(Directly next to the APA Hotel, Roppongi)

Phone: +81-03-6277-7277

HENRY MILLER   BERN PORTER   ROGER JACKSON

DISTINCTIVE COLLECTION OF RARE BOOKS
OFFERED FOR SALE

Published in small limited editions and seldom offered for sale to the general public, Roger Jackson has published the finest Henry Miller and Bern Porter publications ever produced (over 120 separate publications, with over 40 publications by or about Bern Porter). As well as publishing the most distinctive reference compendiums, guides and indexes, profusely illustrated historical records of Henry Miller ephemera and books, including scandalous esoteric and secret information, these publications contain previously unpublished material that cannot be found elsewhere. (One can search the inventory of the several hundred thousand booksellers on the internet and you will not find offered for sale some of these publications.)

Only a handful of institutions possess anything close to a complete archival set of books published by Roger Jackson, among them, Harvard University, Yale University and Ohio State. Three sets are being offered: 1.) THE HENRY MILLER ARCHIVES; 2.) THE BERN PORTER ARCHIVES; 3.) and the combined HENRY MILLER & BERN ARCHIVE (all published by Roger Jackson).

Select individual titles are also available and include these two notable works, both compiled by Jackson:

THE WORLD OF BERN (2002) – this volumes defies description and is the absolute fusion of raw art and published book, must see to appreciate (only 50 copies published).

HENRY MILLER: HIS LIFE IN EPHEMERA 1914 – 1980 (2012) – The finest, rarest and most illustrated esoteric and interesting volume ever produced regarding Henry Miller. This massive volume of 821 pages is absolutely essential for an articulated and total understanding of the works of Henry Miller. Originally published at $995.00, it is extremely rare and not to be found anywhere for sale (only 50 copies published).

For information on pricing contact: dcw0821@aol.com

Nexus: The International Henry Miller Journal is dedicated to the work and life of Henry Miller and his circle (Anaïs Nin, Lawrence Durrell, June Miller, etc.). Issued annually, it contains previously unpublished essays and letters by and about Henry Miller. For current pricing and availability of back issues visit our website at www.nexusmiller.org. To order copies or submit an article (LA format) please contact: Dr. James M. Decker; *Nexus: The International Henry Miller Journal*; 1028 SE Adams #108; Peoria, IL 61602.

Email: nexusjournal@hotmail

Website: www.nexusmiller.org to order by credit card

Made in the USA
Lexington, KY
21 December 2018